IN GOOD FAITH

The growth of faith-based schools, particularly within Muslim communities, has signalled a clear change in direction as a number of religious groups have begun to question the efficacy of 'secular' schooling for all. But why is it that some faith-based schools are regarded as different from others? What makes Muslim and Sikh schools, for example, different from those classified as Anglican, Catholic or Jewish? At the heart of the debate is the question of segregation in terms of race and ethnicity.

This unique book draws on first-hand research to explore these issues and the concerns that the expansion of new faith-based schools will prove to be socially divisive, encourage 'fundamentalism', and incite religious and ethnic tensions. Lord Dearing contributes the Foreword.

To Merv and Will
John, Pavlos and Victor
and Fiona

We dedicate this book to our families for their patience, encouragement
and support whilst it was being prepared

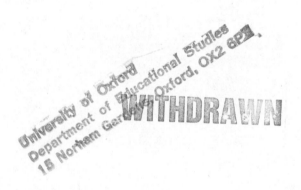

In Good Faith

Schools, Religion and Public Funding

MARIE PARKER-JENKINS
University of Derby

DIMITRA HARTAS
University of Warwick

BARRIE A. IRVING
Canterbury Christ Church University College

ASHGATE

Published by
Ashgate Publishing Limited
Gower House
Croft Road
Aldershot
Hampshire GU11 3HR
England

Ashgate Publishing Company
Suite 420
101 Cherry Street
Burlington, VT 05401–4405
USA

Ashgate website: http//www.ashgate.com

British Library Cataloguing in Publication Data
Parker-Jenkins, Marie
  In Good Faith: Schools, Religion and Public Funding
  1. Church schools – Great Britain. 2. Discrimination in education – Great Britain.
  3. Minorities – Education – Great Britain. I. Title. II. Hartas, Dimitra. Irving, Barrie A.
  371'.07

Library of Congress Cataloging in Publication Data
Parker-Jenkins, Marie
  In Good Faith: Schools, Religion and Public Funding / by Marie Parker-Jenkins, Dimitra Hartas and Barrie A. Irving.
      p.   cm.
  Includes bibliographical references and index.
  1. Church and education – Great Britain. 2. Church schools – Great Britain. 3. Church and state – Great Britain. 4. Education and state – Great Britain. I. Hartas, Dimitra, 1966–
  II. Irving, Barrie A. III. Title
  LC331.P37   2004
  379.2'8'0941–dc22

                                                                                                2004006138

ISBN 0 7546 3350 0 (hbk)
ISBN 0 7546 3351 9 (pbk)

Typeset in Times New Roman by IML Typographers, Birkenhead, Merseyside and printed in Great Britain by MPG Books Ltd, Bodmin, Cornwall

Contents

Foreword

This book is timely.

In a scholarly way, and meticulously avoiding taking a position on whether there should be faith schools or not, in effect this book challenges those, like me, who see such schools as contributing positively to the well-being of society, and as responding to parental choice, to think through, for all faith schools, and indeed for community schools also, the implications of September 11 and the course of events in Iraq for our multi-ethnic and multi-faith society.

Over the centuries it has been the way of immigrants to cluster in communities of those of their own kind for mutual support, linguistic association and to continue inherited traditions and customs; not least amongst these being religious identity. Over the last two centuries these gatherings have been exemplified by immigrations of Roman Catholics from Ireland and of Jews from mainland Europe, with associated concentrations of populations. Since the Second World War we have seen this repeated with major immigration from the Commonwealth nations, of Afro-Caribbeans, Muslims, Sikhs and Hindus, distinguished by ethnicity and colour as well as by religion. This book suggests that while differentiation by religion may not now be a major cause of concern for most people, when this is coupled with differentiation by colour and ethnicity, the potential for inter-community conflict is heightened, as was demonstrated two years ago in some northern towns, where the inherent tensions in the clustering of ethnic groups was aggravated by social deprivation and envy.

Turning specifically to faith schools, the book illustrates the potential for tensions by reminding us of the opposition to state-funded education for Roman Catholics, whose Nonconformist opponents saw it as 'Rome on the Rates'. It reminds us of the struggle of the Jewish community to secure state funding for Jewish schools. With one and a half million Muslims in England and Wales, and over a hundred privately financed Muslim schools and a far greater number of 'after-school' classes to offer Muslim children a grounding in their parental faith and language, it would be inequitable to deny them, if sought, state funding for voluntary aided Muslim schools.

There has been positive support for faith schools from the present New Labour government and it is relevant to note the emphasis currently placed by the Labour and Conservative parties on extending parental choice in schooling. Without doubt there is a demand for faith-based education, and one of the paradoxes of our increasingly secular white Anglo-Saxon community is that the demand for places in church schools has continued to be strong, so strong that the Church of England has adopted a policy of increasing its provision of secondary schools. Muslim and other minority faith parents cannot be denied an equal opportunity.

This poses the inescapable question of how to reconcile legitimate parental choice in education – and the associated wish by a large number of parents for an education for their children that responds to community, religious and cultural distinctiveness – with the need for inter-community understanding, tolerance, respect and good will.

The head teacher of a Church of England secondary school in Oldham, which had received a lot of media attention during the riots, summed up the kind of attitude that is needed if this reconciliation is to be achieved, when he said, 'We are perceived as being part of the problem in Oldham. We want to be part of the answer.' That approach rightly places a clear responsibility on the leaders of faith schools, and this book rightly concludes with its own thoughts on ways ahead, which are as relevant to community schools serving an ethnically or religiously distinct community as they are to faith-based schools.

Lord Dearing
July 2004

Acknowledgements

Our research for this book has involved discussion and correspondence with a wide range of people without whose help we would have been unable to undertake the study. We would like, therefore, to acknowledge a number of individuals and organizations.

For the purpose of the book we conducted research in several faith-based schools. These were representative both of the older religious traditions in England and Wales, and of those which have been more recently established. Whilst our focus was on the new state-funded faith-based schools, we visited a range of schools to provide an overview of issues facing all faith-based schools, as well as those specific to newly funded institutions. They included the following:

Al-Furqan School
Al-Hijrah School
Clore Shalom School
The Guru Nanak Sikh Voluntary Aided Secondary School
Hartshorne Church of England Primary School
The Islamia Primary School, Brent
The North West London Jewish Primary School
The Nottingham Islamia School
St Cyprian's Greek Orthodox School
St Edward's Catholic Primary School
The Swaminarayan Hindu Independent Day School

As well as thanking these schools, we wish also to acknowledge the assistance we received from representatives of organizations with an interest in education who were supportive of our work and who provided additional information, namely:

Meg Buckingham, HMI
Elaine Kennedy, DfES
Marilyn Mason, The British Humanist Association
Idris Sears, The Association of Muslim Schools
Helena Miller, Leo Baeck College – Centre for Jewish Education
Zaki Badawi, The Muslim College, London
Mohamed Mukadam, Leicester Islamic Academy
David Edwards, Derby Diocesan Board of Education

Audrey Osler, Centre for Citizenship Education and Global Studies
Kathleen Wood, the Methodist Church
Rita Price, the Catholic Education Service
Stefan Moroz, Castlebrook High School, Bury
Antonia Kaslelanides, Greek Association Language Enhancement Organization

We are also grateful to Sarah Lloyd of Ashgate Publishing for her ongoing support
of the book; and our research assistant, Michele Wolfe; secretary Stef Lubynskyj;
and indexer Mary Fitzgerald, all of whom have worked with us on previous
projects, and who have been instrumental in the preparation of this book. Similarly,
Paul Weller, Des Hewitt, Doug Briggs, Nick Green and Jane Keeling, Derby
University; Eleanor Jackson, Warwick University; Anne Convery, Nottingham
University; David Gillborn, London University; John Hinnells of Liverpool Hope
University; and Lynn Cotton of Lewis Girls' School, Hengoed Ysprad Mynach,
were all helpful on particular aspects of the work and we wish to acknowledge their
assistance.

Robert Jackson, Professor of Comparative Religions at Warwick University, is
worthy of special mention because he kindly agreed to act as critical friend and
reader for the book, and we are grateful to him for his patience in reading through
the manuscript as it emerged. Similarly, Lord Dearing generously gave of his time
and wrote the Foreword to the book.

While a number of people and organizations have thus been consulted over issues
contained in the study, the opinions expressed are our own; likewise any errors or
omissions.

Marie Parker-Jenkins, University of Derby
Dimitra Hartas, University of Warwick
Barrie A. Irving, Canterbury Christ Church University College
2004

Chapter 1

Setting the Scene

Introduction

Faith-based schools in Britain are not new: those of a Christian tradition have existed for centuries. What is significantly different today is the development of a new type of school founded on an Islamic or Sikh ethos. Such schools see themselves as part of the national education system, yet wish to locate their teaching, learning and practices within a faith-based context. As we move beyond those institutions of a Christian tradition, issues emerge which have provoked fearsome debate about the wisdom of expanding this newer type of school. Historically, Christianity was embedded in the state education system, and Judaism became an acceptable part, but the same may not be said of others. Why is it that some faith-based schools are regarded differently from others? What makes Muslim and Sikh schools, for example, different from those classified as Church of England, Catholic or Jewish?

At the heart of the debate is the question of segregation in terms of race and ethnicity. As faith-based schools continue to grow in number and to represent a wider range of religious beliefs, there is a pressing need to explore the issues that will impact on all schools, religious or 'secular'. There are different levels of diversity in society, for example cultural, socio-economic or those based on special needs and disability. To what extent do faith-based schools mirror this diversity, or indeed wish to? In some geographical locations, community schools are reflective of a monocultural population. Conversely, a number of inner-city community schools are comprised of a majority of non-Christian pupils from minority ethnic backgrounds. If such schools are to respond positively to cultural and religious diversity, what are the challenges they will face? Moreover, will the development of faith-based schools lead to greater social disharmony, reinforce gender stereotyping and provide opportunity for the promotion of narrow religious doctrines? Clearly the development of faith-based schools, particularly those highly representative of ethnic diversity, will have implications for all educational institutions, whatever their religious or philosophical basis. These are some of the issues with which this book is concerned and which are explored with reference to the education system in England and Wales.

Educational research has not involved large-scale enquiries into faith-based schooling in this country. In fact a number of writers maintain that the relevance of faith-based cultures and the academic outcomes from their particular school systems have been largely ignored within mainstream educational study. As such, much of the current political and public debate about these schools has been conducted at the level of prejudice and generalization (Grace 2002b; Francis and Lankshear 2001; Arthur 1995). This is particularly true of minority-faith schools which have significant ethnic representation. Yet state-funded faith-based schools account for approximately one-third of primary schools and one-sixth of secondary schools in England and Wales, accommodating over 7 million pupils (Department for Education and Skills 2003b). Similarly, some religious authorities have not encouraged systematic and critical research of their own schools. For this reason, we have attempted to obtain first-hand evidence gained from visits to faith-based schools, new and old, interviewing practitioners to obtain an insight into the practical issues involved in running a school based on religious principles which is in receipt of public funding.

Our own research background in the area includes previous project work funded by the Economic and Social Research Council (ESRC) (1993–95), the Leverhulme Trust (1995–98), the Department for Education and Skills (DfES) (1999–2000) and the Centre for British Teachers (2001–2003). These studies have been concerned with issues of diversity and opportunity with particular reference to Muslim communities. Whilst this has provided a useful background to underpin this present study, we also undertook research specifically for the book to illustrate and explore issues contained in each chapter. This has involved research of a sample of Church of England, Catholic and Jewish institutions, and we have incorporated perspectives from more recent additions to the educational landscape, namely Muslim, Sikh and Greek Orthodox schools which have joined the state sector since 1998.

We were informed in our study by the work of Poyntz and Walford (1994) who conducted a survey of new independent Christian schools in which 11 institutions were visited and data was collected through questionnaires and interviews. We used the DfES database (2002) to provide a sampling frame and from that we identified the newly funded, faith-based schools. Methodologically this involved visiting ten institutions between 2002–2003 to provide qualitative research from a range of religious perspectives. The focus was on interviewing senior management to explore questions of: religious ethos; cultural background of pupils; admissions policies; community involvement; curriculum issues; special needs education; staff recruitment; school performance; and accountability and inspection. A framework for data analysis was developed to review the information collected from this approach and to help identify emerging categories concerning issues of commonality and difference among state-funded faith-based schools. In addition, we also reviewed school prospectuses, policy documentation and inspection reports from these institutions. A further cohort of faith-based schools and associated organizations, incorporating independent institutions, were also included in our study, to provide an additional database which would enrich our understanding of the field especially in terms of the difference that state funding makes in managing schools of a religious character.

As such, a range of faith-based communities were contacted and generously participated in this study, for example, Church of England, Catholic, Jewish, Muslim,

Sikh and Greek Orthodox educational institutions, the only exception being the state-funded Seventh Day Adventist school which unfortunately did not wish to participate, despite frequent requests. Our particular focus in the book is on the full-time faith-based schools in receipt of public money because this is the category of school the government has signalled its intention to expand. Supplementary schools, such as 'madrassahs' or 'chedarim' which provide instruction in Islam and Judaism respectively, also constitute a type of faith-based schooling, but for the purpose of this book the focus is on full-time education at primary and secondary levels which is supported by state finance.

The book is not, therefore, about religion *per se*: it is about contextualizing education within a religious framework. This is reflected in our use of a wide range of political, social, theological and philosophical literature. By drawing on our evidence-based research we aim to provide an innovative perspective on issues not previously examined, such as the development of schools on Muslim, Sikh and Greek Orthodox lines. It is an applied text in that it is accessible and covers practical issues, but it is also underpinned by theoretical and philosophical perspectives. Our position here is unambivalent: we are not arguing for or against faith-based schools – they are clearly going to exist, with or without government funding. If, therefore, we accept the view that state-funded faith-based schools will remain a feature of the educational landscape for the foreseeable future, we need to look at the emerging challenges they are likely to face. This is of particular relevance for newly funded non-Christian institutions that will be operating within a nationally prescribed system of education. The challenges include their dealings with Ofsted, the delivery of the National Curriculum, and fulfilling parental expectations in terms of the quality and effectiveness of the education they provide. The question therefore is what shape these schools will take in the future: how should they operate; and what challenges might they face? In examining these questions in the book we:

- provide an overview of the development of faith-based schools in England and Wales;
- focus specifically on the emergence of new faith-based schools which may have different values from existing schools;
- explore common issues which have application to all faith-based schools as well as those specific to new institutions; and
- highlight and discuss social and political implications of the expansion of this category of school.

The purpose of the book is to help inform a wide audience: theologians, educationalists, teachers, students, academics, politicians and policy-makers; and to provide insight and understanding of the issues and challenges facing both the school communities involved and the wider educational and political establishments. For parents, faith-based schools are seen as attractive because of the cultural appropriateness of the educational setting and the religious ethos of the institution.

They also provide an alternative to community schools which may be successful academically but which may fail to provide a culturally sensitive model acceptable to some parents. We have written the book to provide an opportunity to reflect on these issues and on broader ones concerning religion, diversity and inclusion, from the point of view of faith-based schools once they receive public funding. By looking at the issues facing these schools we reflect on the changing situation for schools in general: that is, a need to compete with other institutions for resources; to make enrolment more inclusive especially in terms of religious, cultural and socio-economic difference; to ensure high academic attainment of all pupils; and to accept and provide for pupils with special educational needs. By exploring these themes from the perspective of faith-based schools, we also reflect on the changing situation for schools in general.

The new faith-based schools are emerging in a climate of greater parental choice and increased availability of state funding to support choice in education. They will also be operating in the context of what already exists, that is, a tradition of Christian and Jewish schools that have been influential in the development of schooling and in dealings with the state. However, the new state-funded, faith-based establishments, for example Muslim, Sikh and Greek Orthodox institutions, share issues of ethnicity to an extent not experienced by the earlier groups. They provide evidence of how religious diversity is put into practice, especially where there is an ethnic dimension, which gives the issue of funding faith-based schools its more controversial nature.

We are arguing, therefore, that Muslim schools, for example, which constitute the largest group within the new state-funded faith-based school sector, would not provoke criticism if their pupils were predominantly white, and that issues of both race and religion are at the centre of this controversy. For example, a MORI poll conducted for the *Times Educational Supplement* (2001f) reported that 27 per cent of respondents opposed the expansion of faith-based schools, a number which increased to 43 per cent when asked the same question with reference to Muslim, Sikh and Greek Orthodox schools. The debate about the wisdom of providing support for these schools cuts across political alignments, with racism in general – and Islamophobia in particular – featuring as part of the controversy now that a new type of culturally located faith-based school is accessing the public purse (Cush 2003). Ironically, there are a substantial number of community schools which, due to demographics, are highly representative of Muslim communities, yet these are not seen as threatening because they have not been set up deliberately to provide an Islamic education for Muslim children (Department for Education and Skills 2003b).

Exploring Themes of Race, Ethnicity and Culture

Debate about the expansion of new faith-based schools brings to the forefront the issues of race, ethnicity and culture to an extent not demonstrated by the establishment of Christian and Jewish schools. The concept of community and our understanding of the related terms of culture, race and ethnicity have been stretched to include school communities based on such religions as Islam and Sikhism. By the term religious community, we mean here a group of people living in the same locality and/or having the same religion, and sometimes sharing the same ethnic background. In the mapping of minority ethnic populations in Europe, religion has been identified as an important differentiating factor (Rex 1993), and the concept can be drawn broadly in the Islamic sense of the 'ummah' to encompass all Muslims regardless of national borders.

New cultural and religious identities are commonplace in many parts of Europe now as a result of immigration, displacement by war, and those seeking political asylum. As a result of this Diaspora or movement of people, our understanding of 'culture' and how it relates to 'ethnicity' is changing. Culture, which consists of norms, values and specific rules which are learnt through socialization, can be expressed through routine behaviour and symbolic representation (Kirby et al. 1997), and replicated through education. Many fundamental values are derived through teaching (Werbner 2002a) and this is particularly true of the new faith-based schools in our study which use the curriculum, both formally and informally, as a vehicle to transmit cultural heritage and religious identity. We have, within the multicultural West, diverse communities some of which are undergoing change themselves, yet trying to retain their cultural heritage, and very significantly trying to secure toleration of difference from the wider community, and respect for their religious identity.

The construction of identity draws on a number of factors such as ethnic origin and religious belief (Kirby et al. 1997) and it is possible for individuals to have a number of social identities. Most individuals organize meaning and experience in their lives through a primary identity which is fairly continuous (Giddens 2001), but for some people there may be a religious rather than an ethnic boundary around them, a marker which helps to define their sense of who they are, and helps reinforce the strength of their religious belief. Religion is open to interpretation and a variety of expressions are used about what it is to be a Hindu, or what constitutes a Muslim. Religious identity is often more than formal beliefs which distinguish a group: it includes the historical process by which a cohesive community of believers comes to be consolidated and reproduced through a mixture of texts, myths, rituals and symbols often under the direction of a religious leader (Oberoi 1994). Religion can also be used to help a community define itself and maintain its subculture, especially within a dominant cultural group. The centrality of family and places of worship influences identity and acts as a resistance to the erosion of religious boundaries, and serves to challenge the perceived secular and increasingly individualistic society. Within a faith-based school, individuals may feel a greater sense of association with the religious identity of their group than they would in what that group perceives as a secular or non-religious community school.

For some individuals and communities there is an overlap between religion and ethnicity in terms of identity and group loyalty. The importance of an 'ethnic-religious' identity (Young 1990) for different groups is particularly significant and can serve as a major force for political mobilization. Trying to categorize whether it is racial or religious identity which is the major descriptor further highlights the complexity of the situation (Weller et al. 2001), but for faith-based schools religious identity has become a dominant factor for providing community cohesion and mobilizing political activity especially in the struggle for public funding.

Whilst there is huge differentiation between and among religious groups, what is particularly striking today is the importance that religion plays in terms of personal identity (Modood et al. 1997), and how faith-based schools are being chosen by parents who see them as places providing compatibility between the religious values promoted in the home and those practised in schools. The fluidity and multiplicity of issues that communities are dealing with means that there is not a fixed or static sense of culture or religious identity (Giddens 2001), and there are multiple or hybrid senses of identity (Hall 1992) especially for the younger generation. However, members of some ethnic groups see themselves as culturally distinct, and in turn they are seen by the wider society as such. Diversity as espoused through government rhetoric is felt to be important enough to promote and embrace, yet communities fear loss of cultural identity through policies of assimilation and integration (Parekh 2000). Schools particularly are seen as the place where cultural and religious values come into play and identity may be undermined (Miller 2001; Sarwar 1994). It is this perceived undermining of religious identity which has provided the impetus for new groups, particularly those based on Islam, to establish their own schools. What unites rather than divides faith-based schools and their communities is that they all share a desire to perpetuate faith and this is often associated with cultural and linguistic heritage.

New faith-based schools have been established which reflect greater diversity in terms of race and ethnicity than previously experienced in England and Wales, and the role of parents has been central in securing what they see as an appropriate upbringing for their children. This is in the face of a perceived increase in secularization in mainstream society. Parents opt for faith-based schools which they see as the place where the curriculum can reflect and celebrate their cultural heritage and serve as a site for religious worship. They also struggle as a community to seek government recognition and financial support to offset the financial burden of paying school fees, as traditionally provided for schools of a religious character.

Organization of the Book

Throughout the book we argue that the emergence of new, state-funded, faith-based schools is an extension of the tradition afforded other schools established on a religious ethos. It would be unjust to continue to give primacy to those religions which have historically established schools and ignore new additions to the educational landscape which satisfy government criteria. Equality before the law requires equitable treatment for those faith-based schools that have been marginalized in the past by now providing equal access to state funding. Furthermore, the emergence of this new group presents challenges both within and outside the school communities.

To explore these themes in depth the book is organized as follows. This chapter provides a context for the book overall, and an introduction of the key issues and the question of appropriate nomenclature to describe the variety of 'faith-based schools' in England and Wales. Chapter 2 provides an historical perspective of the development of faith-based schooling, detailing the role of the clergy in establishing academic institutions based initially on a Christian ethos, and the subsequent growth in Jewish schools. We move on to highlight immigration and settlement patterns, the Diaspora or movement of peoples in the post-1960 era, and the introduction of new languages, cultures and religion among pupils and their families. Chapter 3 serves as a context, therefore, in which to examine the recent development of Muslim, Sikh and Greek Orthodox schools. International comparisons are also incorporated to see how issues are handled elsewhere, particularly with regards to the development of Muslim schools in the Netherlands and Australia. We then look more closely, in Chapter 4, at the idea of 'community, family and culture' in light of the continuing movement and displacement of populations, the basic right to religious freedom and the extension to choice of school based on religious convictions. Chapter 4 also highlights the alleged failure of the 'common school' to satisfy parent expectations and the increasing advocacy for minority rights in education.

Having established the historical and cultural context of faith-based schools, the next three chapters of the book focus on practical issues concerning legality, accountability and pedagogy. Chapter 5 looks at adaptations within new faith-based schools with regard to the legal framework in which they operate, and issues of accountability in terms of the recruitment of staff, admissions policy and government inspection. We also examine the case presently being promoted by some sections of the media and government, that faith-based schools are academically more successful than community schools, and look at the evidence to support this view. Curriculum matters are then explored in Chapter 6 with discussion of such issues as: the teaching of world religions within a mono-faith school; the inclusion of a Biblical interpretation of 'creationism' within science education; and the meaning of 'citizenship' for pupils who have a dual or multiple sense of cultural identity. These serve to highlight some of the controversies concerning education for children within faith-based schools.

An increasing emphasis has been placed on exploring educational policy, practice and discourse in the context of social justice and human rights. This has stimulated paradigm shifts challenging prevailing concepts of knowledge, children's rights and entitlement to education. There have also developed new and diverse ways of describing and analysing educational experience especially for religious and minority ethnic groups, and the issue of entitlement for pupils with special learning and educational needs. The availability of funding for new faith-based schools means the removal of parental fees and the potential for a more diverse student body to attend, some of whom may require extra support or statementing arrangements. Chapter 7 explores this issue of special needs within faith-based schools, and the requirement to accommodate a range of learning and behavioural needs within a broad understanding of diversity. This presents particular challenges to newly funded, faith-based schools which may not have experience in responding to such diversity of learning needs, nor of adhering to codes of practice concerning special educational needs.

Broader philosophical issues are explored in the penultimate chapter of the book concerning the expansion of faith-based schools, and the extent to which faith-based schools can be seen as leading to conflict rather than social harmony. This is particularly apposite in the light of continuing troubles in Northern Ireland, the September 11 terrorist attacks, the Bali bombings, civil disturbances in northern towns in England during 2001 and the siege in middle school No. 1, Beslan. These events highlight the fact that issues of religious identity, xenophobia and intolerance impact at a global, regional and local level, and that cultural diversity can lead to cultural conflict rather than social cohesion. Concern over segregation of children is explored here, and in particular the claims of 'ghettoized' education that promotes religion in a way that goes beyond exclusivity to that of 'propagandizing' and 'fundamentalism'. These issues lie at the heart of the debates concerning the expansion of faith-based schooling and the hostility shown towards religious communities by some sectors of the wider society. Finally the book ends with discussion of the implications for policy and practice as a result of the proposed expansion of faith-based schools, the role of community schools in responding to cultural difference and the challenges all schools face as they engage with issues of social justice in relation to their local community. If, for example, community schools are failing minority religious groups, is the only alternative the provision of separate faith-based schools, or is a different model of educational provision potentially more responsive to the reality of a multi-faith society?

Terminology

Before we move on to these discussions, it is important to look at the use of language and the shift in terminology, from denominational or church school to that of 'faith school'. Historically, the clergy were instrumental in initiating schooling based along denominational lines, as we shall see in Chapter 2, hence the descriptor 'denominational schools'. Under legislative change providing financial support from the state in 1870, these schools became known as 'voluntary aided' or 'voluntary controlled schools'. Similar terminology was used in the Education Act (1944), and until the turn of the 20th century the names 'voluntary' and 'church' school have been used interchangeably within government documents and in the literature. As a result of the historical development of schools in Britain, all schools incorporate an element of religious education, most notably during the 'collective acts of worship', but some schools are categorized as 'religious schools' and adhere to a particular religious ethos. In *The Way Ahead* (Archbishop's Council Church Schools Review Group 2001), commissioned by the Church Schools Review Group to discuss the future of these institutions, the terms 'church schools', and schools of a 'religious character', are how they are categorized.

The use of the term 'faith schools' to describe this group is of more recent vintage, having gained general currency. The government has declared support for the number and variety of schools within the state system supported by churches and 'other major faith groups' (Department for Education and Employment 2001a, p. 48). We believe that this shift in terminology and conceptualization is significant, suggesting a move to broadening and making more inclusive the potential range of groups reflective of different religious and philosophical traditions. However, 'faith schools' is a very imprecise term and whilst the expression has gained currency in the press, it is a convenient shorthand for a variety of schools: 'church', 'denominational', 'voluntary', 'voluntary aided', 'voluntary controlled', and 'foundation schools'. For the purpose of this discussion, therefore, we will be focusing on state-funded, faith-based schools which provide full-time education at primary and/or secondary level. We are also using the term 'faith-based school' as it more accurately conveys the political spirit of the time in which government is keen to see a growth of this type of school and greater inclusion of minority faith groups.

Chapter 2

Faith-Based Schooling: An Historical Perspective

Individuals may belong to a number of communities during their lifetime, such as family, kinship, school or state, and for some there is also one characterized by their religious belief.[1] For some people, two communities overlap in the form of religion and the choice of school, and decisions concerning membership of these groups are informed by the way in which they construct their lives. The relationship between Church and state has been instrumental in the historical development of public education in England and Wales, and schooling based on Anglican, Catholic and Jewish teachings has been with us for some time. It is important, therefore, to have an overview of this relationship in order to fully understand the contemporary debate concerning the emergence of new faith-based schools. In this chapter we provide an historical perspective of religious schooling in England and Wales, highlighting the role of the clergy in establishing academic institutions based on Christian and Jewish lines, and the use of government funds to support their development. This provides an important historical context in which to set the issue of religious education today and for understanding the present policy to further expand this category of school.

The objectives for the chapter are, therefore, to:

- provide an overview of the involvement of religious groups in the development of a national educational system in partnership with the state;
- highlight arrangements for state funding and the struggle for parity by different faith-based groups as they have established their own schools; and
- discuss the issue of differentiation within faith-based schools in terms of philosophies of education and community support.

We begin by looking at the origins of mass education and the role of the church in initiating formal education for all children.

Historical Context

Educational provision in England and Wales was established on denominational lines dating back to the Middle Ages and faith-based groups have continued to perpetuate this tradition. By the 19th century, major social and economic upheaval due to the direct consequences of the Industrial Revolution called for social policy enactment.[2] Education was considered an important agent of social reform to assist the nation in its economic endeavours. Government at this time was, however, somewhat ambivalent about its role in the provision of educational services. Further, the Victorians were deeply suspicious of government involvement in daily events and feared the growth of state intervention into what had, hitherto, been a purely private concern.[3]

Prior to 1850 what provision there was for educating the 'poorer classes'[4] was by virtue of the charity schools founded by such organizations as the British and Foreign School Society of 1810 and the National Schools established in 1811. The origins of popular education in this country are ensconced in these charity schools, formed as a direct consequence of the 18th and 19th centuries' 'Age of Philanthropy'. Throughout England and Wales the clergy initiated schooling as a means of carving out their evangelical crusade. The Society for the Propagation of Christian Knowledge, for example, attempted to recruit morally upstanding teachers, to assist in this mission. Similarly, teaching associations which flourished in the 1850s were often formed along religious lines, such as the Nottingham Churchmasters Association (Wardle 1976). Other groups were the Welsh Trust, the Gruffydd Jones' Circulating Schools, and the Sunday School Movement which sought to provide education for the children of the poor in their parishes (National Society 2003a). Whilst government began subsidizing education to a limited degree in the form of treasury grants in 1833, it did not assume the role of instigator for educational provision, and universal free schooling was not implemented until the following century.[5] Instead, different faith groups were instrumental in promoting education with a strong inculcation of religious values (Wolffe 1994) and they began a tradition in denominational schooling which has continued to the present day. Furthermore, when the state did choose to venture into providing education for all children, the clergy continued to have influence: indeed, education and Christianity were inextricably linked in the public mind (Tropp 1957).

It is important to note, however, that Church–state relations in matters concerning educational policy and practice has not meant the meeting of two monoliths acting either in conflict or in alliance (Grace 2002a). Rather it is a more complex manoeuvring of interest groups located within both the structures of the state and the Church. As we shall see with reference to Church of England, new Independent Christian, Catholic and Jewish schools, this relationship has been both mutually beneficial and at times acrimonious, especially when the matter of state funding has been involved.

Church of England Schools

The Church of England has been the Established Church of the country since the 16th century and has held a long-time commitment to education. Chadwick (2001) describes this as a balance between:

the 'general' or 'service' role, focusing on its position as the church of the nation and therefore interested in and committed to the education of all the nation's children; and the 'domestic' or 'nurture' role, encouraging pupils in their understanding of the Christian faith and their affiliation to their local Anglican parish communities. (p. 475)

Anglican schools – that is, those established by the Church of England and the Church in Wales – began to expand in the 19th century (Williams 1991; Lankshear 1996). For example, by 1830, 3 678 voluntary schools had been created by the Church of England but some Anglicans were concerned about the implications of accepting government aid. School inspectors were accepted only after the archbishops' veto over their appointment was negotiated for Anglican schools in the 1840 Concordat, a provision also extended to Catholic schools after 1870. (This issue of inspection and accountability will be discussed further in Chapter 5).

The Forster Education Act (1870) established board schools where there was insufficient elementary education. The relationship between the Church and the state took the form of protracted debates, and it was decided that in schools:

established by means of local rates, no catechism or religious formulary which is distinctive of any particular denomination shall be taught. [1870 Act, paraphrased in J. S. Hurt (1979), *Elementary Schooling and the Working Classes 1860–1918*, London: Routledge and Kegan Paul]

This principle, proposed by William Cowper-Temple, was replicated in further education Acts. Church of England schools were often, however, the only ones created in some geographical areas and this monopoly caused tension among the Nonconformists and Dissenters (Larsen 1999) who objected to their children being indoctrinated with the Anglican Catechism. (A similar objection was to be echoed by subsequent generations of parents such as those of the Jewish and Islamic faiths.) In the 19th century, over nine hundred Methodist schools had also been established as part of the wider mission of Churches to provide basic education, along with and sometimes in competition with other denominational schools.

It became apparent that the Church of England and other religious group schools could not be expected to fulfil the needs of a national system of education, and in 1902 the Balfour Act ensured that the new Local Education Authorities, by supporting church schools with local rates, would provide payment for all teachers from state funds. There was an outcry at the time over this, especially with regard to Catholic schools and what was termed 'Rome on the Rates'. Nonconformists, for example, preferred to go to prison rather than pay their rates (Chadwick 2001). Similarly, Methodist groups signalled their dissatisfaction with the ongoing arrangement for faith-based schools and Catholics and Jews felt excluded from 'Anglican Christianity' (Miller 2001). It was only with the Liberal government of 1906 that it was agreed that all state-funded schools should come under public control.

Legislation enacted in 1902 and 1906 established the concept of a voluntary denominational school maintained by government funding existing alongside newly created board schools, the forerunner of local authority county schools and what are today called community schools. This 'dual system' provided for the provision of state funding in order to supplement and assist existing 'confessional schools', that is, ones which promote one dominant religion or 'confession', and which had been established voluntarily by various church groups (Cush 2003). In Wales, for example, the Welsh Intermediate Education Act (1889) created local council schools, to supplement those created by such groups as the British and National Societies along the lines of the English educational system (Roberts and Williams 2003). A range of categories for denominational schools were designated in the Education Act (1944) with various levels of government control and were generally referred to as 'voluntary' schools.[6] It is important, at this juncture, to discuss the different categorizations because they have implications for such things as the level of community involvement in the governance of the school and the nature of religious education provided.

Lankshear (1996) describes a *voluntary* school as one within the state-maintained system which is owned or administered by an education trust, most of which are religious although some originate from secular organizations. The two most common categories are *voluntary controlled*, on the one hand, where the governors no longer provide any financial contribution for the maintenance of the school building, and the school is controlled by the Local Education Authority (LEA) which assumes responsibility for the employment of staff and the school's admissions policy. Further, the teaching of Religious Education (RE) is predominantly non-confessional and multi-faith, but the school ethos and worship are confessional (Cush 2003). *Voluntary aided* schools, on the other hand, provide for the governors to continue being responsible for the external maintenance of the school building and its improvements, with a government grant available towards the cost of the work. The Local Education Authority assumes responsibility for all other payments but the governors are the legal employers of the staff and assume responsibility for the admissions policy (Lankshear 1996). In this case, whilst most of the funding is provided by the state, Religious Education and school worship are 'conducted in accordance with the school's trust deeds' (ibid., p. 33). Funding for staff, building and maintenance was at 50 per cent of total costs in 1944, subsequently increased to 85 per cent, and is now set at 90 per cent as a result of proposals made in 2001 (Department for Education and Employment 2001a). This partnership now consists of links with the national government's Department for Education and Skills (DfES), upon whom schools are dependent for their capital funding, and with local government, (Local Education Authorities) for professional support. Over half of the Church of England schools opted to become voluntary controlled in status, and this in practice minimized their church links (Arthur 1995; Locke 2001).

Arrangements were also made for schools to be designated as having a *special agreement* which contains elements common within both aided and controlled schools. For example, the Local Education Authority may employ the staff, but school worship may be conducted according to the school trust deed. Presently this group constitutes a national total of around sixty-five in number (Department for Education and Skills 2003b). We discuss the legal implications of the different categories of schools later in Chapter 5, but mention should be made here of *City Technology Colleges*, which were established to promote science and technology (Gerwitz et al. 1991; Walford 1991), because there is some overlap with 'religious schooling'. These institutions, which currently number 14, receive a proportion of their funds from central government and from sponsors, usually companies from industry (Department for Education and Skills 2003b). Whilst not designated as faith-based schools or 'schools of a religious character', their sponsorship may result in them promoting a particular Biblical interpretation on certain curriculum matters which we shall explore later in Chapter 6. Overall, the state-funded faith-based schools today are categorized under the heading of voluntary aided, voluntary controlled or under special agreement as provided in the 1944 Education Act. The 1944 legislation is seen as the cornerstone of the partnership between the Church and state and as providing the safeguarding of arrangements for the establishment of a national network of viable schools at primary and secondary levels (Chadwick 2001; Francis and Lankshear 2001; Arthur 1995). Most importantly for this discussion, this statute which confirmed the status of voluntary schools did not specify religious affiliation or which denominational groups were to be included in the scheme. As such there were Jewish voluntary aided schools from this time and the door was open for other religious groups such as those based on an Islamic ethos to subsequently apply for funding, which we shall explore in the next chapter. Specific provisions for religious education were also contained in the Act. The school day was to begin with a collective act of worship, and every state-maintained school was to provide Religious Education according to a local authority agreed syllabus. Further, the subject was to have equal weighting with other subjects in the curriculum, and it could be taught at any time in the school day.

In the post-1960s era, notes Chadwick (2001), there was an increased interest in world religions, cults or traditions other than Christianity:

> in this 'anything goes' culture, the position of church schools came under attack for indoctrinating their pupils into the Christian faith and its morals, and appearing to select middle-class pupils with supportive parents as a result of using primarily church attendance criteria for admissions. (p. 480)

(This argument is still raised with regard to access to some Church of England schools, and we shall be returning to the issue of admissions policy later in Chapter 5.)

The Durham Report (1970) was important for what it said of the nature and purpose of the Church of England schools at this time, arguing forcefully for recognition of their historic contribution to the country's culture and traditions, and serving as an important document for shaping policy throughout the 1970s and

1980s. The document was also important for sharpening the distinction of the functions of these schools, that is, 'inward-looking' to equip children to take their place in the community, and 'outward-looking' in order 'to serve the nation through its children' (Francis and Lankshear 2001, p. 426). The 'service' model, says Chadwick (2001), caught the prevailing mood and church schools flourished:

> even in the more difficult 1980's when pupil numbers fell nationally, church schools generally worked with their LEAS to mitigate the problems of school closures. (p. 480)

During the Thatcher era, faith-based schools continued to be seen as part of a partnership, particularly as they appeared to fit into a market economy model of responding to client demand, and they assumed some element of independence and self-finance. This view was not, however, shared by all Anglicans. With the introduction of Grant Maintained (GM) status for schools, Church of England schools – which at this time represented 20 per cent of all schools – had to compete harder for limited finance available from central government. Other changes were brought about by the Education Reform Act (1988), which introduced a National Curriculum and meant that the Church of England also has to compete for its position in terms of religious education. We will be looking at the teaching of religion later in Chapter 6, but it is noteworthy that the Church of England, along with other groups, felt obliged to respond to what it saw as the undermining of the spiritual dimension of education in the nation's schools from secular proposals. A challenge was launched with the support of Roman Catholics and the Free Churches to safeguard the position of religious education in schools, and the result was an added provision that each locally agreed syllabus should:

> reflect the fact that the religious traditions in Great Britain are in the main Christian, whilst taking account of the teaching and practices of the other principal religions represented in Great Britain (Education Reform Act (1988), London: HMSO, ch. 40).

This had implications for voluntary controlled and community schools, but voluntary aided schools continue to provide Religious Education based on their trust deed. The new legislation made provision for the secular curriculum in faith-based schools to come under the system of national inspection, and RE and collective worship was to be assessed separately by inspectors with approval by the church community.

The influence of faith-based schools continues as the New Labour government promotes parental choice with what it sees as evidence of academic success in league tables. Ministers are interested in identifying the apparent ingredients for this successful 'ethos', and to 'bottle' them for other schools to emulate.[7] Some caution should be used when claims are made about academic success in Church of England schools, and those of other denominations, as this has been challenged on a number of grounds such as parental support and pupil selection, as we shall discuss later in Chapter 5, but the issue of school ethos has been cited as an important consideration (Judge 2002).

Between 1986 and 2002 there were 16 Education Acts and the partnership between Church and state has continued to develop through various reforms and changes (National Society 2003a), but the School Standards and Framework Act (1998) is noteworthy because it contains a number of provisions which bring faith-based school communities substantially into the decision-taking process. The Act created four categories of schools within the state system in England and Wales:

- Community schools (formerly County schools);
- Foundation schools (formerly Grant Maintained schools);
- Voluntary Aided schools; and
- Voluntary Controlled schools.

All community schools must implement the local Agreed Syllabus as a basis for religious education and may not have a 'religious character' (Jackson 2003b). Schools within the other categories may have a 'religious character' based on the school's trust deed or traditional practice. All schools which have a religious character, for example Church of England, may have a collective act of worship reflective of the religious group concerned, but only those designated voluntary aided may have denominational religious education, a point we will be exploring later in Chapter 6. This legislation also aims to make decisions a matter for collective agreement at both national and local levels for the Church to work in partnership with government.

In this favourable political climate, the Church of England has signalled its commitment to maintain and expand its involvement in education (Archbishop's Council Church Schools Review Group, 2001). The General Synod announced in 1998 that 'church schools stand at the centre of the Church's mission to the nation',[8] and this was followed by the establishment of a Church Schools Review Group in 2000 under Lord Dearing in order 'to review the achievements of Church of England schools and to make proposals for their development' (Archbishop's Council Church Schools Review Group 2001, p. 1). As noted in the introduction to our book, the Dearing Report has been influential in setting the agenda for the expansion of Church of England schools, particularly at secondary level where 100 more have been recommended. Traditionally, the Anglican presence has been significantly stronger at primary school level and so this expansion will help offset the imbalance in provision. There have also been proposals for the creation of new 'city academies' in socially disadvantaged areas in Haringey and Liverpool which are sponsored by the Church with financial assistance from local businesses and charitable trusts.

It would seem therefore that the partnership between church and state continues but, cautions Chadwick (2001), 'it would be wrong to suppose that the Church automatically has a permanent role in the education of the future' (p. 486): as demonstrated under the Thatcher era, the Church has felt alienated as a partner in the past. However, it has embraced the New Labour government's general offer of partnership to major faith groups to provide more schools where there is public demand (Department for Education and Employment 2001a). This comes at a time, however, when the Church of England is said to be facing a demise in church attendance, and a decrease in numbers attending Christian Sunday school (Gledhill 1998). The National Society, however, continues to support Christian education for Church of England and Church in Wales schools and to provide guidance in the running of these schools. Since the advent of the Welsh National Assembly, Church in Wales schools are subject to new government and legislative change concerning such things as assessment and curriculum content.

We should also note that within one faith tradition there are schools which reflect different philosophies about education. For example, notes Lankshear (1996), school governors may wish to make it explicit that the central commitment of the school is to provide a Christian education for the children of the members of the denomination. This view of 'Anglican schools for Anglican children' is, according to Brown (2003) in opposition to what he sees as:

> a long and honourable tradition whereby Anglicans have seen their church and clergy as serving the entire community. (p. 108)

Indeed, it is this long tradition of the Church of England and Church in Wales providing education, continues Brown, which has given it privileged access to parliamentary structures and the Establishment, and which gives the schools 'a distinctiveness about them', not shared by other faith-based schools (p. 103).

Another factor of importance in looking at the nature of these schools is the relationship between the church and the school and the amount of time and commitment it is able to offer to an academic institution. Lankshear (1996) adds that a church may also adopt an 'evangelical model' in which it leads acts of worship in the school. Importantly, it is precisely this issue concerning the purpose and ethos of the Church of England school which led to a number of new independent Christian schools being established in the 1970s and 1980s and which adds to the diversity of schooling in England and Wales within the Anglican Christian tradition.

New Christian Schools

The discussion so far has concerned the development of Church of England schools in general, but it would be a mistake to see Christian faith-based schools as a homogeneous group. As with other faith traditions, there is huge differentiation based in part on the interpretation of doctrine. In addition to the 4 800-plus state-funded Church of England institutions in 2003, for example, were are 57 Methodist schools, as well as a smaller number of Central Reform and Quaker institutions (Department for Education and Skolls 2003b). In some cases, dual denominations operate within one school, for example Methodist and Church of England (ibid.). There are also a number of new Christian schools which were established in the 1970s and 1980s as a result of dissatisfaction with the perceived secularism within schools. These schools have also been referred to as 'evangelical schools', but that is misleading as there are Church of England schools which are evangelical in character, a point we will return to later in this section.

Some of the new Christian schools sought government funding under the category of 'Grant Maintained Schools', introduced under the 1988 Education Reform Act. This made it possible for those schools wishing to opt out of local government control to instead be funded by central government. Along with a number of small schools, and Muslim pressure groups, the Christian Schools Campaign representing approximately sixty-five Christian schools attempted to use this legislation to 'opt in' to grant-maintained status. The Christian Schools Trust helped co-ordinate the efforts of some of these schools seeking state support as well as providing in-service teacher training and disseminating curriculum materials (Walford 1995a). They were influenced by policy in the Netherlands which has more generously allowed for state support of schools from a variety of religious and philosophical backgrounds (Dijkstra and Veenstra 2001).

The struggle of new Christian independent schools to receive state funding has been documented by Deakin (1989) who states that whilst the five thousand existing voluntary aided schools at the time provided a useful model of a school system based on a religious community, new Christian schools were established to reflect the wishes of parents. Multi-faith education was criticized as being a part of 'secular humanism' in schools which:

> waters down all the essential ingredients of all the faiths by reducing them to their behavioural and cultural phenomena, and avoiding questions of ultimate commitment. (ibid., p. 7)

Likewise, Walford (1995b) who conducted a survey of these schools states that they were set up by parents or groups dissatisfied with what they perceived as increasing secularization in the majority of schools. Further, they tend to share:

> an ideology of Biblically-based evangelical Christianity that seeks to relate the message of the bible to all aspects of present life whether personal, spiritual or educational. (Deakin, 1989, p. 7)

Walford quotes one parent in his study as saying:

> we believe in a Christ-centred curriculum ... We obviously have Christ and the Bible at the centre of home, and we want them to have the same at school. (Walford 1995b, p. 14)

The number of new Christian schools in the early 1990s was calculated to be nearly ninety and demand for places was 'in the light of evangelical Christianity being (at that time) one of the fastest growing religious groups in Britain' (ibid., p. 8). The exact number is difficult to calculate because of 'the lack of any strict definition of what should count as a new Christian school' (ibid.). Finally, part of the appeal to parents also lies in the stress placed on academic standards, which is a common theme in support for faith-based schools.

As a result of bureaucratic and legal hurdles, however, only 14 managed to achieve GM status (Walford 2001a), several of which were Catholic or Jewish, and they also included two Muslim schools which we will be discussing in the next chapter. These schools are now categorized as voluntary aided under the School Standards and Framework Act (1998). The reason for so few of these schools receiving funding was due in part to the tight financial criteria being applied at the time; some were very small in terms of pupil numbers, and some did not seek state funding.

Within the broad group of independent Christian schools formed since the 1970s there are about sixty 'Evangelical Christian' schools (Walford 2001a). They are run on the lines of strict interpretation of the Bible, and the Genesis version of Evolution. Pupil behaviour is an important part of the schooling that takes place and corporal punishment is seen as having a place in the upbringing of children. These newer centres of learning have on occasion been prepared to take their religious claims to the European Court of Human Rights despite the ban on the use of physical chastisement in any schools in England and Wales (Parker-Jenkins 1999a). Those schools which are independent institutions are not, however, governed by the National Curriculum directives and the legal requirements concerning the Literacy or Numeracy Hours. Conversely, those in receipt of state funding are legally obliged to teach the National Curriculum and we will be exploring this theme in greater detail in Chapter 6 with reference to the teaching of 'creationism'.

Within this new group of Christian schools there is a subgroup associated with the 'Accelerated Christian Learning' approach to teaching. In Walford's survey of new Christian schools, the number of these schools was given as 19, or 36 per cent. This teaching method is described as 'a highly standardized system of individualized instruction' originating from the United States (ibid., p. 22). Information, equipment and materials are supplied for a school to be set up using this approach, and pupils work at their own pace through a series of work packs, seated in separate cubicles which are 'designed to limit student interaction' (ibid.). The appeal of this programme lies in the availability of materials and support to establish a school 'at low cost', and the fact that there is 'little or no teaching experience required by those adults in charge' (ibid.). However, criticism has been levelled at some of these schools through Ofsted reports concerning such things as the lack of resources, a stimulating environment or adequate accommodation (ibid., p. 21). This, states Walford, accounts for the fact that the majority of schools have tended not to adopt this teaching approach.

The new Christian independent schools also differ significantly in terms of governance and admissions. Some schools have an open door policy for pupils, as we noted earlier in this chapter, whilst others cater specifically for children of Christian parents. Some of the schools feel the need to have affiliation with a church body for guidance and support, whilst others see parents as the school managers (Walford 1995b; Deakin 1989). Many of these schools established since 1970 have, notes Walford (1995b), faced financial difficulties forcing them to close, and others have lacked organizational support to promote their interests. He adds that they tend to charge low fees according to the parents' ability to pay, and as their financial situation is often precarious they survive on 'faith'. (In the next chapter we will see a similar pattern in the development of Muslim schools during the same period.) However, the new Christian independent schools, continues Walford, are the result of a grass-roots movement in education stemming from the belief that education is the responsibility of the parent and the Church, and not that of the state.

The new Christian schools also reflect the diversity within the Anglican tradition, and can be seen as an extension of the values of the home (Deakin 1989; Crick 2002). For example, the black immigrant members of the Seventh Day Adventist Church in Greater London, who were predominantly from the West Indies, wanted an educational setting for their children which reflected their beliefs and values as a community (Kapitzke 1995; Valley 1995; Howard 1987). As such the John Loughborough School was established with church leadership and parental support in response to this demand, and it has subsequently been successful in securing state funding (Department for Education and Skills 2003b). As we shall see later in Chapter 4, the heavy influx of immigrants to Britain in the 1950s and 1960s brought in groups of people with a variety of backgrounds, and this created a challenge to existing Church of England schools to adequately accommodate religious as well as cultural difference. Conversely, Walford's 1995 survey highlights an independent Christian school run by a Christian staff in which 90 per cent of the pupils are from Muslim, Sikh and Hindu families who are supportive of the institution and the religious ethos it has created.

Diversity within schools in terms of educational philosophies and student composition is also evident in the establishment of Catholic schools in England and Wales, as we shall see next.

Catholic Schools

There is a shared history between Catholic and Church of England schools, particularly as regards the increasing involvement of the state in developing a national system of education, and the impact of legislative change, as previously noted. Here the discussion will focus on the specifics concerning the history of Catholic schools and the relationship between the Catholic Church and the state.[9]

As with the Church of England, the Catholic Church was instrumental in establishing schools in England and Wales. The major purpose of the Catholic Church in voluntarily establishing schools was to induce children into the faith. Matters of curriculum and staffing policy were considered of major importance, and as such, through legislative provision which we discussed earlier, 'aided status' became the norm for Catholic schools since this allowed them greater freedom from government interference. Grace (2001) adds:

> between the 1870's and the 1970's, despite initial anti-Catholic prejudice, the Catholic hierarchy was able to negotiate a favourable educational settlement in which substantial public funding was obtained without loss of autonomy and mission integrity for the Catholic school system. (p. 489)

These negotiations were guided by three prevailing principles which the Catholic Church was keen to retain: doctrinal integrity, religious management and the importance of Episcopal jurisdiction on educational matters (ibid.). Historically, financial support was also a concern in the establishment of these schools:

> a central issue in extending Catholic schooling to every Catholic child and young person in England and Wales was the struggle to obtain government grants for Catholic schools on a scale which matched those available to Church of England schools. (ibid., pp. 490–91)

Grace adds that compared with many Catholic systems of schooling internationally, the Catholic Church of England and Wales was able to obtain a very favourable educational settlement with the state from the 1870s to the 1970s. Financially this included support for new school buildings, which rose from 50 per cent of total costs in 1936 to 85 per cent in 1975, and the state also met the running costs of all maintained Catholic schools. Importantly:

> after the 1944 Education Act, the Catholic Church, through its educational agency, the Catholic Education Council, enjoyed partnership status with the Church of England, the Local Education Authorities and the state in educational decision-making at national and local levels. (ibid., p. 491)

The significance of this period in the development of Catholic schools in Britain is also noted by O'Keefe (1999) who maintains:

> for the Catholic Church, in its educative role, it signified a shift from the margins of educational endeavour towards a more pivotal role in an enhanced partnership with the state in a publicly funded education system. (p. 224)

Catholic schools were able to offer an education with a Catholic ethos, supported by a curriculum which reflected Catholic values, an admissions policy which gave priority to Catholic children, and the recruitment of staff who practised the faith. As such Catholic primary and secondary schools with voluntary aided status became integrated into the British system and were not associated with the concept of private fee-paying educational provision which has characterized Catholic school education in the USA and elsewhere.[10] This is a particularly important point given the Catholic Church's mission to the poor, a client base which was once mainly Irish Catholic (Hickman 1995; O'Keefe 2000) but which is now more ethnically diverse, for example as a result of refugees settling in England and Wales after the Second World War (Marzec 1988).

It would be a mistake, however, to think that Catholic schools did not have to struggle to gain parity of treatment with Church of England schools or escape criticism during their development. Grace (2001) notes, for example, the historical representations of Catholic schooling as being indoctrinatory and socially divisive. (We will be returning to this theme later, in Chapter 8, with reference to the proposed expansion of faith-based schooling in general.) However, once the concept of funding Church of England schools was established, a precedent had been set to justify extending this funding arrangement to Catholic schools as part of the 'Dual System' of state and church established in 1870, as we noted earlier. Accordingly:

> the privileged role of the Church of England as the Established Church meant that it was the major provider of church schooling and the major recipient of government grants. The strategy adopted by the Catholic bishops was to focus upon the extent of differential funding of Anglican schools compared with Catholic schools. (ibid., p. 492).

Greater equality in provision was achieved as a result of a reduction in prejudice towards Catholic schools, and an increase in the political power of Catholic voters. Catholic communities in England and Wales also financially supported the growth of their schools and:

> especially in the 20th century, the negotiations of the Catholic hierarchy with the elected government of the day were backed by a mutual understanding that behind the bishops' requests for more funding and autonomy for Catholic schools was the Catholic vote. (ibid., pp. 492–3)

(Similarly, the New Labour party solicited the Muslim vote in the build-up to the General Election in 1987, and they in turn looked to the Blair government to make good on its electoral promises and provide government funding for Muslim schools, as we shall see in the next chapter.) By not ignoring the importance of the Catholic voter, or the leadership of the Catholic Church, the state agreed an educational settlement between the 1870s and the 1970s in which public funding was obtained without loss of religious integrity by Catholic schools.

This situation was not replicated in the 1980s and the 1990s when there were policy struggles with the Conservative governments as experienced by the Church of England schools, which we noted earlier. A series of Education Acts between

1980 and 1996 were passed which reflected the fact that the cornerstone of the new political settlement was the market economy (Dale 1989). Again the issue of religious education within a National Curriculum was raised and this was seen by the Catholic community as 'weakening the mission integrity of the system (Grace 2001, p. 494). Government policy at this time was seen as limiting the scope and authority of the Catholic Church in making a contribution to education. The Conservative governments between 1979 and 1994, argues Arthur (1995), eroded the historic rights and responsibilities which had been acknowledged and were continued within the Education Act (1944). This was also exacerbated by the introduction of Grant Maintained schools, which were seen as privileging some schools and weakening Local Education Authorities. Grace says that although this category of school has now been abolished by the New Labour government, the issue has considerable importance in any analysis of Church–state relations regarding educational policy, and the Catholic Church was very active in its lobbying against this development.

In the post-Vatican 11 period, the Catholic school system has a mission of social justice and common good, a moral dimension shared by other groups who reject the image of faith-based schools as being segregated and inward looking.[11] The change in approach to social and religious formation, and the emphasis upon commitment to the common good, within Catholic schooling have been noted in research carried out in the UK by Hornsby-Smith (2000), O'Keefe (1997) and Paterson (2000). Also, a similar pattern in the development of Catholic education has been documented by O'Sullivan (1996) and Feheney (1999) in Ireland, and Flyn and Mok (1998) in Australia. Within the English context, Grace (2002a) conducted research of Catholic schools in Liverpool, Birmingham and London and maintains that post-Vatican 11 Catholic schooling has undergone a considerable transformation, particularly with regard to educational processes, the personal autonomy of pupils, and its relationship with other faiths and wider communities. He concludes that although it is a faith-based system it is entirely compatible with the principles of a liberal education, and a democratic and socially caring society.

As we saw earlier, there are differences within as well as between faith-based schools, and this is also reflected within Catholic schools. O'Keefe (2000) identifies three models of Catholic schools in responding to pluralism today, distinguishing between 'catechesis', 'religious education' and 'evangelization'. (We discuss these themes later in Chapter 6).

We can also describe difference among and within religious school communities, using factors such as ethnicity and socio-economic background. Current debates about faith-based schools tend to suggest that ethnicity lies only within Muslim and Sikh schools but there is also a tradition of ethnic diversity within Catholic schools. O'Keefe highlights the Catholic Church's mission to educate the poor, who were initially of Irish Catholic background, but by the 1970s and 1980s Catholic schools were having to respond to a diversity of cultures within their school communities. In 1986, for example, Cardinal Hume's Advisory Group on the Catholic Church's 'commitment to the black community', raised the need to challenge racist attitudes and to implement programmes to develop mutual respect for different cultural and ethnic groups within Catholic schools, and the wider community. Similarly, in its analysis of Ofsted reports relating to Catholic schools, the Catholic Education Service (1996) argued that in terms of cultural development of their pupils there was a need to fully integrate pupils from other cultures into the life of the school community. An overlapping issue has been that of responding to the needs of children from deprived socio-economic backgrounds. O'Keefe (2000) states that the poor are 'heavily represented now among ethnic minority groups of diverse religious and cultural backgrounds' (p. 130). This is illustrated in a study by the Department for Catholic Education and Formation involving 27 Catholic secondary schools within some of the poorest areas in Britain, in which it was reported that, in a quarter of the schools, children from ethnic backgrounds accounted for 30–70 per cent of the pupil population (Catholic Education Service 1997).

O'Keefe adds that there is considerable variation in the response of Catholic schools to this issue of diversity within the pupil population. Some Catholic schools, she notes, have widened their admissions criteria for pragmatic reasons, often due to falling rolls, but they have not necessarily adjusted their practice, and instead they have tended to pursue a policy of assimilation within the school. Alternatively, a small number of Catholic schools have, in accepting children of other faiths, taken a principled decision to develop policies in response to the reality of a more diverse pupil population. So, within Catholic schools, we can talk about cultural diversity within the Catholic pupil body, and within the Catholic school itself. *The Catholic Schools and Other Faiths Report* (Catholic Education Service 1997) acknowledges the tension which can exist for Catholic schools on this matter, and suggests that there can be different valid approaches used by Catholics in different parts of the country. Three approaches are recognized: to offer 'hospitality' to Sikh, Hindu and Muslim children whose parents are seeking a faith environment for their children's education; to see Catholic schools as 'servants' to the local community and at the service of other religious communities, particularly in socio-economically deprived areas as we noted above; and thirdly, to see such schools as a place for 'encounter, dialogue and partnership' between the Catholic community and other religious groups.

As a consequence of the increasing heterogeneity of pupils in Catholic schools in the last few decades, there has been wide debate as to what is the appropriate role of Catholic schools (O'Keefe 2000; Zipfel 1996). The difference of opinion ranges from those who fear that to open up Catholic schools to non-Catholics is to run the risk of undermining the character of the school (Kelly 1986), to those who feel that it is possible for Catholic schools to be seen as witnessing to Catholic educational values in a new and innovative way (McLaughlin 1996). O'Keefe (2002) concludes that:

Catholic schools, true to their highest ideals, are well placed to offer an education rooted in a vision ... which transcends religious, ethnic and cultural groups. (p. 132).

This forms part of the challenge facing Catholic schools, which, like Church of England schools, are having to redefine themselves and their mission within and beyond the school community (Catholic Education Service 1998, 1999, 2000; Conroy 1999; Longmore et al. 2000).

As well as this adaptation by some Catholic schools to accommodate non-Catholics, such institutions are also perceived as providing high academic attainment, as are other faith-based schools. (We will explore this point in more detail in Chapter 5.) Moreover:

> the fact that the British Prime Minister and his wife have committed their children to the Catholic schooling system has brought added status to the whole enterprise. (Grace 2001, p. 497)

Today in the UK there are over two thousand Catholic schools, which stand alongside Church of England schools as a central feature of faith-based schools,[12] accommodating 9.8 per cent of children of school age (Lankshear 2003). Oona Stannard, Director of the Catholic Education Service, rejects the idea that Catholic schools are not inclusive and maintains that they are very much reflective of the areas in which they are situated (Stannard 2001, CES 2003).

Statistically, the next largest faith group which has established schools in England and Wales is that based on Judaism, which we look at next in terms of the efforts of communities to provide education for their children, and the changing notion of religious pluralism within the educational system.

Jewish Schools

The Jewish education system in the UK can be traced back to the mid-17th century, when day schools were established along with synagogues. This followed the readmittance of Jews into England in 1656 (Romain 1985), and the early establishment of Jewish day schools, notably the Creechurch Lane 'Talmud Torah School' in 1657, and the 'Gates of Hope School' in 1664 (Black 1998). The importance of education within the Jewish tradition goes back much further, however:

> when Jacob and his family journeyed to Egypt, his son Judah was sent on ahead to establish a house of training. (Genesis 46:28)

As we saw earlier in the chapter, there was an urgent demand to meet the need for an educated workforce in the 18th and 19th centuries, and the establishment of Jewish schools such as the 'Jews Free School' in 1732 helped to respond to this call (Black 1998). The National Society (1811) and the Christian Sunday School Movement, also noted earlier, opened schools close to the early Jewish settlements. As a result, within some Jewish communities:

> there was great concern that these children would be at risk of losing their Jewish heritage and identity, through compulsory study of Christianity and the New Testament. (Miller 2001, p. 502)

Such was the perceived threat of missionary zeal by Anglicans that by 1850 Jewish schools were established in all areas across the country where there were Jewish communities. Financial support was not automatic, however, as the government of the day was not persuaded that 'the religious requirements of the Jewish schools closely matched their own' and so state funding was withheld, as it had been initially withheld from Catholic schools (ibid., pp. 508–509).

Changes were brought about by the work of a pressure group under the leadership of Sir Moses Montefiore to gain a share in the grants awarded to denominational schools, with provisors based on the daily teaching of the Old Testament and government inspection. As a result:

> in 1853, the Manchester Jews' School received state funding, putting the Jewish schools on an equal basis, for the first time, with other denominational schools. (ibid.)

Where Jewish pupils were in attendance in non-Jewish schools, their parents were free to withdraw their children from Religious Education classes, as they are still able to do today.

A wave of immigration from the 1880s to the First World War resulted in large numbers of Jews arriving from Eastern Europe. This contributed to an increase in the community to around a hundred thousand Jews living in England, which carried with it obvious implications for the education system (Miller 2001). The influx helped sustain pupil numbers in the Jewish voluntary schools and in some cases caused an increase. For example, the Jews Free School rose in pupil numbers from 2 500 in 1870 to around four thousand in 1900 (Gartner 1960; Black 1998). The Local Education Authority 'Board School' also saw an increase in pupil numbers, and in some cases, such as Castle Street School in the East End of London which was heavily populated by Jewish communities, 95 per cent of the student body in 1883 were of the Jewish faith.[13] (Interestingly, the very areas of immigration of the Jews, for example the East End of London, are the same areas which are now heavily populated by Muslim children, mirroring the pattern of immigration and the composition of community schools.[14])

The balance increasingly shifted away from attendance at Jewish voluntary schools to the Board Schools. For example, in 1880, nearly 60 per cent of Jewish school-age children were in Jewish schools (Black 1998), but by 1894 the number was under 50 per cent, and by 1911 there were less than 25 per cent (Miller 2001). This demise can be encapsulated by the fact that, by 1945, 'only 2 of the 7 State aided Jewish schools that had existed in London were still functioning' (ibid., p. 503). Ironically, whilst the Jewish education system in Britain had reached a low point in terms of Jewish education during the Second World War – only 20 per cent attending full-time Jewish schools – the Jews in Britain constituted 'the only intact surviving Jewish community in Europe' (ibid., p. 504). Assimilation rather than integration became more prevalent:

> Judaism became something that happened at home – maybe through the marking of the Sabbath and major festivals … as well as keeping the Jewish dietary laws, and the supplementary schools were increasingly expected to provide a Jewish education which had decreasing connection to the lives that the pupils were in practice leading outside the Synagogue classes. (ibid., p. 505)

As we saw earlier, the 1944 Education Act continued the practice of providing state aid for faith-based schools, but British Jewry failed to capitalize on the situation. The reason for this demise in Jewish schools was due in part to the ideology and process of integration, which was seized upon by many Jews and other immigrants as a way out of poverty. As such:

> acceptance of the Jewish children into an Anglicised way of life meant far more than learning how to speak English. It also included teaching the young people to adapt to English usage in speech and in manner, in culture and in principles, in such a way as to enable them to integrate successfully into the wider English community. (ibid., 2001, p. 503)

'Pride in being Jewish' and the adherence to Jewish traditions and practices were still encouraged, often through 'chedarim' or supplementary schools taking place in synagogues and classes attached to Board Schools, which were often funded by Jewish philanthropists. The system of 'supplementary' education has existed alongside day schools and different ethnic groups have used this system as a way of maintaining their own cultural heritage.[15] For Jewish children, this tended to take the form of classes three or four times a week with lessons in Hebrew, Yiddish and Jewish knowledge. (When we look at the development of Muslim education in the next chapter we will see a replication of this approach with the use of the mosque for instruction in Arabic and the Islamic way of life.)

Shifting demographic patterns and reduced family size also contributed to the decrease in the number of Jewish children attending Jewish day schools. By 1939, 'the entire pupil population of the Jewish day schools in Britain had dropped to below 3,000' (Miller 2001, p. 504). After the war, efforts were made by the Joint Emergency Council for Jewish Religious Education to organize supplementary education across the country. Statistically, 360 centres had been established by 1942 accommodating 10 500 pupils and this number was augmented by the Progressive Jewish movements which co-ordinated a separate system for over two thousand children (ibid.). The Reform Synagogues for Great Britain, the Masorti, and the Union of Liberal and Progressive Synagogues are generally known by the umbrella term 'Progressive Movements', as opposed to Orthodox or ultra orthodox (Miller and Shire 2002). As such it would be more correct to talk about different Jewish communities which provide support for the development of a range of Jewish faith-based schools. Due to immigration, there is also now a rich cultural heritage from different European communities, most notably the Ashkenazi (European Jews) and the Sephardi (Middle Eastern Jews), and major Jewish centres established in London, Leeds, Birmingham and Glasgow reflect this cultural diversity (Schmool and Cohen 1998).

The development of a Jewish identity is today supported by the role of the 'shul' or synagogue, the 'chedarim' or supplementary school, and Jewish day schools, both independent and state-funded. Research has demonstrated the importance of these influences on families, whether from Orthodox or Progressive communities, in interpreting the process of nurture in the Jewish tradition (Diamant and Cooper 1991; Jackson 1997). As with many faiths there are differences in interpretation and adherence to religious texts, and communities can loosely be placed on a spectrum from what can be called 'Orthodox' to 'Liberal'.[16] In terms of Jewish school communities, our research revealed a slightly different set of descriptors, ranging from 'ultra Orthodox', to 'Liberal/Progressive', with a group in the middle identifying themselves as 'modern Orthodox' and/or Zionist. Where individuals and communities position themselves on this spectrum is governed in part by the test of adherence to the 'halacha' or the rules. In terms of schools, therefore, the question 'what is a Jew?' is as important a question as 'what is a Jewish school?' Once you establish the former, you people the institution accordingly. Judaism is passed down from parents and there is an 'Orthodox' interpretation of Jewish identity (Klein 1979; Trepp 1980). For some, the religious background of the mother is pivotal to the bestowing of a Jewish identity, and having a non-Jewish parent does not take this away.[17] The Liberal Jewish movement, however, maintains that Jewish status can be passed through either parent. The ethos of Jewish schools reflect this orthodox/liberal continuum, with the North West London Jewish Day School, for example, describing itself as 'modern orthodox', and the Akiva Primary School as 'Progressive'.[18] The common link between them, regardless of nomenclature, is their commitment to Judaism, which is promoted through the choice of curriculum.

Support for more Jewish schools came from the Jewish Educational Trust. This was spearheaded in 1971 by Chief Rabbi of the United Synagogue, Lord Jakobovits, with the aim of raising the profile of Jewish education within its own community (Sacks 1994). Two new schools were built in the 1970s, and funds for teacher training were raised. Numbers have increased in recent times and statistically it is calculated that there are now over two hundred and fifty supplementary and day schools altogether (Schmool and Cohen 1998), 90 of which provide full-time education (*Times Education Supplement* 2003g) and 32 are in receipt of voluntary-aided funding (Department for Education and Skills 2003b). In their study of Jewish institutions, Schmool and Cohen (2000) reported there were nine Reform day schools, seven Zionist, 24 Strictly Orthodox and 70 mainstream Orthodox (p. 21). Miller and Shire (2002) give the number of primary day schools supported by Reform, Liberal and Masorti movements as three, which accounts for 5 per cent of Jewish children in day schools, and there are in addition nine nursery schools supported by these groups. These schools differ considerably, however, in their engagement with other religious communities and other faith-based schools. Short (2003) conducted a study of the way Jewish schools approach cultural diversity. He found that at primary level, particularly among those schools established by the Progressive rather than the Orthodox communities, there was a willingness to engage in multicultural issues and to teach about other faiths. Conversely, at secondary level he reported that only one out of the five schools in the study incorporated multicultural education and the teaching of other faiths with any degree of seriousness. Rather the focus was on instilling knowledge about the Jewish tradition and the nurturing of a Jewish identity and consciousness. A number of reasons for the resurgence of support for Jewish education are given by writers in this field, such as the needs to counteract the trend of assimilation and influences of the wider society; to ensure a strong basis of learning in the Jewish tradition; and to offer an alternative to other local options, providing a high academic level of education (Miller 2001). This development has been supported by philanthropic efforts resulting in the establishment of a National Jewish Agency (later replaced by the United Jewish Israel Appeal) aimed at raising the level and profile of Jewish education in Britain (ibid.). Along with other faith-based groups in Britain at the end of the 20th century, such as those based on Islam, there has been an increase in day school attendance. In 1975, approximately eleven thousand children aged 4–18, received full-time Jewish education, and by 2000 the number had increased to 22 650, representing 55 per cent of the total number of Jewish children in the UK (Rocker 2000).

There has also been a growing conviction by Jewish communal and education leaders that the continuity of Jewish life is dependent on the perpetuation of intensive Jewish education (Miller 2001; Schmool and Cohen 1998). Full-time Jewish education is seen as having the advantage of 'thickening' (Alexander 1995) or intensifying links with Judaism. As such, enculturation into Judaism and the possibilities for 'thick' Judaism to occur are vastly increased and children may leave primary and secondary school with 'a strong sense and secure understanding of who they are in Jewish terms and how they relate to both the Jewish and secular worlds' (Miller 2001, p. 507). Other groups also cite this factor in explaining the increase in support for faith-based schooling: that is, a desire by parents to provide for their children a strong foundation of religious identity, which they believe cannot be carried out within a community school. Furthermore, supplementary schooling was found to be inadequate to sustain and perpetuate religious heritage, a point also noted by Schiff (1988) with reference to the Jewish community in New York. Along with this there is the desire to strengthen links with synagogues and other Jewish communities, and to prevent what Chief Rabbi Jonathan Sacks (1994) refers to as the loss of an integrated Jewish life due to the trends of assimilation. Collective action was, therefore, used to challenge and counteract what was seen as the prevailing trend towards assimilation, and to prevent 'deculturalization' or loss of cultural identity. As such, Jewish schools are now chosen by some Jewish parents because they are seen as promoting 'a strong sense of who they are as Jews and how they relate to both the Jewish and secular world' (Miller and Shire 2002, p. 3). When we look at the growth of Muslim schools in the next chapter, we will see a mirroring of this desire to retain religious identity, and parental dissatisfaction with community schools in terms of school ethos and academic standards.

As with Anglicans and Catholics, the Jewish community has experienced periods of tense relations with the government, such as during the Thatcher era, but there has of late been both a resurgence in support for Jewish schools and a more positive relationship with the state. This has been instrumental in the development of the Jewish school phenomenon, notes Miller, and the opportunity to provide a Jewish ethos within a day-school context. For example, in Jewish schools there is scope within the curriculum for the teaching of Hebrew, the centrality of Jewish texts, life cycle, festivals and 'shabbat' prayer, values and knowledge about Israel. There is also a general aim to encourage academic excellence, and in some schools there is comparative religious education, and exchange programmes with different faith traditions, although this varies according to the nature of the Jewish school as we discussed earlier. (The issue of teaching other faiths within a mono-faith school is discussed later in Chapter 6.) One governing principle is that:

> pupils, parents and staff all learn in an environment that holds 'tikkun olam' – concern for the betterment of all society – as one [of] its highest aspirations thus contributing to British life in general and Jewish life in particular. (ibid., p. 6)

The 'secular' curriculum in state-aided Jewish schools embraces the National Curriculum, whilst apportioning some percentage of the day to Jewish Studies and Hebrew. Single-sex instruction for physical education and sex education may take place, as it does in many community schools. Importantly, curriculum such as sex education is usually taught acccording to the principles of 'sneeut', or modesty. (Similar issues concerning choice of curriculum governed by levels of decency are also part of the Muslim school ethos, as we shall see in the next chapter.) Interestingly, policy on admissions is often based on Orthodox or Liberal interpretations of the faith which we highlighted above, and some Jewish schools see 'inclusion' in terms of providing access to all Jewish children and converts, such as that furnished by the 'Pluralistic' schools. Conversely, the King David School in Manchester is only 30 per cent Jewish in terms of pupil composition, according to its 2003 Inspection Report, due to a dwindling Jewish population in that location. (Policy on admissions to faith schools and government inspection will be explored in more detail in Chapter 5.)

Jewish institutions are open to scrutiny and accountability: assessment is from inside in the form of a 'pikuach' inspection conducted through the Jewish community and in keeping with the Education Act (1988) governing religious as opposed to secular inspection. As such, Jewish schools are subject to the same rigour of inspection through Ofsted as other schools. In addition, the Jewish Studies curriculum is inspected through 'pikuach', to comply with government regulations. The Board of Deputies of British Jews produced a framework on explicit Jewish values of the school (Miller 2001). Felsenstein (2000) notes the general improvement in the inspection of Jewish schools, but, as with other educational institutions, there have been instances of less than favourable reports.[19] It is argued that children educated within a voluntary aided Jewish school have a greater exposure to a sustained Jewish education, but not all the teachers are of the Jewish faith (Miller 2001). As we shall see in the next chapter, the same situation exists in the staffing of Muslim schools, where there is often a reliance on non-Muslim teachers, who normally have faith or who are sympathetic to faith-based schooling.

There is a perception that Jewish full-time schools excel academically, as other faith-based schools are said to, and again the reason for this is far from simple, but tends to be rooted in issues of pupil selection and parental support. (We explore these issues in greater detail in Chapter 5.) Recent government initiatives that are potentially useful to Jewish communities in the further development of their schools include the School Standards and Framework Act (1998), which provides for new educational establishments of 'a religious character', and the Green Paper (Department for Education and Employment 2001a), which, we noted in the previous chapter, indicates a positive policy towards the development of faith-based schools of all denominations, and therefore the opportunity for the establishment of more Jewish schools.

As Jewish day schools continue to develop, they face challenges in adapting to a fast-changing political, social and educational environment (Valins, Kosmin and Goldberg 2001), and responding to the needs of pupils, their communities and the wider society. Another challenge vital to the further development of Jewish schools is the question of relevant curriculum materials, and, in particular, adequate teacher training. In the past Jewish schools have experienced similar difficulties as other faith-based schools in recruiting and retaining qualified staff of their faith. The increasing demand for Jewish schooling will mean that teacher training will be a central feature of the strategy to promote Jewish identity and to professionalize Jewish education to ensure cultural continuity (Valins, Kosmin and Goldberg 2001). The Leo Baeck College – Centre for Jewish Education, for example, is attempting to respond to this need and trains rabbis and teachers, providing courses in Hebrew, Jewish studies and curriculum development, and postgraduate courses in Jewish Education offered in conjunction with London Metropolitan University.[20]

Present-day support for Jewish schooling suggests that these institutions will flourish and continue to be part of the educational system. They have been established through the procedure of obtaining voluntary aided status following the traditional pattern afforded Church of England and Catholic schools, and they face similar challenges in maintaining their position and in choosing to expand. As we have seen there have been shifting trends and levels of commitment to the concept of full-time Jewish education, affected by demographic patterns, the perceived inadequacy of supplementary education and concerns about assimilation into a British Christian society. However, Jewish schools report specific problems concerning anti-semitic violence and vandalism. The Community Security Trust, which monitors anti-semitism, has requested that address details of Jewish schools are not placed in the public domain as, for example, through online inspection reports (*Times Educational Supplement* 2003g). As we shall see in the next chapter, other faith-based schools, such as those based on an Islamic ethos, have also experienced hostile reactions from the wider community.

At this point it is useful to consider, historically, the shifting nomenclature used to describe these schools based on a religious doctrine, highlighted in the introduction to the book, as new groups become part of the educational landscape.

From 'Denominational' to 'Faith-Based Schools'

In the discussion so far we have seen how the clergy have been instrumental in initiating schooling based on denominational lines, hence the descriptor 'denominational schools'. Under the legislative change of 1870, religious groups could not afford to meet the educational needs of the country, and voluntary aided or voluntary controlled schools were given financial assistance from the government based on Anglican, Catholic and Jewish lines, as noted throughout the chapter. Similarly, this terminology was used in the 1944 Education Act, and confirmed in the 1988 Education Reform Act. Up until the 21st century, the terms 'voluntary' or 'church' school have been used interchangeably but they are not synonymous: there are a few voluntary schools that are not religious foundations, and there have been some voluntary aided Jewish schools since 1944, as we saw earlier. Another description is a school of 'religious character', clarified in the School Standards and Framework Act (1998) as an institution which has at least one governor representative of the interests of the religious group concerned, and which has school premises operating for the benefit of the religious group or is providing education according to the tenets of the faith group.

The use of the term 'faith schools' has gained currency since the report 'Schools Building on Success' (Department for Education and Employment 2001a), as we highlighted in the previous chapter, which declared its support for 'the number and variety of schools within the state system supported by the churches and other major *faith groups*' (p. 48, emphasis added). This shift in terminology and conceptualization is significant because it suggests a broadening of groups beyond those of the Christian and Jewish tradition, to other major religious traditions such as those based on Islam and Sikhism. Moreover, the move to broaden the potential scope for other groups, such as new religious movements, through a more inclusive nomenclature reflects the political spirit of the time and the government's unwavering support of this category of schools of a religious character. The shift in terminology is also consistent with the ideas of theologians and academics such as Smith (1978), who in deconstructing the concepts of 'religion' and 'religions', argues that they are 'confusing, unnecessary and distorting' (p. 50), and prefers instead 'faith' and 'tradition', which are seen as better tools to explain the spiritual dimension of life. Although not without its critics, this conceptualization has gained both political and academic support.

Further, in defining what we mean by a 'faith-based school' that description offered by the Humanist Philosopher's Group is a useful starting point, as an institution which:

> intentionally encourages its pupils to have a particular religion and which regards such encouragement as a significant part of its mission. (Humanist Philosophers' Group 2001, p. 8)

Faith-based schools are often governed by an admissions policy selecting predominantly those who follow or who are supportive of their doctrines and are normally funded in part by a religious organization. Importantly:

> the *defining* feature of religious schools ... is that they attempt to instil particular religious beliefs in their pupils. (ibid.)

Another way of describing this function is that of 'religious nurture' as opposed to 'religious education'. Hull (1984) explains this distinction as religious education being non-dogmatic, and religious nurture being the transmission of religious culture from one generation to another. So, looking back at this historical perspective on the development of schooling in England and Wales, voluntary aided and voluntary controlled schools would normally provide religious nurture, whilst county or what we today call community school, are institutions which provided religious education. Jackson (1997) notes this distinction as both conceptually and institutionally important, whilst Smart (1964, 1971) describes religious nurture as 'confessional', and religious education as 'educational'. However, the distinctions are not always so sharply focused. For example:

> church schools may or may not be religious, though in practice almost all of them are. Conversely, a school could be religious without being owned or run by a religious organisation. (Humanist Philosophers' Group 2001, p. 8)

From our research of Muslim schools, for example, we interviewed parents who stated their objection to the local community school because their perception of it was that of a Christian school, which they saw as having an evangelical approach aimed at undermining their children's religious heritage. We will be returning to this point in the next chapter, but here we conclude our discussion on the shifting nomenclature used for faith-based schools by remarking that no one term adequately conveys the range of schools now being encouraged to develop, but for the purpose of our discussion we are using the term 'faith-based school' to include all those educational institutions which aspire to inculcate religious beliefs into children, and to perpetuate a particular style of life. This definition could include a lifestyle based on philosophical convictions, and many of the 'isms', such as humanism, could well be included. For the purpose of this discussion, however, our focus is on those establishments of a religious ethos and which in their school mission go beyond making available religious education to providing religious nurture in schools, and which are in receipt of state funding.

Conclusion

Schools in England and Wales were initially established by the Church of England and the Catholic Church in order to make formal education available for all children. By the end of the 19th century it was apparent that the clergy alone could not provide sufficient schools to ensure an educated workforce for the country, which, as a consequence of the Industrial Revolution, was seen to be of increasing importance. The government became involved in providing universal education and a dual system developed whereby the state provided financial support for those schools founded by religious groups as well as creating a national system of 'Board Schools', the forerunner of today's community schools. The 1944 Education Act confirmed this arrangement and financial support was also extended to schools established by Jewish communities, signalling that the foundations had been laid for incorporating different religions within a common school system. As such, faith-based schools are now a significant feature of the educational landscape, and their relations with external agencies mean that those which are now state-funded do not sit on the margins of the educational system but instead act in partnership with government. This has been underpinned by ongoing legislation throughout the last century, and faith-based schools have struggled to survive and to maintain their influence in the educational system, sometimes in the face of hostile governments. That is not the case today as a New Labour government has given clear signals that schools of a religious character are a valued part of the educational provision in the country and their numbers are to be expanded with state support. This is a move welcomed particularly by the Church of England which is looking to create more schools in this favourable political climate.

Although they have experienced criticism in the past, Church of England, Catholic and Jewish faith schools have a culture which has matured in many ways in terms of engagement and dialogue with the wider community, and they have struggled to overcome discrimination and to be accepted as part of the national education system. Prejudice towards faith-based schools has and continues to be a fact of life, and this can be particularly forceful when the community members are highly representative of visible minorities. It is the development of new faith-based schools in Britain, based on Islam, Sikhism and Greek Orthodoxy, which forms the basis of the next chapter, and where we will begin to identify and highlight the overlapping issues of race, ethnicity and religion.

Notes

1   See Rowe (1992).
2   Wood (1960).
3   Curtis and Boultwood (1966).
4   Wardle (1976).
5   Armitage (1964).
6   See, for example, Francis (2000) and Simpson (1992).
7   *Times Educational Supplement* (2001a) and *The Guardian* (2002b).
8   General Synod (1998), as cited in *The Way Ahead* (Archbishops' Council Church Schools Review Group 2001), p. 1.
9   See also Judge (2002), Albisetti (1999), Grace (2002a) and Pittau (2000).
10   See, for example, Bolton (1991).
11   See also Daly (1995), Morris (1994), Marks (2001) and Sander (1997).
12   See Hornsby-Smith (2000).
13   Miller (2001).
14   See Department for Education and Skills (2003b).
15   See, for example, Hall et al. (2002).
16   For more on this theme see Borowitz (1985) and Gillman (1993)
17   See Marmur (1994).
18   Grateful thanks to Susan Brehans, Deputy Head Teacher at North West London Jewish Day School, and Helena Miller, Director, the Leo Baeck College-Centre, for information provided in this section.
19   See, for example, Keiner (1996).
20   The Leo Baeck College – Centre for Jewish Education, London N3 2SY.

Chapter 3

The Emergence of New Faith-Based Schools

The expansion of faith-based schools can be seen as part of a government strategy to extend provision of a category of schools which it sees as being successful in terms of parental support and academic attainment. In the last chapter we looked at the early faith-based schools in Britain dating back to the 17th Century, and their relationship with the state in building a national system of education. We also saw how there have been waves of immigrants to Britain, such as Jewish communities from Eastern Europe, and how this has impacted on the development of schooling. In the post-1950s era there has been further migration, this time from the Caribbean, Asia and East Africa particularly, and this has led to the establishment of several new faith communities in the West. Here we look at the growth of new faith-based schools emerging from these communities: that is, those established in the last 20 years which mainly serve the children of first- or second-generation immigrants, and which have succeeded in obtaining state support since 1998. In the development of these academic institutions there have been a variety of schools, such as Sikh and Greek Orthodox and those established by Muslim communities.

The objectives of this chapter, therefore, are to:

- illustrate the growth of full-time faith-based schools in England and Wales with particular reference to Muslim, Sikh and Greek Orthodox institutions;
- explore the religious background, demographics and community involvement in the establishment of these schools; and
- highlight their efforts as communities in seeking to obtain government funding as voluntary aided schools.

We begin with the development of Muslim schools which are by far the largest group among the new faith-based schools.

Muslim Schools

There has been little research conducted on the private sector of education and religious schooling in general, as we noted in the previous chapter, and Walford (2000) notes that 'none has examined Muslim schools as a specific group'(p.9). In this discussion we draw on our own research in this field, and that of small, individual studies which have been conducted into Muslim schooling.[1]

The history of Muslim schooling in Britain has been associated with the struggle for parity with other faith schools, along the lines of that afforded to Catholic and Jewish institutions. As Hewer notes (2001b), there have been Muslims in Britain for centuries, but issues of accommodation within the educational system did not arise until the post-1950's migration period. In addition, the obstacles Muslim communities have faced have been magnified because their supporters are predominantly representative of ethnic minorities, and this wave of immigration raises 'complex issues of colour, race and religion' (ibid., p. 515). (We will be looking at these overlapping issues of race and religion in the next Chapter.)

Muslims are the largest religious minority in Britain, followed by Jews, Hindus and Sikhs (Weller 1997). There have not been definitive statistics on Muslims living in Britain and estimates have been drawn from questions relating to ethnicity. For example, using the 1991 Census and other statistical sources on demographic and social details, Anwar (1993) attempted to calculate the number. This survey was the first British census which included an ethnic question. It was based on nine categories: White, Black, Caribbean, Black Other, Indian, Pakistani, Bangladeshi, Chinese and 'Any Other' ethnic group. From this question on ethnicity, coupled with information on country of birth, calculations were made to determine group sizes. The ethnicity question was useful in attempting to obtain a figure, because of the two categories of peoples originating from predominantly Muslim countries: Pakistan and Bangladesh. The majority of Muslims in Britain are from these countries and are sometimes described as 'visible minorities', easily identified by dress and skin colour, but there are also other minority groups including British converts to Islam.

Today the 'official' number of Muslims in Britain is given as just over one and a half million based on the 2001 Census returns.[2] Among this number there are variations based not only on national grounds but also on sectarian differences. The general public is probably aware of the Sunni and Shia sects among adherents to Islam, especially since recent events in the Middle East, but this oversimplifies the Muslim communities since there are other major sectarian divisions (Joly 1989; Robinson 1988; Lewis 1997; Hewer 2001a). Speaking languages such as Bengali and Urdu, these UK groups are further differentiated by regional affiliation, occupation, customs and traditions. As a result of association with the textile industry, Muslim communities have been established in the Midlands and northern towns such as Bradford, Blackburn and Oldham. (A similar pattern of development took place in the establishment of Jewish schools, highlighted in the previous chapter.) Outside England, there are concentrations of Muslim communities in Glasgow, Cardiff and Swansea.

Sarwar (1994) calculates that around half a million Muslims in Britain are children of compulsory school age, and this figure is likely to increase.[3] The Association of Muslim Schools suggests a figure of around 350 000 pupils who are predominantly of Pakistani, Bangladeshi, Indian and Somali backgrounds.[4] In Birmingham, for example, Hewer (2001b) states that the Muslim population represents 11–12 per cent of the total population, and 24 per cent of the school population is Muslim. There are implications in terms of educational policy at local and national levels and, he continues, it is predicted that 'the Muslim population of Britain will at least double before it reaches demographic stability' (p. 516).[5] For some Muslims who see themselves as struggling to define their identity in Britain the education system provides a focus for academic success, but at the same time parents aspire to keep their children faithful to Islam. This generates discussion over educational provision in this country, within both the state system and the independent sector.

The ideal environment to promote the Muslim identity and faith is believed by some to be within a separate school system, a view shared by other faith-based groups. Islam is not simply a world religion but is also regarded as an all-embracing way of life requiring submission to God or Allah, and adherence to religious principles which lead to harmony, and happiness in the hereafter or afterlife (Ashraf 1993). Education begins in the home before formal education at school, and parents see their role in this matter as a duty and a privilege to ensure their children develop an Islamic consciousness (Haneef 1979). There is also a focus on preserving the tenets of Islam within the context of the 'ummah' or community, rather than as an independent nuclear or single unit.

In all aspects of life, Muslims are provided with guidance through religious texts and community interpretation of the holy scriptures (Asraf 1993). Written in Arabic, the Qur'an is the holy book of Islam containing 114 chapters (or 'surahs') and 6 236 verses (or 'Ayaat'), which Allah revealed to the Prophet Muhammad in the seventh century (Sarwar 1992). It is from the Qur'an that the words 'Muslim' and 'Islam' are used, and five basic duties are practised by Muslims, known as 'the five pillars of Islam' (ibid.). In many matters of life, Muslims describe things as being 'halal' which means permissible, or 'haram' which means forbidden (Sarwar 1994). This distinction is used with regard to food, behaviour, dress and social activities, and helps shape an Islamic consciousness in the young. (Similarly, we noted codes of moral conduct and behaviour in the previous chapter with regard to the raising of Jewish children.) For supporters of Muslim schools, the curriculum, both formal and hidden, should ideally reflect an Islamic orientation (Anwar 1982; Hulmes 1989; Modood et al. 1997), and it is argued that the rights and duties of Muslim children are supported best within these schools (Haneef 1979). However, not all Muslim parents argue this: many support community school education and make use of supplementary classes outside of their homes or in the madrassah.

Some Muslim commentators maintain that separate schools are not intended to disunite society but to preserve their pupils' Islamic identity. Independent and government-financed Muslim schools are thus permeated by an Islamic ethos supporting their 'unshakeable faith' (Halstead 1986). This also applies to early education settings where, in some areas of Manchester for example, parents are opting for all-Muslim nurseries because they wish to reinforce their children's sense of religious identity (Holmes, Jones and McCreery 2002). Muslim children, it is argued, are better British citizens as a result of separate schools, providing a moral compass, and instilling a new sense of morality into society. Separate schools provide for parents who feel their children are caught in a situation of 'culture clash', whereby the whole ethos of British state schools and educational policy is seen as inconsistent with their way of life. Sarwar (1983) and Modood et al. (1997) highlight the importance of cultural identity for Muslims, and the fear that their community is threatened by the undermining of cultural consciousness. (As we saw in the previous chapter, the resurgence in Jewish schools was also said to be attributed to the fear of cultural loss.) Muslim parents thus aspire to keep their children faithful in the face of perceived Western materialism and permissiveness.

Muslim Schools or Schools for Muslims?

From our research of Muslim schools in Britain and elsewhere during the last decade, we have found that in terms of full-time education, both state funded and independent, there are both 'Muslim schools', and 'schools for Muslims', and it is important to distinguish between the two. In the former case, the intention is to develop an entire ethos consistent with religious values, rather than in the latter case, which aspires to being fully 'Muslim' in nature but which in reality tends to be a school characterized by a shared religious identity but one which does not go much further in terms of developing curricula and ethos, often due to staffing and financial difficulties. The availability of state funding can help offset these difficulties and help create an ethos more consistent with religious considerations. For some people, the term 'Islamic school' better describes this desire to develop a school along the lines of Qur'anic scriptures, with a strong nurturing of an Islamic ethos which permeates the school curricula both formal and hidden. Within such schools, there are no areas of the curriculum which are essentially 'secular' subjects, as every area of study should be taught from an Islamic perspective. There is, therefore, an underlying, distinctive epistemology: 'the relation of all created Beings and things ... is given and immutable' (Hewer 2001b, p. 522). (We will be looking further at curriculum matters in faith-based schools later in Chapter 6.) Also, modesty in attire forms an important part of the dress code, as we saw in the development of some Jewish schools, and although provision has been made for this in community schools, there are still cases of Muslim girls being prevented from wearing the 'hijab' or headcovering.[6] (Objection by schools to the wearing of the 'hijab' has also taken place in France and Germany because it has been seen as a political as well as a religious symbol.)[7]

Generally, the curriculum has been defined as a transmission of culture (Lawton 1980), and within Muslim schools there is a desire to emphasize an Islamic culture and see this embedded in the teaching and ethos of the school (Parker-Jenkins

1995). Furthermore, education is seen as a driving force in Muslim communities, amply supported by Islamic texts such as: 'My Lord, increase me in knowledge';[8] 'Oh my Lord do not let the sun set on any day that I did not increase my knowledge';[9] and 'No gift among all the gifts of a father to his child is better than education.'[10] As such, Muslim schools strive to focus on the great value placed on the acquisition and pursuit of knowledge in Islam, as well as on practical matters such as the religious obligations of prayer and fasting. The desire to strive for both academic pursuit and religious obligations was also seen within the Jewish school tradition, detailed in the previous chapter.

It is calculated that full-time Muslim schools, both independent and state funded, provide education for around 1 per cent of an approximate population of 300 000–500 000 Muslim pupils in Britain (Berliner 1993; Sarwar 1994; Association of Muslim Schools 2003). Varying in number of pupils from approximately five to 1 800 on roll, Muslim schools coincide with the establishment of Muslim communities around the country, such as in the London, Leicester, Birmingham, Kidderminster and Dewsbury areas. Relying on community support, they are seldom purpose-built and instead operate above a mosque or in disused schools, invariably connected to one or more mosques based on sectarian divisions, as mentioned earlier. They are also established in homes and similar buildings by concerned parents and community leaders.[11]

The first independent Muslim school was established in 1979 (Dooley 1991), and currently, there are over a hundred in Britain which serve the needs of children whose parents are financially able and willing to pay.[12] The Association of Muslim Schools, which was formed in 1992 to provide co-ordination and advocacy for these institutions, cites the present number as 111 which includes two each in Scotland and Wales. All are Sunni with the exception of one Shia school, which reflects the fact that only 10 per cent of the Muslim communities in Britain are Shia.[13] The figure can only be given approximately, for these institutions open and close randomly due to financial insecurity, as we saw in the last chapter with regard to the establishment of new independent Christian schools. In 1989, for example, the figure cited was 15 (Midgeley 1989; Parker-Jenkins 1991), and by the early 1990s the number quoted was in the area of twenty (*Islamia* 1992; Raza 1993). Given that Muslim schools rarely operate on economic grounds or charge economic fees, Hewer (2001b) suggests they are best described as 'community-based' schools dependent on support from the community, teachers and administrators. They include a collection of single-sex schools for girls and boys at both primary and secondary levels, and there are also boarding schools and seminaries (Midgeley, 1989; Rafferty, 1991; Association of Muslim Schools 2003).

In terms of demand for Muslim schools in Britain, Hewer has pinpointed four basic reasons. First, they are seen as providing a safe educational environment. Secondly, the curriculum incorporates faith-based principles which ensures that an Islamic ethos permeates the school. Thirdly, specialist training in Islamic 'religious sciences', in addition to general education, is also seen as an important opportunity so that boys particularly can be educated as potential religious leaders. Finally, the concern with raising academic achievement has also been a reason for their growth, especially among pupils of Pakistani and Bangladeshi background, who have been found to be performing significantly below the national average (Department for Education and Skills 2003b). Similarly, Hussain (1996) and Mustafa (1999) point to the holistic approach to education that accommodates faith and a positive learning environment, and which they feel characterizes Muslim schools.

Single-sex schooling has also been part of the appeal of Muslim schools. Under section 36 of the Education Act (1994), it is the duty of the parent of every child of compulsory school age to cause him/her to receive efficient full-time education suitable to his/her age, ability and aptitude, either by attendance at school or otherwise. The term 'or otherwise' refers to home tutoring or education within the private sector. Instances have arisen where Muslim parents have failed to ensure their daughters attend school because of an ideological opposition to co-educational schooling, and court proceedings have ensued (Barrell and Partington 1985). Single-sex education continues to be an aspiration for some Muslim parents, who see the phasing out of such schools as contrary to their interests (Modood et al. 1997). In Bradford, the Muslim Parents Association was formed in 1974 to represent the Muslim view on this issue, and from this time a number of independent Muslim schools were founded along single-sex lines and in accordance with Islamic principles (Barrell and Partington 1985; Osler and Hussain 1995). Feversham College in Bradford is a case in point (British Muslims Monthly Survey, 1999b). More recently, Muslim schools for boys have been established to accommodate the wishes of Muslim communities who have expressed a need for single-sex schooling for their sons as well as their daughters (*Islamia* 1994).[14] In the absence of schools promoting an Islamic faith, Muslim parents have opted for alternative faith-based schools, such as those run on Anglican or Catholic lines, which are seen to be supportive of both moral education and single-sex schooling (Centre for the Study of Islam and Christian–Muslim Relations 1985; Nielson 1987). Others have struggled to pay the fees of private Muslim schools, hopeful that one day this financial requirement will become unnecessary.[15]

The Struggle for State Funding

The thorny issue in granting voluntary aided status to Muslim schools has been that, unlike previous denominations, this new group has been perceived as predominantly of a 'visible minority'. Racial segregation, as well as religious apartheid, appears to contradict government rhetoric on fostering multiculturalism. Furthermore, these schools have been criticized as potentially creating education ghettos, and developing a situation in which diversity is unhealthy, as argued in the aftermath of the Oldham riots and the terrorist attacks of September 11 in America.[16] (We will be returning to this point later in Chapter 8.) Notwithstanding the issue of 'voluntary apartheid' (National Union of Teachers 1984), as funding was not forthcoming for this minority faith group until 1998, there has been an equality before the law issue. In the previous chapter, we saw that voluntary aided status brings with it grants towards capital costs of the buildings, 90 per cent of running costs, and 100 per cent of teachers' salaries. Figures provided in 1991 by the Department of Education and Science (now the Department for Education and Skills) demonstrated that approximately one-third of maintained schools fell within the voluntary aided category and were denominational in character. Collectively, they have been described as a mixture of 'religious and secular education, with the state paying the schools' running costs and 85 per cent of their capital expenses, while governors and church leaders control the curriculum' (Durham 1989, p. 12).

Today in England and Wales there are over seven thousand faith-based schools or schools of a religious character and of this figure 35 per cent are primary and 16 per cent are secondary (Lankshear 2001; Department for Education and Skills 2003b).[17] The majority of these are Church of England and Catholic, but as we saw in the last chapter the relevant legislation has meant that it is theoretically possible for other denominations such as Jewish schools to apply for funding and to be supported by the state. Some of these schools have also experienced discrimination in the past. For example, there have been a number of claims raised by Catholic schools over equitable allocation of funding for school transport.[18] However, until 1998 this group of faith-based schools in England and Wales was devoid of any of an Islamic nature and Muslim communities vigorously expressed their dissatisfaction with the situation.

Prior to 1998, several independent Muslim schools[19] tried unsuccessfully to be afforded voluntary aided status. They boast long waiting lists and have been increasingly clamouring for public funding along the lines of other faith-based schools in Britain (Halstead 1986; Parker-Jenkins et al. 1998). For example, Feversham College in Bradford (formerly the Muslim Girls' Community School) worked its way through the relevant stages of the procedure, having obtained support from the local education authority (British Muslims Monthly Survey 1999b). In a policy statement on multicultural education, the opposition Labour Party signalled its general support regarding voluntary aided status for Muslim schools Labour Party (1989). Similarly, Baroness Cox unsuccessfully attempted to introduce the Education Amendment Act, which would have extended eligibility for public funding to independent schools providing an alternative religious ethos to existing state schools. More recently, the Education Act (1993) contained provision for the government support of schools formed by voluntary groups. The door therefore appeared to be open for Muslim schools to receive state finance and this was realized in 1998, as we discuss next.

The struggle to obtain government funding for Muslim schools spanned 15 years in total as applications were repeatedly turned down, sometimes for spurious reasons. For example, a letter of enquiry in 1983, followed by a formal application in 1986, by the Islamia School in Brent was rejected in 1990 (*Times Educational*

Supplement, 1998a). Judicial review of the case resulted in the Secretary of State being ordered to reconsider his ruling. The application was again rejected, this time in 1993 on the grounds of surplus places in local schools. It was argued that the same reason did not obtain for other faith-based schools being granted funding in the same geographical area. Islamia made attempts again in 1995 and waited three years for a response, which resulted in grant-maintained status being approved and state funding made available after 15 years of struggle. More specifically, notes Hewitt (1998), the move came '14 years and five Secretaries of State after the first naïve approach by Islamia School' (p. 22). Prior to this, Muslim schools remained 'the only ones to have been consistently rejected for public funding' (Lepkowska 1998). Judge (2001) notes that their:

> heroic efforts in establishing from their own resources their own schools, in communities which were generally underprivileged, strengthened their case, in reason and justice, for securing an equitable measure of State support for some of those schools. (p. 469)

During a visit to the Islamia School, Prince Charles paid a similar tribute, saying:

> I really do believe that the Islamia school is an important model and it will be interesting to see how many more develop in the future. You are ambassadors for a much misunderstood faith. You have much to tell people in a secular society like ours. (British Muslims Monthly Survey 2000a, p. 1)

For the Al-Furqan primary school in Birmingham, a four-year struggle took place to satisfy the criteria and receive funding. It was established by a group of parents who originally educated their children at home (Hewer 2001b). Redundant office buildings were subsequently found, and the project benefited from the commitment of a group of Muslim women who wanted their children to be educated to a high standard and in an Islamic environment. As a result, the school has flourished 'on sound educational provision', and due to the dedication of staff and parents, pupils achieve 'well above average attainment levels at the end of primary education' (ibid., p. 519).

Like many other Muslim schools, Al-Furqan boasted long waiting lists and has struggled to survive, charging fees which have been one-third of those of the average independent school.[20] Being oversubscribed like the Islamia School, Al-Furqan School also enrols children from a variety of ethnic groups.[21] Islamic values permeate the curricula, and the National Curriculum and Arabic are offered in both schools. The admissions policy allows children from all faiths to attend, but enrolment is normally 100 per cent Muslim. Al-Furqan was one of the first Muslim schools to be state funded and is now designated as a voluntary aided school (Department for Education and Skills 2003b).

The first two Muslim schools to receive public funding were initially designated as 'grant-maintained schools', but subsequent legislation of the Education Standards Act (1998) placed them in the 'voluntary aided' category and as such they enjoy parity of esteem with other faith-based schools in the country. As we noted in the previous chapter, the struggle by Muslim schools was part of a campaign by other independent schools to obtain state funding (Walford 1995b; Deakin 1989), and voluntary aided rather than voluntary controlled status allows a school more control over the nurturing of a religious ethos.

The Al-Hijrah Primary and Secondary School in Birmingham, which also receives state funding under the voluntary aided category, has from the beginning admitted boys and girls 'in parallel but separate classes' and with different break times (Hewer 2001b, p. 520). (We will see a similar arrangement used in Dutch Muslim schools later in this section.) Along with most other Muslim schools, they teach Arabic and Islamic studies, as well as Urdu. Al-Hijrah School:

> sees itself as a potential centre of excellence in which curriculum material can be developed for other Muslim and LEA schools and which can educate the leadership of the next generation. (ibid., p. 520)

Significantly:

> great emphasis is placed on the moral ethos of the school and the governors, staff and parents are determined that this will not be lost in the shift to public funding. (ibid.)

Of the 100-plus independent Muslim schools created in England and Wales during the last 20 years, some have gone on to become well-established institutions such as the Nottingham Islamia School,[22] the Leicester Islamic Academy,[23] Al-Muntada Islamic School in London,[24] and the Manchester Islamic High School for Girls,[25] and among these there are also applications submitted for voluntary aided status which would allow them to develop further, especially in terms of curriculum options and staffing levels. As we saw with reference to the development of Jewish schools, the position of the teacher in a Muslim school is not that of 'neutral communicator', but 'the committed embodiment of the message being taught'Hewer (2001b, p. 520). Again, this places huge demands in terms of staff recruitment, an issue shared by Catholic schools of late which strive to employ practitioners who are committed to the faith.[26] (The teacher as exemplar of faith is also discussed later in Chapter 5 with regard to legal issues in faith-based schools.)

The decision to provide state funding for this group of schools now serves as a milestone, as Muslims in Britain have seen their previous applications rejected in the context of increasing 'Islamophobia' (*Dialogue* 1997; Runnymede Trust 1997) and fear of 'Fundamentalism' (Yuval-Davis 1992). Statistically, there are five Muslim schools which are state funded, under the voluntary aided category, along with approximately five thousand Anglican, two thousand Catholic, 32 Jewish, two Sikh, one Greek Orthodox, and one Seventh Day Adventist schools (Valley 1995), which, as we saw in the previous chapter, fall under the voluntary aided and voluntary controlled headings (Department for Education and Skills 2003b).

Whilst state funding has now been awarded to some Muslim schools, the majority of the existing independent Muslim schools charge low fees, and, notes Walford (1995b), 'they are in poor quality buildings and lack many facilities that would be common in state schools' (p. 7). They tend mainly 'to serve relatively poor families who have strong religious beliefs and object to the secularist (if not anti-religious ethos) that they perceive to be prevalent in state schools' (ibid.). As with other religious groups, they struggle to find sufficient trained staff, and they do not have to follow the National Curriculum, but may utilize any teaching method provided it offers a broad and balanced curriculum.

It is not the case, however, that all Muslim parents want Muslim private schooling for their children: some do not wish to see their children educated in ideological isolation and instead look to state schools to accommodate their needs. There is no coherent view among Muslim parents in this instance, as with parents of other faiths, about the need for their children to attend a faith-based school, or whether spiritual matters can be left to the family and attendance at religious services. Differences of opinion were highlighted by Taylor and Hegarty (1985), and the Swann Report (Swann 1985) cited Cypriot Muslims, for example, who were mostly opposed to separate schooling. Similarly, Bradford's first Asian Lord Mayor was quoted as saying, 'I don't want separation in any form, what we want is accommodation of our cultural needs, especially in the education system.'[27] This contrasts markedly with the argument proffered by organizations like the Muslim Education Trust, which suggests that there are a sizeable number of Muslim parents who want government funding for separate schools (Cumper 1990). It would be wrong to assume, however, that support for and against separate Muslim schools falls entirely along ethnic lines, for, as in other religious groups, there are wide differences of opinion on this issue.

The issue of state funding for faith-based schools has generated continual debate in the last decade, caused, among other things, by the decline in Christian intake and the clamouring for financial support for Muslim schools. Critical re-evaluation of the religious clauses of the 1994 Education Act with a view to dismantling all denominational schooling is a possible solution to the problem, as raised in previous studies (Swann 1985; Commission for Racial Equality 1990). This is clearly unlikely to be an option as such a move would provoke angry responses from Anglicans and Roman Catholics, who, as we saw in the previous chapter, have historically held voluntary aided status within a dual system of education (Lustig 1990). But, it was argued, we either provide equal access to state funding for all qualifying religious schools, or we embrace a 'common school' for all. (Halstead 1986; Parker-Jenkins 1995). (We will be looking at the future implications of the development of faith-based schools later in Chapter 9.)

Muslims, like other religious groups, are also developing educational provision beyond school level. Not only are there several Muslim colleges or seminaries teaching what may be called strictly 'Islamic' texts, such as the Qur'an and the collections of the Prophet's sayings, as well as languages,[28] but there are also several courses which have been established to produce Muslim teachers, for example at the Selly Oak Colleges in Birmingham (*Times Higher Education Supplement* 2001), and through the School Centred Initial Teacher Training (Postgraduate Certificate in Education) partnership which was run by the Association of Muslim Schools and validated by the University of Gloucestershire (Association of Muslim Schools School Centred Initial Teacher Training 2000). Muslim institutions are also participating in degree-awarding courses, for example Loughborough and Portsmouth (*Times Educational Supplement*, 2001b); the Markfield Institute of Higher Education in Leicester offers postgraduate courses in Islamic Studies up to doctoral level;[29] and since 1991 a four-year B.Ed programme with a specialism in religion based on Islamic and Christian studies has been offered by Selly Oak Colleges/Birmingham University (Hewer 1992). Such developments suggest that an embryonic infrastructure is emerging which supports Muslim educationalists and encompasses both the 'separate' and 'mainstream' sectors. This reflects developments by other religious groups in the country and is a pattern which is repeated elsewhere, such as in Germany and the Netherlands.

Muslim schools particularly have been the focus of controversy in the expansion of faith-based schooling but, as we saw in the last chapter, Catholic schools in the past have also been criticized as authoritarian and socially divisive:

> if misrepresentations of Catholic schooling can exist in political and public debate, it suggests that misrepresentation of the contemporary schooling systems of other faith schools can also exist. (Grace 2002b, p. 8)

Muslim communities are presently particularly vulnerable to attack both verbally and physically as a result of the war against terrorism, an issue we will return to in Chapter 8.[30]

Muslim schools also see themselves as raising academic attainment in what they feel is a preferred environment because:

> pupils there do not suffer from being in a minority, nor from elements of racism that may remain in local authority schools. Parents, staff and the community place a high level of expectation on students in Muslim schools, and students thus affirmed generally raise their attendance level. (Hewer 2001b, p. 524)

As a result of receiving government funding, some Muslim schools are also able to provide access to a wider student body, particularly those whose families are unable to pay school fees, but the majority of Muslim children are educated in state-funded community schools.

At this juncture, it is interesting to refer to the situation in the Netherlands because a significant number of Muslim schools have been established there with state support. Unlike Britain, the Dutch system provides government funding to a wide diversity of school types based on both religious and philosophical principles. Walford (2001a) is useful here because of his comparative study of Muslim schools in England and the Netherlands. He describes the Dutch educational system as one in which:

> state-provided schools do not identify with a particular religion or outlook and are open to all religions and beliefs. (p. 531)

As a result, two-thirds of all primary and secondary pupils are taught within private schools. The diversity is such that as well as Muslim and Hindu schools, there are a number of ideological as well as religious traditions represented, such as Humanist, Steiner and Montessori schools.

In terms of immigration, 700 000 immigrants and refugees from Islamic countries have settled in the Netherlands, which constitutes about 4.5 per cent of the population. They are predominantly from Turkey and Morocco (Sunier and van Kuuijeren 2002), and as with England there have been settlements in large cities such as Amsterdam, Rotterdam and Utrech with, consequently, the development of 'Dutch Islam' (Bartels 2000). (We will be looking at the issue of post-1960s immigration and its impact on education policy later in the next chapter.) The first Dutch Muslim primary school was opened in 1988, and today Dutch Muslim schools operate at both primary and secondary levels. As with the British situation, only a minority of parents opt for separate Muslim schooling for their children. Again this choice is due to a desire to ensure a religious ethos is maintained and to ensure a greater coherence between what is being taught at home, in school and in the mosque. Moreover:

> separate schools allow religious beliefs and practices to be taken into consideration in all activities in school, and enable activities which are found in other schools which are considered undesirable to be excluded. (Walford 2000, p. 6)

This has implications for the selection of reading books and texts which may 'refer to explicit sexual activity or put dubious moral frameworks' (ibid.). In Muslim schools, the appropriateness of music education has been challenged (Scarfe 2001), and the representation of living beings in art classes (Parker-Jenkins 1995). Similarly, Muslim schools can provide the teaching of Arabic, and the Islamic contribution to such things as science and architecture. The inclusion and exclusion of particular subject matter in the curriculum is found in Muslim schools in the Netherlands and England (Walford 2001b) and is also a feature of Muslim education in other countries, for example in Australia (Donohoue Clyne 2001).

The Dutch provision of separate schools for religious minorities means an extra cost to the state in terms of teachers who have to be qualified and paid at the agreed national rate. Also, compared with England, more is known in the Netherlands about the academic performance of Muslim schools.[31] For example, in 1999 the Dutch Inspectorate produced a report on 'Islamic First Schools' which came from its regular inspection of 14 of them.[32] It was concluded that the quality of education was no worse than in other schools with a similar high percentage of immigrant children, and in some subjects such as maths it was significantly better. As these schools are also in their early stages of development, there is the potential for increased academic attainment. For example, some relatively new Muslim schools in England and Wales which are not in receipt of public funding have been found to perform well in league tables.[33]

Equitable access to funding has for a long time been a keystone of the Muslim school movement in England and Wales, as highlighted earlier, and thus far five out of 100-plus schools have been given access to state funding since 1998. Conversely, in the Netherlands the idea of equity has been firmly established, and, at the theoretical level, funding on an equal basis with other schools has been legally provided since 1917 and is readily available for religious minorities (Walford 2001b). Furthermore, Dutch Muslim schools tend to receive more funding than the average school because they are eligible for an extra allowance as a school where a pupil is from an ethnic group or 'whose parents have not been educated beyond the pre-vocational level' (ibid., p. 11). Such is the support for religious schools in the Netherlands that, unlike England:

> it is almost inconceivable that any parents should pay for schooling (beyond the costs of 'extras in many schools') or that a group of parents should start such a school. (ibid., p. 8)

Recognizing that there is a trade-off between state funding and freedom over pedagogy means that not all faith-based schools wish to enter the state sector in England and Wales. However, in the Netherlands, none of the Dutch Muslim schools in Walford's study appeared to have considered becoming a fee-paying independent school. Even in the face of gradual secularization within the state-maintained sector, there is an acceptance of such things as attainment targets, and a belief that Dutch Muslim schools will 'maintain the faith' despite government regulation (ibid., p. 9). Muslim schools, both here and in the Netherlands, tend to be oversubscribed; however, a key difference is that:

> in England but not in the Netherlands, separate Muslim schools have been linked to the separation of girls from boys as well as the separation of minority ethnic origin children from the majority. (ibid.)

In terms of single-sex education, this fact is corroborated by our research into Muslim institutions in this country, but some of the schools would challenge the view that they do not have a cultural mix of pupils.[34]

Due to a shortage of trained Muslim teachers, Muslim schools in both countries are staffed with non-Muslim teachers. For example, in a Dutch report, only 20 per cent of teachers in Dutch Muslim schools were actually Muslim (Van Onderwijs 1999). Another shared similarity is that of media attention. Both school communities have experienced Islamophobia, particularly in the aftermath of September 11, and in the Netherlands in the wake of the death of Pim Fortuyn in

2002.[35] As a backlash to this event, there is said to be an increasing political shift to the right in the Netherlands, and less tolerance for the wearing of the 'hijab' in some schools, a key aspect of school dress for many Muslim schoolgirls.[36] Added to this have been accusations in the Netherlands that some of their schools have been linked to militant Islamic organizations (Walford 2001b). This is one of the major concerns in the controversy about the expansion of Muslim schools, alongside the general issue of 'Islamophobia', a point we shall return to in Chapter 8.

Thus far we have been looking at the establishment of Muslim schools, both here and in the Netherlands, and the desire by communities to develop schools reflective of Islamic principles and to receive government support. The expansion of these institutions to over a hundred in number in the UK has been a significant sociological event, with a proliferation of different kinds of Muslim schools. Initially it was cultural conservatism which provided the impetus for the creation of Muslim schools, but access to state funding and the longevity of some of these institutions of over twenty years have led them to be outgoing and confident in their dealings with the wider community. There are around eight more applications pending from Muslim schools seeking state funding, and collectively they have been working to raise the level of professionalization in their schools and to raise academic performance among pupils, a fact well demonstrated in the academic league tables.

Next we look at another type of school new to the educational landscape in this country which has also sought state funding, that based on Sikhism.

Sikh Schools

The majority of Sikhs living in Britain are of Punjabi ethnic origin whose families arrived in the 1950s and 1960s, but the historical roots of Britain's Sikh population go back to Victorian times, and to the 1920s when small groups were employed in seaports (Ballard 2000; McLeod 2000). Some Sikhs came from former British colonies, and, as a result of their serving in the British forces in the First and Second World Wars, there was also migration to Britain after these conflicts (Brah 1996; Weller 1997; Shackle et al. 2001). Elsewhere there are large Sikh communities in Canada and the United States. The Sikh community in Britain is just over 390 000 according to the 2001 Census, which relies on 'self-designation' in reaching this figure. It is classed as the largest Sikh community outside the Indian subcontinent, with particularly substantive numbers in London, Leeds, Birmingham, Bradford, Wolverhampton, Coventry, Leicester and Cardiff (Weller 1997; Ballard 2000; Helweg 1986). Sikhs in Britain often retain close religious, political, economic and cultural ties with their Punjab homeland, and there has been a replication of patterns of religious and social life (Tatla 1999). Employment in textile mills and foundries particularly in outer London and the West Midlands was commonplace for the early immigrants. Further, the right to wear a turban as a symbol of their religious identity formed the basis of a number of campaigns in the 1960s and the 1970s, for example for motorcyclists (ibid.).

The first 'gurdwara' place of worship to be opened in Britain is recorded as being in Shepherd's Bush in 1911 (Weller 1997, p. 605). Today there are also national, regional and local organizations within the umbrella 'Network of Sikh Organizations' developed by Indarjit Singh to support co-operation between the different groups (Singh 2000). The community language is Punjabi and the scriptures are in Gurmukhi script, but Sikhs from East Africa may also be familiar with Swahili, Urdu and Hindi (Singh 2000; Weller 1997). As with the other minority ethnic groups we have discussed there is considerable differentiation among Sikhs on social, economic and linguistic lines (Nesbitt 1994). One of the key unifying factors, however, is said to be the shared outrage at the storming of the Golden Temple in Amritsar by Indian troops in 1984 as the Temple was regarded as the 'symbolic centre of Sikhdom' (Cohen 1996a, p. viii). Support for religious 'revivalism', with an emphasis on Sikh identity and religion, among some Sikh communities has been steadily growing as it has among their Muslim and Hindu counterparts (Ballard 2000), but there have been divisions, for example, correspondinge to caste in Leeds (Kalsi 1992) and in Coventry (Nesbitt 1994). Further, different strategies of adaptation have ensured that there has, and continues to be, no single way of being a British Sikh. For:

> although Sikhs in Britain take a great deal of pride in their distinctive heritage, Sikh behaviour is anything but uniform. (Ballard 2000, p. 138)

Most British cities have at least one 'Gurdwara'. These are supported by families which have joined their menfolk from the Punjab, although today most Sikh children are UK-born. (This pattern of reuniting families is one we saw earlier in the case of Muslim communities.) As well as being sites for religious revival, the local Gurdwaras are used for social gatherings, marriages and influencing 'a Sikh social and moral order' (ibid.). Further 'revivalistic' processes have not only been confined to the religious forum of the Gurdwara, for Sikh families continue to maintain their cultural heritage. For example, some Gurdwaras have 'gatha' (sword-fighting) classes. This would not have been the experience of 1950s Sikh settlers, but has more to do with self-definition associated with the Khalistan movement of the 1980s (McLeod 1997). Further, as we saw with reference to Muslim communities, there is an emphasis on family honour or 'izzat', clearly stipulated duties of sons and daughters, and the perpetuation of patriarchal values among many groups (Tatla 1999).

Sikhism is based on 'dharam' or appropriate behaviour which is also referred to as 'Khalsa Panth' meaning 'path of the pure ones'. The religion is underpinned by the teachings of the ten 'Gurus of Sikhism', and the first of these was Guru Nanak who was born in the 1649.[37] The word 'guru' within an Indian context signifies a teacher, often a spiritual teacher, but the ten Sikh gurus are seen significantly as 'the mystical "voices"' of God (McLeod 2000). As with Islam, there are also distinctive practices and traditions in Sikhism. A 'Sikh' is defined as: 'one who believes in Akal Purakh (the one immortal God)'; the teachings of the ten Gurus; the 'Amrit Pahlul' or the Sikh form of initiation; and who has allegiance only to the Sikh religion (Weller 1997, p. 608). Sikhs are also monotheistic, believing in one Being who is known by a variety of names such as Nirankar. Prayers are said at home or recordings listened to by congregational acts of worship as a means of supporting each other in their religion. There is a belief among Sikhs that their religion should permeate everyday life and act as a guide, a view shared by all faith communities. Further, equality of the sexes is stipulated in the Gurus' teachings as it is in Islam, although cultural rather than religious conventions may militate against this in reality.[38] This is a complex matter, and McLeod (1997) argues that, as a religious system, 'orthodox Sikhism teaches that women are completely equal to men in all respects' (p. 241), but that Sikh history and communities present a different impression as 'power rests with males and patriarchy indisputably rules' as it does elsewhere (p. 249).

A part of the distinctiveness of being a Sikh is taking 'amrit', that is, undergoing an initiation, and wearing the five articles of faith. These are associated with the 'Khalsa', and are more commonly known as 'the five Ks' because the Punjabi word for each of these begins with the letter 'k'. These five articles have deep spiritual significance and the wearing of them indicates adherence to Sikhism. 'Kesh' refers to uncut hair and 'is one of the outwardly distinctive signs of Sikh identity' (Weller 1997, p. 611). 'Kangha' or a small comb is worn in the hair and signifies 'orderly spirituality'; 'kara' is a steel bracelet used 'as a reminder of the universality of God and a symbol of religious allegiance'; 'kachhahera', an undergarment which must be no longer than knee-length, signifies 'modesty and moral restraint'; and 'kirpan', a sword, 'represents a readiness to fight in self-defence or in the protection of the weak and oppressed' (ibid., p. 611).

McLeod (1997) is useful here for his summary of 'who is a Sikh?'. He defines a Sikh as a person who reveres the ten Gurus, and acknowledges the sanctity of the Gurdwara and the role of the Gurdwara in expressing the anti-caste ideals of the Gurus. A Sikh observes the rituals and personal obligations which include 'the five Ks', highlighted above, and especially the prohibition of hair-cutting. These undertakings may form part of an initiation into the 'Khalsa', the religious order established by the tenth Guru, Guru Gobind Singh, at the end of the 17th century. As such they are termed Amrit-dhari Sikhs, or if they have not undergone initiation but accept the fundamentals of the faith, they are regarded as Kes-dhari Sikhs. Observant Sikhs bear an outward physical appearance, notes McLeod:

> the turban stands out and it is by his distinctive turban that an Orthodox Sikh is easily recognized. (ibid., p. 213)

Self-designation' also has a bearing on 'who is a Sikh?', and is an important factor in identity, even if a formal initiation has not taken place or external appearance does not denote 'orthodox' Sikhism. Further, although the vast majority of Sikhs are Punjabis or of Punjabi descent, there is no objection in principle to people from other ethnic groups or cultures converting to Sikhism and becoming members of the Panth or Sikh community. Overall, Sikhs see themselves as 'heirs to a history and a fund of tradition which they regard as a continuing source of guidance and inspiration' (ibid., p. 227).

Cohen (1996a) maintains that such social markers are 'a deliberate display' demonstrating that:

Sikhs do not want to go down the paths of assimilation or unthinking integration. (p. vii)

(However, this is to generalize, as there are many different perspectives among Sikh communities as to how they maintain cultural heritage, an issue we shall return to in the next chapter). Guidance on the wearing of 'kirpans' has been given in terms of the carrying of a knife for religious purposes, and for health and safety reasons at school.[39] Another point of distinctiveness is the use of the religious name 'Singh' or lion for Sikh men, and 'Kaur' or princess for Sikh women. Initially this was intended to indicate equality and to remove the concept of 'Zat' or class, which was and still is traditionally indicated by people's family names, but it is a mistake to assume that all people with the name 'Singh' are Sikh: the situation is more complex for the practice was in use in India before the rise of Sikhism (Weller 1997). As such, it is a religious principle in Sikhism that caste has no religious significance, but the role of social gatherings in Sikh communities still exists and, in practice, many Sikhs add their family name. We look at the contested boundaries around Sikhism as a religious and an ethnic group in the next chapter, and the legal protection against discrimination; however, it is worth noting at this point that there are still indications that many British Sikhs have a strong sense of distinctiveness (Ballard 2000). The wearing by many men, and a few women of the turban, the importance of the family and kinship networks, and the significance of religious identity have remained central aspects of life for many Sikh communities. As well as reproducing many of their cultural and religious values there is still for many Sikhs a relationship with the Punjab, and an increasingly global communication and networking with Sikh communities around the world. Further, the Sikh diaspora has revitalized social and religious norms, and, as with other minority ethnic communities, there are emerging new Sikh identities, especially among the younger generation. This has been made easier by the use of the Internet, which serves as a way of connecting communities and families who are geographically dispersed (Tatla 1999),

Supplementary classes have also been established for Sikh children, providing instruction in the Punjabi language, and in 'kirtan' or devotional music (Nesbitt 2000). 'Gurdwaras' are used not only for worship, but also for religious education, political mobilization, and a variety of social activities for young children and the elderly (Barrow 1995). Similarly, efforts to support linguistic and cultural maintenance, especially for Sikh children, have taken place in Canada and the United States (Tatla 1999). Unlike Muslim groups, Sikh communities in Britain have established only one full-time school, the Guru Nanak School in Middlesex,[40] which is believed to be the only Sikh school, not only in this country but in Europe.[41] The institution was originally an independent school founded by Sant Amar Singh Ji who had established several institutions in India. Formally opened in 1993, there are now a primary and a secondary section to the school. A sixth form was added in 1995 in partnership with Handsworth College, Birmingham and the first student intake was 13 pupils who had previously performed badly at GCSE level elsewhere, and who went on to take GNVQ and 'A' levels in the school. Demand for the school came from parents in the community who were said to be concerned about 'drugs, indiscipline and declining moral standards'(Guru Nanak Sikh Secondary School, *School Prospectus 2001–2002*, p. 2).

A campaign was launched to seek voluntary aided status for the Guru Nanak School in 1997, and with the support of the community, parents, political parties and the local authority, London Borough of Hillingdon, it achieved this goal in 1999 becoming the first Sikh voluntary aided secondary school. Both sections of the school, primary and secondary, are now in receipt of government funding and they stand as the only maintained Sikh schools in the state sector (Ofsted Report 2003; Department for Education and Skills 2003b).

The School's overall aim is:

> to provide a happy and outward-looking school, within which all the pupils work hard to realise their full potential intellectually, morally, physically, personally and socially and in which the Sikh religion is fostered. (Guru Nanak Sikh Secondary School, *School Prospectus 2001–2002*, p. 4)

The full National Curriculum is taught and, in keeping with a school of religious character, the pupils are instructed in the principles of their faith, in this case Sikhism. Education in the mother tongue also forms part of the curriculum as well as the implementation of Sikh principles:

> doing the Nitnem (prayer) daily, showing respect for adults, showing respect for other religions, caring for the elderly and the underprivileged, [and] showing humility. (ibid., p. 4)

In terms of pupil numbers, the school consists of 220 primary age children and 350 eleven- to eighteen-year-olds as of February 2003. The majority of these pupils are bilingual in Punjabi and English, and their families migrated from India, Africa and Afghanistan. Overall, the student body consists of 99 per cent second- and third-generation Sikhs, with one pupil each from the Muslim, Hindu and Catholic religions now registered, and a Buddhist pupil scheduled to begin in the academic year 2003–2004. Admission for Sikh pupils is contingent on formal confirmation of religious adherence from any of the 'gurdwaras' in Hillingdon or neighbouring boroughs. Currently, the proportion of pupils with special needs is 13.3 per cent of the total school population, below the national average, and only one has a statement of needs. As with other faith-based schools in this chapter, the Guru Nanak Secondary School is positioned well in league tables and due to parent demand the school is set to expand significantly; for example, the sixth form doubled its pupil strength from 40 to 81 in 2003–2004.

Another characteristic shared with other faith-based schools is that the staff of the Guru Nanak School are practising adherents from a variety of religions. Thirty per cent are Sikh and 70 per cent are non-Sikh, with slightly more female teachers than male. After voluntary aided status was awarded to the secondary institution, all unqualified staff obtained 'Qualified Teacher Status' through an arrangement between Manchester Metropolitan University and Uxbridge FE College, Hillingdon.[42] The school was also supported by a retired head teacher and the Local Education Authority in obtaining the policy and structural knowledge it needed once it had achieved voluntary aided status. As a result of state funding, the school has also received financial support for expanding and upgrading the facilities in the post-1999 period. Interestingly, all the major religions are represented on the school's governing body, which is more common in community rather than faith-based schools, and there is strong rejection of the view that new schools of a religious character are pursuing a policy of indoctrination or serve as a place where fanaticism takes place. (We shall be looking at allegations of indoctrination and fanaticism later in Chapter 8.)

There has been a close and successful relationship with the Local Education Authority and the many stakeholders in the first Sikh school to be established within the educational system, first during its independent status and subsequently as a voluntary aided institution. More recently this has resulted in a successful Ofsted inspection which reported:

> this is a very good school: students achieve very well because they are keen to learn and taught well in a harmonious environment. GCSE results are well above average. Sixth form results match national expectations and are improving. The ethos is strongly positive, underpinned by the shared values of the Sikh faith and excellent leadership. (Ofsted Report 2003a, summary report, page 1)

As the Guru Nanak School looks to expand it has secured its position as the only Sikh school in the state sector, having responded to parental demand to establish an institution, and successfully having obtained support from the wider community. Given that it is the only school (divided into primary and secondary sections) based on a Sikh ethos we cannot draw generalizations, but the institutions demonstrate the variety of state-funded schools providing a religious education. Similarly, the third and final type of faith-based school we will be looking at in this chapter is also unique in its financial status and religious ethos.

Greek Schools

Greek schools have been established in England and Wales to accommodate the religious and cultural needs of Greek communities. The Greek Orthodox religion has roots in the Byzantian tradition, but there has also been a two-way influence shared with the Russian Orthodox Church.[43] The Greek community in Britain consists predominantly of Greeks and Greek Cypriots, many of whom emigrated to the country in the post-Second World War period.[44] In terms of ethnicity, the recent Census does not cite the number of Greeks living in Britain, and they are instead clustered within the category 'Other White'.[45]

As with other immigrant communities, Greek communities have created schools in order to maintain their cultural heritage. The ideological underpinning for these establishments is to support the cultural life of Greek communities in terms of the Greek language, the Orthodox religion, and traditions and customs. As such the function is not purely academic: the social dimension plays an important part of the school experience. The Greek government is involved in sending teachers from Greece to support teaching and it pays for their salaries, whilst the local Greek communities tend to support the school infrastructure, supplying buildings, which in many cases are part of the local Greek church. Parents may also contribute small amounts of money for resources. The largest number of Greek schools have been established in the London area whilst other regions are Birmingham, Manchester and Kent.[46] These reflect the settlement of groups in the various areas (Kotsoni 1990), and their wish to perpetuate cultural identity through the education of their children.

Most of the Greek schools in the United Kingdom operate on a part-time, supplementary basis. As we noted in the previous chapter, supplementary education is established by communities to provide additional education alongside full-time compulsory education. Within Greek schools supplementary education lessons normally take place twice a week, and are run by such organizations as 'the United Forum for Greek Education in the United Kingdom'.[47] This group consists of a number of separate bodies, such as the Central Education Council of the Greek Orthodox Archbishopric of Thyateria and Great Britain, the Federation of Educational Associations of Greek Cypriots in England, and Independent Greek Schools of Britain. Collectively they support approximately one hundred and ten schools, three of which provide full-time education.[48]

Part-time, supplementary education continues to be used by Greek communities to actively maintain the Greek language and tradition but recently steps have been taken to be more proactive in maintaining cultural heritage. This development is due in part to the perceived inadequacy of the mainstream and supplementary school systems to accommodate parental expectations. The Greek Association Language Enhancement Organisation (2003) was formed in 1995 by representatives of the existing Greek community schools of South London and has as an overall objective:

to satisfy the needs and aspirations of children and parents who wish to maintain and develop a Greek cultural linguistic and religious identity.[49]

This aspiration found expression in the foundation of St Cyprian's Primary School which is seen as a place where the core cultural elements can be provided for 'a more developed sense of identity'.[50] The Greek language is integrated into the life of the school and the Greek Orthodox religion underpins the school ethos. What we see evident here is the close relationship between community language and religion, as demonstrated earlier in our discussion of Muslim and Sikh schools.

St Cyprian's opened in 2000 as the first Greek Orthodox primary school in the country, and is designated as voluntary aided under the auspices of the Archdiocese of Thyateria and Great Britain.[51] The school's governing body is representative of the Greek Orthodox church, the Cyprus High Commission, The World Federation of Overseas Cypriots, Greek banking groups and local Greek families.[52] There are currently 122 pupils on roll aged 3–11 and in a recent inspection report (Ofsted Report 2003b), it was stated that, in addition to the National Curriculum, the school provides a daily lesson in Greek for each class, and has quickly established a distinctive ethos that reflects the traditions of the Greek Orthodox faith. Additional staffing is provided by the Greek and Greek Cypriot Education missions, particularly for extra-curricular teaching of the Greek language, dance and music.[53]

Just over half of the pupils in the school are Greek: the remaining numbers are representative of 'white and black British, and black Caribbean communities', and first languages include Russian, Spanish and Cantonese.[54] This is a pattern we saw replicated in Catholic schools, discussed in the previous chapter: the enrolment of children of other faiths and cultural backgrounds in addition to pupils belonging to the school's religious group. Interestingly 'attainment on entry is below average' and 'the proportion of pupils on the special needs register, over 25 per cent, is well above the average, with a significant number of these pupils said to have behavioural problems'.[55] (We will look at the issue of responding to special educational needs within faith-based schools later in Chapter 7.) The school is seen as offering a 'second chance' to those children who have not realized success in other schools, and as such this challenges the general assumption that all faith-based schools are highly selective in terms of pupils' academic competence, a point we return to in Chapter 9.

As a new school St Cyprian's has only just begun to establish a reputation within its own community and beyond. This is reflected in the inspection report which noted the success of English and Mathematics, for example, which is above the national trend in Years 2 and 6; but the school performed less well in such areas as information and communication technology. As with other faith-based schools, St Cyprian's does not recruit all its teachers from its own religious group, and in our research we have observed that difficulty in staff recruitment has a bearing on a school's ability to deliver the National Curriculum satisfactorily in all subject areas, especially in its early stages of development and in new learning technologies.

The Greek Orthodox faith forms the basis of the school's collective acts of worship, with contributions from members of the Archdiocese of Thyateria and Great Britain. Respect for other religious and cultural traditions is demonstrated in the celebration of such events as Divali and Chinese New Year, an approach we noted in use in other faith-based schools. The development of spirituality is highlighted in the school's mission statement:

> religious education will form an integral part of the daily life of the school ... [and] pupils will experience their religion as a lived reality.[56]

As such, the school displays paintings, symbols and artefacts which draw on the Greek Orthodox tradition. The local Greek community is used as a resource and there is a programme of visits to Greece and Cyprus which are seen as useful for widening the experiences of pupils, and for promoting learning in history and geography.

What we see here is a similarity of provision between all the faith-based schools discussed in this chapter: community support for establishing a religious education; a faith tradition reflected in the formal and informal curriculum; the incorporation of community languages; and the overall aim to strengthen children's religious identity.

In the discussion so far we have focused on examples of new faith-based schools which are in receipt of state funding, and the Guru Nanak School and St Cyprian's Greek school stand out uniquely as the only ones from their communities to be in this category. Brief mention should also be made of the Swaminarayan Independent Day School, also unique, for not only is it the first Hindu day school in the UK (Weller 1997), but also it is again believed to be the only one in Europe.[57] Opened in 1991 in Neasden, London, the Swaminarayan School accommodates approximately four hundred and eighty pupils, divided into a preparatory school, two and a half years of age to eleven, and a senior school providing education up to sixth form level. The pupils in the Swaminarayan School are predominantly second-generation Gujirati speakers, and the school community can be seen as part of the Asian society in Britain which has been through the processes of migration (Coward et al. 2000; Modood et al. 1997). As the only Hindu school in Britain,[58] and operating as an independent school, the Swaminarayan School lies outside the principal focus of this book. It is, however, an example of a further faith-based school which has been recently created in response to parent demand for an institution which aims to provide both a religious ethos and high academic performance.[59] The vast majority of Hindu children in this country are educated within the state system, which is augmented by supplementary education provided by Hindu communities, and there appears to be little development to change the situation. This may be due to Hindus in Britain constituting a relatively smaller population than, for example, the Muslim population: that is, 558 000 as opposed to one and a half million (Census 2001). It may also signal a lack of demand by Hindu parents for separate schooling, and an expectation that their children's religious and academic needs can be met in the community school.[60] To date, no full-time Hindu day school has received public funding, unlike those of the Islamic, Sikh or Greek Orthodox traditions, nor are any applications for financial support pending.

Conclusion

The new faith-based schools based on Islam, Sikhism and Greek Orthodoxy have followed in the traditional footsteps of Christian and Jewish communities in securing state funding. This was achieved due to parent demand and community support in establishing academic institutions which not only thrived, but in many cases performed well academically. In the case of Muslim schools, this achievement was a struggle secured after 15 years of repeat applications to successive governments. For the Sikh and Greek Orthodox schools, strong support from the Local Education Authority and the wider community meant that their success was achieved in less time. With state funding under the category of voluntary aided, these schools have been able to develop further the provision of education along religious lines and to nurture faith, both formally and informally, which is reflective of their communities. Despite evidence of a decline in religious adherence, and an increasing trend towards secularization in the West, religion remains for many a significant marker of their personal and communal sense of identity, and some religious groups and institutions, such as those based on Islam and Judaism, claim an increase in numbers and support. The emergence of new faith-based schools instigated by minority ethnic communities demonstrates the promotion of diversity in education which has changed the existing social order in England and Wales.

So far we have looked at a range of faith-based schools, both old and new, and what they all share is a commitment to community, and a strong sense of religious values and tradition. It is these shared concerns of community, family and culture which form the subject of the next chapter, where we will explore in detail the overlapping issues of race and religion which characterize many of the new faith-based schools.

Notes

1 Parker-Jenkins (1990, 1991, 1992, 1996); Parker-Jenkins and Hartas (2000); Parker-Jenkins and Haw (1996, 1997); Parker-Jenkins, Hartas, Irving and Barker (2002); Walford (2001b); Hewer (2001b) and Osler and Hussain (1995).

2 See Weller (2003) for an in-depth discussion on interpreting the Census results in terms of religious affiliations.

3 Figures can only be estimates given the difficulty of identifying the number of Muslims in England and Wales, and accounting for those who did not complete the Census returns or who were not eligible to do so. Hewer (2001b) also discusses the age profile of Muslim communities and attempts to calculate those of school age.

4   Idris Sears of the Association of Muslim Schools, 23 September 2003.
5   Ballard and Kalra (1994).
6   *Time Educational Supplement* (2002m) and www.muhajabah.com/islamicblog/veiled4allah.php
7   *Times Educational Supplement* (2002k).
8   The Qur'an, 20:14.
9   The Haddith (sayings of the Prophet).
10 Ibid.
11 See Hewer (2001b).
12 *Times Educational Supplement* (2001b); Association of Muslim Schools (2003).
13 Weller et al. (2001).
14 See also Archer's (2001) research on Muslim boys and issues of schooling.
15 See for example, the case of Leicester Islamic Academy, 'Schools resist faith newcomer', *Times Education Supplement*, 29 November 2002, p. 14, and 'Islamic academy seeks cash', idem, 15 November 2002, p. 4.
16 *Times Educational Supplement*, (2001b, 2001d, 2001f, 2001h).
17 Department for Education and Skills, statistics website (2003b).
18 Barrell and Partington (1970). See also 'Bus fare change rattle clerics', *Times Educational Supplement*, 31 October 2003, p. 15.
19 The traditional distinction between schools in Britain should be noted. 'Public' schooling refers to a non-maintained school relying mostly on parents' fees and recognized as a charity. The term 'independent' can equally be used here. A 'private' school is normally one owned by one or more individuals and run for private profit. Muslim schools in Britain have tended to fall into the 'independent' category. In common usage, 'independent' and 'private' are often used interchangeably but the official definition of non-state-maintained school is 'independent' and is therefore used throughout the book.
20 See *Times Educational Supplement* (1998a).
21 Al-Furqan School, *School Prospectus (2003–2004)*.
22 The Nottingham Islamia School, nottingham.islamiaschool@btinternet.com
23 Leicester Islamic Academy, 320 London Road, Leicester LE2 2PJ.
24 Al-Muntada Islamic School, London SW6 4HW.
25 Manchester Islamic High School for Girls, Manchester M21 9FA.
26 See *Times Educational Supplement* (2003a).
27 Halstead (1988), p. 52.
28 Ibrahim Hewitt, head teacher Al-Aqsa Primary School, Markfield Conference Centre, Markfield, Leicester, 24 October 2001.
29 Ibid.
30, *The Guardian* (2003b) and *The Sunday Times* (2001)
31 See Whitty (1997) for a general review of school efficiency issues.
32 Walford (2001b).
33 See for example, Nottingham Islamia School; see *Nottingham Evening Post* (2003).
34 For example, Islamia Primary School in Brent has more than 23 different nationalities represented in its school.
35 *The Guardian Education* (2002).
36 *The Sunday Times* (2003a).
37 Weller et al. (2001).
38 See also Drury (1991).
39 Department for Education and Employment and the Home Office (1997).

40 For more on Guru Nanak see Nesbitt and Kaur (1999).
41 Senior management at the Guru Nanak Senior School who through personal interview, school policy papers and Ofsted documentation provided us with information for this section of the chapter.
42 Teacher Training Agency (2002).
43 See Mavrogordatoson (2003), Kallistos (1995) and Binns (2002).
44 See Hutchinson and Smith (1996).
45 NationalStatisticsOnline-Census (2001).
46 Greek Schools in the UK.see html
47 Ibid.
48 Ibid.
49 Greek Association Language Enhancement Organisation (GALE) website (2003), www.theodoru.freeserve.co.uk/greekcyp/schools.htm
50 Ibid, and senior management at St Cyprian's Primary School.
51 St Cyprian's Greek Orthodox Primary Voluntary Aided School, *School Prospectus (2003–2004)*.
52 GALE website.
53 St Cyprian's, *School Prospectus (2003–2004)*.
54 Ofsted Report (2003b) *St Cyprian's School*, p. 5.
55 Ibid.
56 St Cyprian's, *School Prospectus (2003–2004)*.
57 Senior management of the Swaminarayan Independent Day School and literature from Shree Swaminarayan Mandir, London NW1O 8JP, www.swaminarayan.org
58 See Nesbitt and Henderson (2003).
59 See Independent Schools Inspectorate website 2002/isi.org.uk
60 Jackson and Nesbitt (1993) is particularly useful in providing background information on Hinduism and Hindu children in Britain.

Chapter 4

Community, Family and Culture

The significance of 'community' in the lives of individuals and families, and the impact of culture in shaping values, have been themes permeating our discussions so far. Here we examine in more detail the importance of cultural tradition in shaping religious identity through community and school involvement. We will also be tracing the ideologies of assimilation and integration in Britain and the ways in which these policies are seen to reduce and undermine cultural heritage within communities. We examined schooling established by Christian and Jewish traditions in Chapter 2, followed by the growth of schools based on Islamic, Sikh and Greek Orthodox traditions in Chapter 3, all of which are hugely diverse between and among themselves in terms of cultural heritage. Here we look at the importance of cultural heritage which permeates these schools, and the advocacy of their rights in what is seen as an increasingly secular society.

The importance of strong relationships between teachers, parents and pupils in securing educational gains is well documented (Bastiani 1989; Wolfendale 1992). However, it is important to recognize that culture and ethnicity are likely to impact on the effectiveness of strategies employed to achieve this (Bhatti 1999). 'Culture' can be interpreted as encompassing all major aspects of life, and within the social sciences there are a number of debates concerning its meaning and relevance, as well as that of other related concepts, such as 'community', 'family', 'ethnicity' and 'identity'. In order to highlight the complexity of these overlapping concepts and how they relate to faith-based communities, in this chapter we will:

- examine the concept of community and the associated terms of family, culture, ethnicity and identity;
- discuss the nature and significance of religious identity, and of religious communities;
- highlight the fundamental human right of freedom of religion and belief;
- consider the overlapping issues of religion and ethnicity; and
- explore the tension between assimilation and multiculturalism as government policy aims to accommodate newly arrived immigrant groups within the school system.

It is particularly important at the outset to provide a brief definition of key terms, before we go on to explore the concepts and associated theories in greater depth, and we begin this section of the chapter by discussing what we mean by 'community'.

Community

History demonstrates clearly the importance of religion in the lives of individuals and communities, and the importance of 'faith' in shaping personal identity. Such is the significance of faith that, over the years, freedom of religion has been recognized as a fundamental human right. We begin by looking at some of the critiques of the broad term 'community' within the social sciences, in preparation for looking later at the concept with reference to religious groupings.

Sociological discussion of the concept of 'community' has, note Taylor et al. (2002), been marked by a great deal of confusion and disagreement, and what we know for certain is that 'community has no single, fixed meaning' (pp. 386–7). For example, Hillery (1955) identified 94 different definitions of the word in which the only point of agreement was that community has to do with people. Newby (1980) noted, however, that the variety of definitions normally consists of three themes: a social system or set of relationships; a fixed locality; and the quality of relationships or 'spirit' of a community. The term also conjures particular images, add Taylor et al., such as a subcultural community, that is, a subgroup sharing the values of the wider society but in addition maintaining possession of its own cultural identity. This may also be described as an exclusive community involving relationships with both 'insiders' and 'outsiders'. However, this is to present a one-dimensional model because within communities there is differentiation in terms of socio-economic class, sectarianism, gender and patriarchy. Indeed, notes Werbner (2002b), a community may be struggling to deal with the wider community whilst at the same time being at war with itself.

Communities may be the place where meetings, ceremonies, weddings and rituals take place, and identities are reproduced through these exchanges in the community sphere. They are also important for providing an alternative and empowering space outside the national public sphere (Bourdieu 1985), for dissent and the mobilizing of social movements (Gilroy 1993). A further aspect of the creation of a strong or cohesive community is the involvement of particular organizations such as the mosque, synagogue, temple or church in terms of providing a focal point for group cohesiveness. Importantly, notes Werbner (2002b):

> ethnic and religious movements resemble other new social movements...in fostering alternative identities and lifestyles which are submerged in the invisible spaces diasporic groups create for themselves, far from the public eye. Within these spaces they debate and argue over moral, political and existential issues affecting their group. (p. 16)

Occasionally, communities mobilize on a large scale, as for example that of British Muslims in response to the Rushdie Affair. In this instance there may be an invigorating and renewing sense of identity within the community as a result of political activity. We must also note that even on these occasions when the wider society sees large-scale mobilization, there may be dissent within the communities themselves: 'culture, tradition, history and community are the products of processes of argument' (ibid., p. 17). As such, Werbner continues, there are also 'new popular cultural spaces beyond the mosque and community elder politics', demonstrating further the heterogeneity of communities negotiated from different positionings (p. 22).

Giddens (2001) talks about the opening up of communities today and the impact of technology on communication systems whereby the social phenomenon of 'globalization' intensifies worldwide social relations and interdependence. As such, the development of new networks and of new social and economic systems impact on daily life, and mean that communities are unlikely to remain remote, isolated or unaware of events on a global scale. Interestingly, some sociologists challenge whether there is such a thing as community any more, along the lines of that entity encapsulated within Tonnie's theory of 'gemeinschaft', that is, a simple, traditional society based on an homogeneous culture with shared norms and values. Instead they argue that the concept is in fact an idealized unit which has now been eclipsed or lost altogether due to the disappearance of 'close-knit communities' (Taylor et al. 2002). There are, nevertheless, still groups of people who do have some of the characteristics deemed to constitute communities in terms of shared territory, shared values and a shared 'spirit', and for whom the concept is still relevant. This is very much reflected in the religious communities we discussed earlier in Chapters 2 and 3, which have a sense of values and purpose which is shared by the associated families who choose faith-based schools.

Family

The significance of the family unit within communities in perpetuating cultural heritage is important to note as throughout our discussions we have seen that it is families which in many cases have helped to establish and support faith-based schools. Further, studies of religion and community demonstrate the key role played by the family in reinforcing values and traditions of their subculture, and maintaining their differences from the dominant culture in which they live (Harvey 2001).

Kirby et al. (1997) maintain that 'the family is often considered by non-sociologists to be one of the few "natural, institutions in society" ', and people consider that healthy families are intrinsically a good thing (p. 235). Further:

> it is considered 'ideal' that the family should consist of two parents of different sexes and one or more children – preferably of their own. (ibid.)

These writers add that this ideal or 'normal' family is reinforced by media images, but that what constitutes a family varies widely within and among different culture groups in our society. We noted earlier the impact of change on daily life, and

Giddens (2001) maintains that nowhere is this more apparent than in our personal and emotional lives:

> over the past several decades, Britain and other Western societies have witnessed shifts in family patterns that would have been unimaginable to earlier generations. (p. 172)

He adds that the diversity and forms of households are due to a number of reasons: people choosing to remain single; the rise in the divorce rate; the growth of lone-parent families; and the development of 'reconstituted families' which come together as a result of remarriage. Yet for some groups the family continues to be an important part of their culture and the raising of children is not contemplated outside of marriage or traditional arrangements, as we noted earlier in Chapter 2 with reference to some Jewish communities. Similarly, in Islam family and community are significant aspects of religious life and the primacy of the family unit is stipulated within its teachings (Haneef 1979).

Husain and O'Brien (2001) state that:

> the importance of faith, family and community continue to be a challenge in a secular and increasingly individualistic society. (p. 15)

They drew this conclusion from their study of Pakistani communities in Britain in which they researched issues of family dynamics, and generational and gender differences. Once changes in immigration law in 1971 shifted the emphasis from single men to family unification, the migration of women increased and the settlement of families in Britain. The strength of kinship ties among Pakistanis to their family networks in Pakistan has been documented by Ballard (1990), but with the migration of women and the creation of a family base in Britain the myth of an eventual return to their country of birth ended. Husain and O'Brien also explored different levels of family networks and kinship ties in different groups, and found:

> while Sikhs and Hindus are barred from marrying close kin, Muslims are permitted and often encouraged to do so. This has led Pakistanis to create self-contained and somewhat closed and isolated communities based on an extensive system of inter-related members, while Hindus and Sikhs have had to look outwards to non-related community members to create cultural and social structures. (p. 19)

This may account for the difficulty experienced by some groups in engaging with the wider society, and, therefore, the importance of maintaining difference based on cultural and ethnic background (Harvey 2001; Peters 2001; Sherkat 2001).

Culture and Ethnicity

New cultural identities are now commonplace in many parts of Europe as a result of immigration, displacement by war, and those seeking political asylum. We need here to explicate what we mean by the concept of 'culture', which we highlighted in Chapter 1, and how it relates to that of 'ethnicity'. Whilst at a simple level ethnicity may relate to a person's place of birth or historical place of origin symbolized by visible signifiers such as colour, dress, lifestyle or birthplace allegiance, culture reflects a more complex expression of a sense of belonging. Bilton et al. (1981) define culture as 'those ideas, techniques and habits which are passed on by one generation to another – in a sense, a social heritage. This learned behaviour, or social inheritance, of any society is called its culture' (p. 10).

They add that it is the possession of a common cultural heritage and the ability to pass it on to others that is a distinguishing feature of human beings:

> humans are humans because they share with others a common culture, a culture which includes not only the artefacts of its living members but also those of past generations. This is the heritage awaiting those as yet unborn. (ibid.)

Similarly, Kirby et al. (1997) state that culture consists of norms or specific rules, and values or general principles which are learnt through socialization rather than through instinct:

> culture is expressed through routine behaviour and through language, visual work and other forms of symbolic representation. (p. 374)

Further, notes Parekh (2000), culture can be regarded as 'a system of beliefs and practices in terms of which a group of human beings understand, regulate and instruct their individual and collective lives' (p. 34).

Both Kirby et al. and Parekh define culture in a holistic way, seeing it as permeating all aspects of individual and collective living rather than more narrowly expressed as great works of art or literature, for example. Moreover, note Kirby et al. (1997), there is a religious dimension as:

> in most societies, the influence of religion through history means that many fundamental values are derived through religious teaching. (p. 374)

This would be particularly true of the school communities we have been discussing.

Werbner (2002b) is useful here in her examination of 'culture' because it helps us begin to explore the connection with ethnicity. She maintains that:

> only by analysing specific social situations can we grasp the contingency of culture and identity as they are negotiated by ongoing moral, aesthetic and political disagreements and discourses. (p. 7)

She gives, as an example, the position of South Asians:

> just as Westerners carry their debates with them wherever they settle, so too South Asians have carried their cultural disagreements into the diaspora. (ibid.)

This helps explain why there is a lack of consensus among religious groupings about such things as appropriate dress or the position of women in society. She adds that the representation of a 'seamless, ''whole'', homogeneous culture' is false but that within the nature of 'culture' it is also possible to find 'commonalities across differences' (pp. 8–9).

A feature of the new European landscape is the diversity of people, characterized by place of origin, skin colour and a personal sense of identity. Werbner (2002b) maintains that:

> the massive scale of transnational cultures founded by post-World War II immigrant-settlers and refugees in the postcolonial, post-imperial West has disturbed earlier modernist conceptions of the nation as culturally homogeneous. (p. 9)

As such we have, within a multicultural society, diverse communities some of which are undergoing change themselves, yet which are trying to retain their cultural heritage and, very importantly, trying to secure toleration of difference from the wider society. This manifests itself in a number of ways, politically, economically and aesthetically, and, for the purpose of this discussion, educationally, in the support for faith-based schools as part of the process in perpetuating cultural traditions and heritage.

The importance of an 'ethnic-religious' identity for different groups is particularly significant and as Young (1990) notes it can also be a major focus of group politics. Trying to categorize exactly whether it is racial or religious identity which is the major descriptor highlights the complexity of the situation. Furthermore, whether or not a group feel that religion is the central issue of identity, the wider society may have its own perception. For example, 'religion is not seen as intrinsic to identity as opposed to the case where race is' (Weller et al. 2000, p. 71). The law has been criticized for privileging 'colour' within policy documents, and, as we shall discuss later in this chapter, the limited anti-racist policy of the 1980s has also been found wanting because it interprets race and racism in terms of colour only, and polarizes the world into two groups of black and white with little or no reference to religion or cultural heritage which may also include issues of 'ethnicity'. Further, the word 'culture', as we saw earlier, is also not unproblematic and 'the relationship between religion and culture is difficult to unpack' (ibid., p. 72).

We have now introduced the concepts of ethnicity, race and religion and it is important to begin to analyse these overlapping terms. Ethnicity 'involves kinship, a sense of belonging, a common history and a desire for group continuity alongside religion, culture and language' (Schlesinger 2003, p. 113). Modood et al. (1997) argue that ethnic assertiveness arises out of feelings of not being respected and a need to challenge existing power relations, not just to ensure toleration of difference but also to secure 'public acknowledgement, resources and representation'. Likewise, Ball et al. (2000) state:

identity is socially and culturally 'located' in time and space and inflected by rejection, displacement and desire. (p. 24)

'Ethnicity' is a factor which can help give people a sense of belonging and which provides both individuals and groups collectively with a shared sense of identity, and in reality this translates as constituting 'the cultural practices and outlooks of a given community of people that set them apart from others' (Giddens 2001, p. 246). Further:

> members of ethnic groups see themselves as culturally distinct from other groups in a society, and are seen by those other groups to be so in return. (ibid.)

This is true of many of the communities in our study who have a strong sense of cultural distinctiveness, particularly as it manifests itself in religious belief and practice.

In distinguishing between 'race' and 'ethnicity', Smooha (1985) explains that a racial group is composed of people who are believed to share the same biological make-up while an ethnic group is identified by cultural practices and traditions. Taylor et al. (2002) document the development from the 19th century of 'racial types' classification to explain differences between people. It is also important to note that 'race' may be used as a social construct to which meanings are attached and as a basis for identifying differences which carry negative consequences (Kirby et al. 1997). Anti-colonial and anti-racist arguments have contributed to the generating of a new vocabulary in which the term ethnicity has increasingly replaced that of race, particularly since the 1960s, and has been used to acknowledge positive feelings of belonging to a cultural group (Guibernau and Rex 1997). We should also explain that the term 'minority group' is sometimes used in this instance, but it does not just infer a statistical reference to population size, but that, sociologically, 'members of a minority group are disadvantaged as compared with the majority population and have some sense of solidarity, of belonging together' (Giddens 2001, p. 248). Also, the term 'minority ethnic' group is increasingly being used:

> ethnic minority or minority ethnic are terms of convenience. Both are used to refer to people who are identifiably different to the ethnic majority because of their parent's or grandparent's origins. Sometimes these differences are barely apparent. Sometimes they are obvious because of language, accent, dress or religion. (Dadzie 2000, p. 90)

However, the move away from the term 'ethnic minority', which infers a kind of marginalization, to that of 'minority ethnic', suggests the inclusion of all groups in society, visible or non-visible in terms of skin colour or ethnicity.

In our discussion of what we mean by 'ethnicity' we should note that there is little consensus about the concept, as with that of 'community', and it is a hugely contested area. For example, there are a range of theories as to the origins of ethnicity (Weber 1961), about the link between ethnicity and politics (Cohen 1986), and about ethnic groups and boundaries (Barth 1969). The 'ethnic cleansing' which took place in the former Yugoslavia demonstrated most starkly the level of hatred which can exist between different groups, and the perception of different ethnic groups being 'inferior' to others (Bennett 1995). Some writers suggest that as more people are now involved in a global economy we should transcend the term ethnicity towards that of 'real communality', preserving the best in multiculturalism with a commitment to social equality (Castles 1996). However, this belies the power and resilience of ethnic groups as a social force.

Interestingly, there are legal requirements which determine what constitutes an 'ethnic group'. Under British law, for example, a group may only qualify as an ethnic group if it is able to fulfil specific criteria. These were noted in *Mandla v Dowell Lee* (1983) as a long, shared history, and a cultural tradition of its own. Further, a common geographical origin, a common literature peculiar to the group, a common language, a common religion and minority status were also included in the definition. Under these criteria, Sikhs, for example, may legally constitute an ethnic group as we noted in the previous chapter, whilst Muslims do not. This type of deliberation has led to what some see as unfair treatment in terms of discrimination due to the inability to fulfil legal criteria (Weller et al. 2001). Further, this imprecise model negates the huge differentiation within an ethnic group, nor does it acknowledge, note Taylor et al. (2002), that cultural boundaries are difficult to map and are always shifting. We cannot be sure that there is uniformity within a group with total commitment to core values, and Gilroy (1987) cautions against the use of 'ethnic absolutism'.

To summarize so far, there are different dimensions of communities and ethnicity, and a number of different characteristics may be identified to demonstrate the distinctiveness between ethnic groups, such as history or ancestry, language, styles of dress and religion. The fluidity and multiplicity of issues that communities are dealing with means that there is continual change and not a fixed sense of reality. The concept of 'culture' has also been perceived as a fixed category with a stable understanding of 'ethnicity', which is not applicable to contemporary society and which is also continually subject to changing social construction.

Importantly, Giddens (2001) states that ethnic differences are wholly learned, 'a purely social phenomenon that is produced and reproduced over time' (p. 246), and, through socialization, young people assimilate the lifestyles, beliefs and values of their communities. As we have noted in the previous two chapters, some faith-based schools serve as a site where ethnic as well as religious values are learned, for example through the teaching of community languages. Further:

> for many people ethnicity is central to individual and group identity. It can provide an important thread of continuity with the past and is often kept alive through the practice of cultural traditions. (ibid.)

He continues that the broad term 'ethnic' is applied to such things as clothes, music and neighbourhoods, but that using 'ethnic labels' in a collective manner risks producing tensions in society between 'them' and 'us'. The sense of common loyalty may be increased as a result of the experience of discrimination and prejudice. Whilst 'ethnicity' is most often associated with minority groups, we are all ethnically located (Hall 1992), as we shall discuss later, and the 'indigenous' population also has characteristic aspects of life.

Edward Said's work *Orientalism* (1978) is very useful here for his insight into how academic traditions have perpetuated stereotypes and cultural assumptions in the representation of 'other cultures' and have applied Western concepts to describe non-Western situations. In so doing, the politically stronger cultural group defines weaker groups. There is also, according to Said, a tendency to perceive people as 'us' and 'them', and to essentialize the 'other' in terms of 'the Oriental mind'. This can be seen in the form of writing in terms of generalizations about, for example, Hinduism, and omitting the heterogeneity among its groups. If we are not careful we engage in static images of cultural groups and fail to acknowledge the dynamics of experience.

Anthropologists have looked at the issue of difference between and within cultures and the potential for 'culture clash' for those born of one ethnic background and brought up in another. Watson (1977) described this as being caught between 'two cultures'. More recently, work by sociologists such as Stuart Hall (1992) points to the need to understand that cultural identity is not static, it is a dynamic process, and we need to be aware of the shifting nature of new ethnicities, and the dual and multiple senses of reality for some people. In Europe there has been an increase in political activity and political consciousness, with heated debate about the relationship between national and religious identity. The language of identity is used a great deal by Muslim activists, for example, as they seek to maintain their cultural heritage, illustrated by the work of Yusuf Islam and Lord Ahmed (British Muslims Monthly Survey 1999a, 2000b).

This leads us to raise the question, are minority groups expressing themselves more politically, and is it about ethnicity, and religion as a subsection, or, as is often the case for Muslims, the other way round? What is the relationship between the two? These are the sort of questions we need to consider in order to understand the complexity of the issues concerning culture, ethnicity and religion. There are overlapping issues of identity inclusive of religious, cultural, ethnic and personal factors. Further, when we attempt to decide upon majority and minority rights, especially in the allocation of government funding, there is a need to consider how we can fairly accommodate different majority and minority combinations.

It is important, therefore, to see that a person's identity can be constructed in terms of either or all of religion, race or ethnicity. Although we may think of ethnicity in terms of colour, we are all, as Hall (1992) says, ethnically located. He argues that there are new ethnicities and multiple senses of reality in evidence in the UK, and this holds true elsewhere in Europe (Lewis and Schnapper 1994; Nielson 1995; Modood and Werbner 1997). The identities of young people within minority ethnic communities are more hybrid than those of their parents or grandparents

(Cummins 1996). For example, this hybridity can be demonstrated in the case of children who may be Pakistanis but who may also consider themselves to be Muslim, Punjabi and British. Interestingly, there is a view that religious identity will diminish in forthcoming generations, especially among newly arrived groups. This argument has been expressed by many Muslim writers such as Sarwar (1994) who fear their religion will disappear in three generations, and that it is particularly undermined by community schools. Similarly, as we saw in Chapter 2, this fear of loss of religious identity has been cited as an important reason for the expansion of Jewish schools in the last two decades. Cultural pluralism can have a double effect, allowing individuals to connect freely as committed Jews or Muslims, but also allowing them to lose easily all or most aspects of their faith and become what Schiff (1966) refers to as 'deculturalised'.

Certainly adolescence is a time when young people wish to belong with their peers, and may therefore pull away from their religion, seeking out alternative ways of belonging. Yet in Britain and France we see cases of young people being more politically aware than their elder siblings and being prepared to stand up for their religious rights, for example in the wearing of a 'hijab' or headcovering and in being ready to discuss their faith in a variety of forums. Older generations were prepared to accept situations the new generation may not (Modood and Werber 1997; Sarwar 1994). Among some young people there is a discernible move away from becoming more 'Westernized' to a position of being politicized about culture and identity, and finding a comfort zone personally and communally. Sometimes this comes from more progressive elements in a community who are prepared to challenge conservative perspectives, and who try to exercise choice which they feel is still consistent with their interpretation of identity and appropriate lifestyle.

Identity

The construction of 'identity' draws on a number of factors such as gender, age and social class. Kirby et al. (1997) state that identity is shaped by the process of socialization whereby individuals become aware of the knowledge and values of the culture in which they are born, and that this process is ongoing:

> the human personality is dynamic rather than fixed, and develops as it is exposed to socializing experiences throughout life. This is how our sense of our own identity, or who we feel ourselves to be, is constructed. (p. 374)

Similarly, Giddens (2001) notes that, broadly speaking:

> identity relates to the understandings people hold about who they are and what is meaningful to them. (p. 29)

He adds that sociologists also describe identity as 'social identity', that is, the characteristics attributed to people by others, and these markers place individuals with others who share the same attributes, such as Catholics or Sikhs. Further, it is possible for an individual to simultaneously have a number of social identities reflecting that person's life. However, he maintains that:

> while this plurality of social identities can be a potential source of conflict for people, most individuals organize meaning and experience in their lives around a primary identity which is fairly continuous across time and place. (ibid)

Importantly, says Giddens, shared identities, that is, those predicated on a set of common goals, values or experiences, can form an important base for social movements. This could be said of some Jews and Muslims, for example, who, as we saw in Chapters 2 and 3, established schools based on their shared identity.

Alternatively, 'self-identity' or personal identity 'refers to the process of self-development through which we formulate a unique sense of ourselves and our relationship to the world around us' (ibid., pp. 29–30). In this case, it is the individual's constant negotiation with the outside world which helps form his or her sense of self, and 'the process of interaction between self and society helps to link an individual's personal and public worlds' (ibid., p. 30). Giddens argues that people are today less bound by inherited rules and conventions, they are inclined to be more socially and geographically mobile, and identity is therefore more multifaceted and less stable. Whilst this would be true of multiple senses of identity, such as being British, Muslim, female and Urdu speaking, for some individuals one characteristic, that is, religion, may remain the key factor of identity, serving to define *who* they are.

Having provided an introduction to the broad sociological concepts of community, family, culture, ethnicity and identity we now focus more specifically on the concepts of religious identity and religious communities, and how these relate to faith-based schooling.

Religious Identity

For some people there may be a religious rather than an ethnic boundary around them, a marker, which helps to define their sense of self. With ethnicity and religion we need to distinguish between self-ascription and description by others, as there are issues in relation to both types of designations. Religion is open to interpretation and therefore a variety of expressions are used about what it is to be a Hindu, or what constitutes a Muslim. Furthermore, of the variety of characteristics we could use to describe ourselves, such as age, height, education, profession or skin colour, religion has been noted as of primary importance in the construction of identity and a key component of self-description. For a definition of 'religious identity' Oberoi

(1994) is useful for he suggests that it is more than the formal beliefs which distinguish a group, and includes:

> the whole historical process by which a cohesive community of believers comes to be consolidated and reproduced through a fusion of texts, myths, symbols and rituals with human bodies and sentiments, often under the aegis of religious personnel. (p. 4)

These symbols, myths, texts and rituals of religion only become meaningful, however, when different groups of people interact with each other and are persuaded that what they are doing is of deep significance.

In a study in Britain, Modood et al. (1997) noted that 'a growing number of white people have no religious affiliation' (p. 298). This contrasted with the behaviour of South Asian groups, for example, who they found strongly embraced a number of religious traditions such as Islam, Hinduism, Sikhism and Christianity. (We should again note that concepts such as 'Hinduism' are recent and Western in origin). The researchers also found that 'the primacy of religion in South Asian identities is owed at least partly to community relations as much as to personal faith' (ibid., p. 299). As such, in discussing religious identity there is not an easy way of providing categorization. This is particularly so because of the overlap between religion and culture. There is an assumption that 'race', which is not the same as 'ethnicity', identifies faith, but this need not necessarily be true. For example, the word 'Muslim' cannot automatically be associated with 'Asian'. Likewise, not all Asians are Muslims: many embrace other religions, such as Hinduism, Sikhism or Christianity.

Some people may not wish to be labelled primarily by their ethnic background, such as 'Asian Christian', but rather their identity as a Christian may be what is of foremost importance in their sense of self. Importantly, note Modood et al.:

> the most common expression of ethnicity is not what people do but what people say or believe about themselves. (ibid., p. 332)

We should take this point further and add, 'and in which context they are in when they say it', for there is also a contextual aspect to identity (Barth 1969). Therefore, within a faith-based school, individuals may feel a greater sense of association with religious identity than in a community school.

Religious identity is also connected to people's sense of feeling. People describe themselves as 'feeling Jewish' or 'feeling Catholic', whether they are born into the religion or adopted (Weller et al. 2000). Religious identity may be closely linked to religious study, especially for those in the process of converting to a faith. For others it may be 'all they have ever known' (ibid., p. 17). Thus, self-description is primarily an expression of 'whom one belongs with', of membership or what might be called an 'associational or community identity' (Modood et al. 1997, p. 332).

In his study of Manchester Jews, Schlesinger (2003) echoes the significance of religious identity and the importance of support within a community to ensure a 'sustainable Jewish identity'. Similarly, Lawton (2000) states that Jewish continuity lies in producing ideas, values and behaviours which are transmissible to future generations, and which are connected with the Jewish religion and tradition. As well as transmitting this cultural heritage through Jewish schools, as we saw in Chapter 2, this objective is actively promoted through the work of Jewish Cultural Centres around the country. What is particular to the Jewish group which cannot be shared readily with mainstream society is described by Schlesinger (2003) as follows:

> the centripetal forces that pull Jews towards each other have to do with a shared history, background, location and attitudes to life. These are powerful forces: they can embrace even secular Jews. (p. 23)

An interesting point here is the suggestion that religious identity can compel group membership even when the individual follows a life predominantly secular or devoid of religion, and as such religious identity may be characterized as having different levels of adherence rather than total conformity. However, a common factor is the desire to have one's religious identity recognized, and to be treated with dignity as an individual and as a member of a community.

We should also add that the questioning of identity by younger generations in various communities has led to a distinction being made between nationality, ethnicity and religion (Husain and O'Brien 2001). The matter of nationality is normally easy to resolve by virtue of birth or citizenship acquired through the naturalization process. Allegiance to the 'old country' origin of the first generation may fade, but in the case of South Asian Muslims, for example:

> whether one is British Pakistani or British Muslim is a difficult discussion, particularly when the boundaries of where ethnicity ends and religion begins is unclear. (ibid., p. 23).

Self-designation or self-description is likely to be the only way forward, as we suggested earlier, and the conflation of ethnic and religious boundaries means that for the younger generation 'the notion of being Pakistani is separate from that of being Muslim' (ibid.). Further, 'often their rejection of parental traditions has taken them not towards Western mores which would lead to communal alienation but to a religious doctrine cleansed of cultural impositions' (ibid.).

In some cases, Husain and O'Brien argue, politico-religious movements have taken advantage of disaffection by forming youth groups to provide a base of resistance in Britain and other European states, encouraging 'a religious identity which supersedes national and ethnic allegiances' and which is in part 'a reflection of the constant prejudice and discrimination against visible minority ethnic individuals' (ibid., p. 24) by the majority ethnic community. Islamophobia, for example, has been documented by the Runnymede Trust (1997) who observe that:

a deep dislike of Islam is not a new phenomenon in our society. What is new is the way it is being articulated today by those sections of society who claim the mantle of secularism, liberalism and tolerance. (p. 11)

Further, 'not only are minority ideological beliefs often disregarded but also the historical heritage and rich cultural traditions of ethnic groups is rejected for a globalisation of religious belief' (Husain and O'Brien 2001, p. 25). As a result, in this struggle or process 'many liberal Muslim voices are silenced and others become unwitting defenders of "Islamic" practices and policies which they do not support' (ibid.).

Further afield, Saeed and Akbarzadeh (2001) suggest that second- and third-generation minority ethnic groups such as Australian Muslims are adding a new layer to their identity:

> they are developing a certain bond with Australia, which in most cases is not at the expense of their Islamic and ethnic heritage. Their Australianness complements and puts into perspective their Muslim identity and their ethnic traditions. The result may be a hybrid Islamic identity based on commitment to the secular norms of Australian society and Islamic/ethnic traditions. (p. 5)

Importantly they add that the sense of ownership and social responsibility among Muslim Australians is tied to the extent of their inclusion and participation in mainstream society, and that the shifting nature of group loyalties should not be taken as un-Australianness but as an affirmation of the country's diverse cultural heritage. Similarly, Webber (1994) in his review of Jewish identity in Europe argues that the constituents of identity change over time and place, and that there is no single Jewish identity. He maintains that lifestyle and social and cultural frameworks are of increasing significance compared to worship and religious practice.

Baumann (1996) suggests not only that identities are fluid but that individuals operate, often consciously, with multiple identities, developing or selecting the one which is seen to be the most functional or useful at a particular time. This is what Nielsen (1995) calls 'situational identity choice'. So a child in a classroom may be perceived as Muslim at school, British or German at home, or simply an adolescent in the playground. Yet, as we discussed earlier, ascription and identity need to be looked at from angles of self-description. Likewise, in the case of Muslim communities, the 'patterning of religious-cultural differentiation may disappear with the loss of provincial and national identification by younger generations of Muslims who may also acquire English speaking Imams' (Husain and O'Brien 2001, p. 19).

Communities themselves are under constant change as they seek to adapt to living as a minority in Britain, and individuals, for example women and British-born younger-generation members within communities, may also challenge the status quo. This contradicts a common assumption among Europeans that identity is a 'fixed non-moveable entity', and European institutions have tended to respond to the development of immigration and ethnic minorities with policies based on 'mono-identities' within religious communities.

Religious Communities

We introduced the concept of community earlier and here we discuss the term as it relates to that of religious groupings, and the basic freedom of religion and belief. By the term 'religious community' we mean a group of people living in the same locality and/or having the same religion, and in some cases sharing the same race or ethnic background. Rex (1993) maintains that:

> it has become increasingly clear that in any mapping of the ethnic minority populations in Britain and Europe religion is an important differentiating factor. (p. 16)

The concept can be narrowly drawn to refer to a small group of people living dependently or co-dependently, or, notes Werbner (2002b), as in the Islamic sense of 'ummah' it can be constructed to incorporate all Muslims throughout the world regardless of national borders. Rex (1993) adds that religion has the ability to divide groups which have shared geographical, national and linguistic origins, such as Indians, who are divided between Hindus, Sikhs, Muslims, Christians and others. Or, he argues, religious affiliation may serve as a unifying factor joining together individuals of different ethnic and national origins, for example Catholics and Jews.

The strength of belief, and indeed the strength of opposition to religious beliefs, have been documented in a number of ways. Hinnells (1997) explains:

> religions have often been deeply involved in political matters, in cultural developments, they have been used to legitimate, suppress or inspire regimes, philosophies and artistic movements. Religious institutions have, for good or for ill, dominated or undermined secular establishments of many kinds. It is not possible to understand the history of most, if not all, countries without knowledge of the religions which have flourished there and influenced, moulded or corrupted both leaders and masses. (p .3)

As we discussed earlier, the Diaspora or movement of people around the world has meant that new religions, languages and cultures have been introduced into this country and other Western states. For example, South Asian religions such as Hinduism and Sikhism all have sizeable presences in the West, and this has added to the religious landscape of society (Coward et al. 2000; Lipner 2000; Knott 2000). Some groups may belong to several different diasporas or multiple diasporas, for example Asian, Muslim, nationalist Pakistani and Punjabi. As such there may be a 'hybrid diaspora', which has an impact on the religious community and self in terms of shaping identity (Werbner 2002b).

When we talk about religious traditions, there are no clear-cut categories but instead a huge differentiation of people under the umbrella terms.[1] Despite research demonstrating a decline in religious adherence and a trend towards what is loosely called 'secularization' (Cox 1996; Smart 1968; Smith 1978; Gallagher 1997), there is also evidence of an increase in religious activity among some groups, for example Islamic revivalism, and the growth of 'alternative' religions in the West (Hinnells 1997).

Britain has one of the most religiously diverse populations in the European Union, and each religion itself has a high level of diversity in terms of traditions, histories, languages and culture.[2] Statistically, Muslims are the largest religious minority in Britain after Christians, as noted in the previous chapter, followed by Jews, Hindus and Sikhs (Census 2001). Smaller groupings exist such as Buddhists, Jains, Zoroastrians, Baha'is and Pagans. Members within these religious communities share common beliefs and practices, but, notes Weller (1997), 'there are also significant differences of tradition, organisation, ethnicity and language' (p. 23). Further, within each of these religious groupings are a range of minority communities whose relation to the majority is either distinct and/or disputed.[3] There is also fluidity in the boundaries between different religious traditions; for example, within the religious practice of Chinese communities there is evidence of Taoism, Confucianism and Buddhism in intermingled form (ibid.). Pagans and people from new religious movements, often labelled by the media as 'cults', are also an increasing part of religious pluralism (Weller et al. 2001), and followers of New Age spiritualities are also evident in our landscape, as are Humanists, agnostics and atheists. (We will be looking at how this translates into practice, concerning religious acts of worship in schools, later in Chapter 6.) In short, whilst Christianity remains the UK's main religious tradition in terms of the size of its following, there is a wide spectrum of beliefs and practices, and plurality is to be found in varying degrees elsewhere in Europe. Finally, for all these groups there is an expectation that they will have the freedom to practise their religion and beliefs as a basic human right.

Freedom of Religion and Belief

It is useful to consider what we mean by 'freedom of religion and belief' as this is fundamental to the efforts of communities in establishing their own institutions, such as schools. The capacity to believe is a defining feature of human beings, and it is a characteristic which has found expression in religions and ideologies throughout history. Most countries recognize freedom of religion and have laws which relate to this freedom, but there are varying degrees of the right in terms of principle or practice. The United Nations Declaration Of Human Rights states:

> everyone has the right to freedom of thought, conscience and religion; this right includes freedom to change his religion or belief, and freedom, either alone or in community with others and in public or private, to manifest his religion or belief in teaching, practice, worship and observance. (Article 18)[4]

Protection of this freedom is not restricted to religion but also extends to atheism and the right *not* to profess any belief. It also covers freedom of thought, conscience and personal convictions, and a commitment to belief whether manifested as an individual or in a community with others. Importantly, freedom of religion is wide-ranging and does not refer to traditional world religions only. As such, new religious organizations or religious minorities, highlighted above, are entitled to equal protection. In reality, however, the right to freedom of religious belief may only exist as rhetoric, and in practice there can be intolerance shown by the state, individuals and among religions, for example in leaving a religion, in joining a religion, or through the experience of 'mixed marriages'.

Clarification of terminology is useful here for 'religion' is commonly interpreted by the UN declaration as being broad in scope rather than the narrowness of historical interpretation, and it incorporates freedom of 'thought and conscience'. The concept of 'beliefs' is also a broader category than religion, and can incorporate political and ideological views, as well as spiritual or moral views on life. The word 'faith' which we have used throughout our discussions is often used by religious groups themselves and refers to a way of life rather than a hierarchical structure. We should note, however, that it is a Western term and is less commonly used, for example, in Eastern religions. Faith groups share a 'truth', a knowledge that they wish to share with others and through which they examine their own problems, and those of society in general. Faith groups' understanding of inclusion and the global nature of religion mean that throughout history they have spanned many cultures. Faith, identity and culture are interrelated with subtle layers of meaning, and 'cultural heritage' is maintained differently by different groups, a point we will return to later in the chapter.

Conversely, 'secular' means not concerned with or related to religion, and for many people in society life is secular and they do not themselves have a religious identity. For the religious adherent, religious obligations may have to be negotiated in school and at work. As such, individuals may feel that in some way they are involved in a 'trade-off', whereby they are expected to choose parts of religion, and not change what they are but change what they do at certain times. This has direct implications for children at school, and is a reason why some families opt for faith-based education. There is perceived to be a difficulty, at times, of secular educationalists understanding religious educationalists, and vice versa, in some cases challenging whether there is any place for religion in school. But this is to oversimplify the situation: there are secular teachers of religion, and the place of Religious Education in the school timetable is not contested or undermined in all community schools. Further, despite the differences between religious and secular teachers, there tends to be a shared consensus on the critical place of moral values in the educational process, and understandably those responsible for community schools are offended by the assumption that this may be absent in their schools.

Parents have the right to raise their children according to their religious convictions or conscience, passing down religious belief from one generation to another in the home without interference by the state. This is reflected in European law as follows:

> no person shall be denied the right to education. In the exercise of any function which it assumes in relation to education and teaching, the State shall respect the right of parents to ensure such education and teaching in conformity with their own religious and philosophical convictions. (The European Convention on Human Rights and Fundamental Freedoms)[5]

In school, children have the right to receive education in matters of religion or belief which are in conformity with the wishes of their parents. (We will be looking at the issue of religious education in more detail later in Chapter 6.) Importantly, the state is not obliged to provide schools which meet the religious beliefs of parents, but instead to respect the liberty of parents to establish schools which reflect their religious beliefs.

Traditionally, religious communities have been pivotal to the establishment of schools, as we saw in Chapter 2, and in countries like Britain, the Netherlands and Australia they have looked to the state for financial support. Rights are not absolute, however, but are subject to time and circumstance, and so in this case, for example, the rights of the parents are balanced by the requirement that religious freedom must not be injurious to the child. In addition, the child should have access to education that protects against intolerance, and encourages a respect for the beliefs of others. The United Nations Convention on the Rights of the Child, for example, stipulates that there must be respect for the child's right to freedom of thought, conscience and religion as the child gets older. (We return to the issue of children's rights as opposed to parents' rights later in Chapter 8.)

There is a distinction in law between the right to have religious convictions, an unconditional right, and the freedom to manifest those beliefs. The concept of freedom of manifestation of belief can cover a broad range of activities such as the building of places of worship, the displaying of religious symbols, and the choice of religious holidays and days of rest. Furthermore:

> the observance and practice of religion may include not only ceremonial acts but also such customs as the observance of dietary regulations, the wearing of distinctive clothing or headcoverings, and the use of a particular language customarily spoken by a group, the practice and teaching of religion, the freedom to choose their religious leaders, priests and teachers, the right to establish seminaries or religious schools and the freedom to prepare and distribute religious tests or publications.[6]

In interpreting this right, Boyle and Sheen (1997) state:

> it is in this sphere of collective activities that religions in particular are likely to have to relate to the law and government administration; this is where many complaints arise over bureaucratic obstruction or failings of the state. (p. 7)

Countries which are a party to the United Nations Convention are obliged to secure religious freedom, to eliminate discrimination, and, as with any other right, this is dependent on 'the rule of law' in a democratic society. There should be a harmonization between religious law and international human rights standards, to accept the reality of religious belief in different cultures. Restrictions placed on the right to manifest religion or belief are measures to prevent propaganda for war or the advocacy of national, racial or religious hatred. Interestingly, freedom of religion includes the right to believe that one has exclusive truth and that what others believe is lacking in truth. However, under international standards people should not be treated less favourably because they do not share your beliefs and, as such, differences of belief should not render you more vulnerable to discrimination. In reality, however, this is precisely what happens in many parts of the world when discrimination and intolerance are justified by reference to the inferiority or falsity of opposing beliefs, whether religious or non-religious.

One final point on the concept of religious freedom is the right to choose and change religious commitment. International standards state clearly that there must not be coercion in matters of religion, a view shared by many faiths. It is within this right to change one's religion that people choose to convert to a religion into which they were not born, but which subsequently shapes their religious identity and their role in the community, a point we return to later in the chapter.

Schools, particularly, are the place where differences in religion and values come into play. Britain has a tradition of religious pluralism and the church involvement in education goes back several centuries, as we saw earlier in Chapter 2. In Germany, through its 'Basic Law', there is a guarantee of the right to religious worship, organization and teaching, and children have traditionally received instruction in Catholicism and Protestantism whilst the state is 'religionsneutral' (Nielsen 1995), although this is now undergoing change. In France, state schools have followed a secular tradition except in private, Catholic schools (ibid.). Elsewhere, the curriculum has been opened up to include knowledge of world religions, a pattern followed in Sweden and Norway and one being replicated in faith-based and community schools in Britain. Very importantly, schools have assumed a major responsibility for inculcating ideas of citizenship, which may conflict with the expectations of parents. Ironically, when Churches have been involved in schooling, for example in Germany, France and the Netherlands, they have also been perceived as largely secular in nature in contrast with the religious consciousness of families, especially among newly arrived communities. Accordingly:

> for the immigrants and ethnic minorities, on the one hand, the school is the passport to the upward social mobility and material success of their children. But it is also the forum in which they perceive their core values as being most open to subversion. For them the school is a threat at the very same time as it is a necessity. (ibid., p. 8)

It is this perceived subversion of core values in society in general, and in schools specifically, which can be the source of tension.

Islam, for instance, is a good example of how an increased sense of politicization within some Muslim communities has signalled a change 'from a passive to an active factor of identity' (ibid., p. 15). This may be demonstrated through dress, and non-Muslims are often understandably confused when Muslims from different cultural backgrounds are themselves divided on such issues as appropriate attire where there is no overall consensus. (A similar difference of opinion concerns the choice of curriculum at school, as we shall see later in Chapter 6.) This has led to schools trying to identify which elements of cultural life, for instance fasting and prayer times, are essential to a sense of religious identity; and which aspects of life can be moderated. There is the undeniable mixture of religion and culture within a child's background: where does one end and another start? Some Muslims, either through education or other personal circumstances, may feel more comfortable in engaging with the wider community than others. As such:

> across the continent young people in growing numbers are beginning to explore ways of redefining or even re-inventing Islam in ways which can function constructively in the European and political environment. (ibid., p. 16)

There is also a representation among the children of Muslim immigrants in countries like France, and they are engaging in 'a critique of traditional Muslim practices regarding social and family structures' (ibid., p. 17). This lead from the Muslim intelligentsia is evidenced by the work of Ramadan in Switzerland, Modood in Britain and Said in the United States, about the bias demonstrated by the media in handling issues of religious identity. Ramadan's work is also useful in highlighting the process from a passive to an active identification with Islam, and from one culturally bound towards a 're-acculturation' in which awareness of shared concerns, sometimes even a perception of a shared fate with the Muslim universal community or 'ummah', has strengthened support. Similarly, Baumann (1996) examines how various definitions of 'culture' and 'community' are mobilized by different sectors of a local society, the religious leaderships, the extended family, youth groups, local government and local agencies of central government. Moreover, sectors within the local community have repositioned themselves to benefit from the resources being distributed by 'the holders of power' according to such selected definitions. This would be true in Britain of Muslim, Sikh, Greek Orthodox and Seventh Day Adventist communities, which are now accessing state funding for their schools.

One of the measures of religious adherence is also the frequency of attendance at places of worship. Rules governing the need to attend church, temple, synagogue or mosque vary within and among different groups. For Muslims, for example, there are also differences of opinion about whether women should worship at the mosque or in the home (Sarwar 1992). Other groups, such as Hindus, may have their own private shrines at home (Kanitkar and Jackson 1982; King 1984; Knott 1986). Places of worship may also be used for educational purposes, as we noted in the previous two chapters, and elders at these places of worship may be asked to confirm attendance of the family and child, which in some cases is essential for admission to a faith-based school. So what we see is that within religious groupings there is no consensus as to whether attendance at places of worship is obligatory and whether in fact religious adherence has to be demonstrated by such attendance. This has become a very contentious issue for admission to some Church of England schools, however, where proof of church attendance by both the child and the family is required in order to secure a place in the school (*Times Educational Supplement* 2003l).

Mention should also be made of the role of converts in promoting religion. Some would argue that 'revert' rather than 'convert' is a better descriptor because it is the process of reverting back to an intended state (Weller 2001). In Britain, for example, there have been a number of converts to Islam, the most famous of whom is Cat Stevens. Now known as Yusuf Islam, he has for the last few decades provided leadership in the establishment of successful Muslim schools, and he has been an important spokesman for the community. In Germany, notes Nielsen (1995), native German Muslims have provided significant leadership. Indeed, 'more than any other European country, German Muslims have played a crucial role in the establishment of Islam' (ibid., p. 14). There are over five thousand converts to Islam in Germany and they have been particularly important in supporting the construction of purpose-built mosques in the 1980s, such as the famous Islamic Cultural Centre at Alstar Lake in Hamburg, and in Aachen and Munchen (ibid.).

Similarly, Donohoue Clyne (2001) states that, in Australia, many of the founders of the first Muslim schools have also been converts to Islam and therefore aware of the values underpinning local government. Silma Buckley (1991) is probably the most well-known Australian convert as she waged a long and successful battle against local government to obtain state funding for her private Muslim school. Overall, therefore, these converts have provided leadership, as in Britain, and they have been able to mediate with German and Australian society, often establishing constructive relations with government and other religious groups.

The idea of converting from one faith to another is not a new phenomenon, but those living in the West who choose to convert to religious traditions from the Indian subcontinent often find that they are also absorbing cultural difference. Indeed, the version of the faith they are converting to is likely to be shaped by the cultural background of their new religious community, and this raises issues for them about the nature of the religion they have chosen and its ethnic content. As such, where there are converts in a religious community there is not necessarily a shared history but a shared religious identity, which binds them.

To summarize so far, self-description about identity is primarily an expression of whom you belong with, of membership of a community. This may extend to preference for schools based on one's own religion or to choosing a particular religious instruction in school. The concept can also be used to provide a unifying perspective through which we can gain a fuller and more integrated understanding of social activity and collective identity: a localized affair, which may be a matter of individual conduct, or a social group characterized by huge diversity with little commonality or expectation of conformity in terms of religious adherence. Religion can also be used to help a community define itself and maintain its subculture, especially within a dominant cultural group. This is sometimes achieved through marrying within the faith in order to prevent assimilation and loss of faith, and also to avoid alienation. Groups may also use their distinctive dress or language to reinforce their separation from mainstream society, to retain their difference and sustain their values. The centrality of family and place of worship also influences this sense of identity and acts as a resistance to the erosion of their religious boundary, serving to challenge the perceived secular and increasingly individualistic wider society in which they find themselves.

Religion and Ethnicity

So far we have looked at religious identity and religious communities, and one of the key issues which has emerged is the overlap between religion and ethnicity and what some writers describe as 'ethnic-religious communities'. Some religions have congregations consisting of large numbers of visible minorities, such as Muslims, Sikhs and Hindus, and there is often a degree of overlap between religion and ethnicity in the way they conduct their lives, and in the way they are treated by others. The experience of implicit or explicit racism may be part of their experience, as well as religious bigotry. Furthermore, it is not always clear whether religion or ethnicity is the dominant characteristic affecting people's understanding of themselves, and their personal sense of identity. Religion and ethnicity are complex and difficult to define or separate, as we have seen in our earlier discussion, yet both are potential causes of discriminatory treatment. In a study conducted for the British government on religious discrimination it was found that some religious people as a matter of principle make no distinction between their religion and their ethnicity or race (Weller et al. 2000). Others have a strong wish to do so. Also, people representing religions with a high proportion of minority ethnic members see a clear overlap between religious and racial discrimination. With particular reference to Muslim communities, it was found that they 'suffer from colour, racial, ethnic and religious discrimination' because 'racists cannot analyse between race and religion' (ibid., p. 13)[7]

Claims of unfair treatment on the basis of religion are often made by groups that include a substantial proportion of people who also suffer discrimination on the basis of ethnicity.[8] This confusion can be seen in public policy where, for example, ethnic-religious groups, like Jews and Sikhs, as we noted earlier, are directly covered by the Race Relations Acts (1975, 2000).[9] This protection has not, however, been extended to others, such as Muslims, who can sometimes be covered by 'indirect discrimination' provisions in the legislation, but the courts have not been consistent in their interpretation of this clause. An awareness of religion as a dimension of equal opportunities is evident in the policy of some organizations, but current law does not extend to include discrimination on the basis of religion.[10] Muslim communities, for example, have struggled to obtain state funding for their schools in the face of what they felt was discrimination and a failure to receive equitable treatment compared with other religious communities (Parker-Jenkins 2002).

Minority ethnic communities and their faith-based schools do not fit easily into current theoretical paradigms, particularly as they relate to the construction of identity.[11] There is a need for theoretical and methodological innovation to clearly articulate differing accounts of the issues regarding equal opportunity and equal access to resources. The work of Tariq Modood is particularly helpful here because of his extensive study of ethnicity in the UK. Researching into diversity and disadvantage for the Policy Studies Institute, Modood et al. (1997) raised the question, 'how do ethnic minority people think of themselves?'. They found in their survey that most of the second-generation Caribbeans and South Asians, for example, were uncomfortable with the idea of 'British' being anything more than 'a legal title'; in particular, 'they found it difficult to call themselves ''British'' because they felt that the majority of white people did not accept them because of their race or cultural background' (ibid., p. 331). Importantly, they also noted the contrast between African-Asians and Indians on the one hand, and Pakistanis and Bangladeshis (most of whom are Muslim) on the other, in relation to a number of factors, such as preference for religion, for single-sex schools for daughters, and for schools of one's own religion. For example, some Muslims expressed their support for single-sex girls' schools based on Islamic principles and the researchers found 'a higher degree of cultural retentiveness or conservatism among Pakistanis' (ibid., p. 325).

Also of relevance to this discussion on the theorizing of race and ethnicity is the work of Paul Gilroy. He challenges general assumptions underpinning anti-racist policy, and his book *There Ain't No Black in the Union Jack* (1987), examines shifting notions of race, nation and power, and the failure of British government on both sides of the political spectrum to articulate anti-racism in a manner which is inclusive. He highlights conceptual weaknesses in existing policies, and argues for a wider, more theoretical and dynamic understanding of race and racism. Echoing Giroux's view that there are no fixed boundaries, Gilroy (1987) maintains, 'the culture which defines the groups we know as races, is never fixed, finished or final. It is fluid, it is actively and continually made and re-made' (ibid., p. 80). This is well captured in the novel *White Teeth*, which explores the shifting nature of cultural identity in three families in Britain over three generations (Smith 2000b).

In challenging existing paradigms on identity, therefore, we need to be aware of broader and more dynamic concepts of ethnicity, for, as Modood (1989) argues:

> neither Muslims nor other religious-ethnic minorities will be understood unless current race philosophies are re-evaluated. The beginning of that understanding is the

appreciation of the centrality of religion to the Muslim, and perhaps also to the Sikh and Hindu, psyche: that it is of far more importance and central to self-definition than 'race' or than can be allowed for by the black-white view of the world. (p. 284)

Finally, with regard to the issue of access to public resources, which forms a central theme of this book, it is also useful to give some thought to how we conceptualize 'equality'. In their conclusion to the Fourth National Survey of Ethnic Minorities in Britain, Modood et al. (1997) highlight a shift in understanding, from equality in terms of cultural assimilation, to one of political recognition:

> equality is not having to hide or apologise for one's origins, family or community but expecting others to respect them and adapt public attitudes and arrangements so that the heritage they represent is encouraged rather than contemptuously expected to wither away. (p. 358)

This would be particularly true of the development of Muslim and Sikh schools. Furthermore, equality is conceptualized in two ways: the right to assimilate to the dominant culture in the public sphere and toleration of one's difference in the private sphere; and the right to have one's difference recognized and supported in both the public and private spheres. There is clearly a potential tension here and these researchers conclude that change can only come about 'through finding and cultivating points of common ground between dominant and subordinate cultures as well as new syntheses and hybridities' (ibid.). The important thing, they maintain, is that the burden of change, or the costs of not changing, should not be placed on one party only.

Broadly, theoretical perspectives underpinning the issue of faith-based schools established by minority ethnic communities fall into the category of shifting economic, social and cultural contexts, within which religious and ethnic minority individuals and communities operate. As we have seen so far, they draw on race, culture and difference (Donald and Rattansi 1992), 'the politics of difference' (Young 1990), and on what Modood (1992) refers to as the difficulties of being accepted by the majority group, and the implications of this in terms of limited access to resources, which influences education provision. Also, as we have noted, under the Race Relations Act it is not illegal to discriminate on the basis of religion *per se*; yet there are overlapping factors of identity, which are inclusive of religious, cultural, political and personal factors. Modood et al. (1997) suggest that:

> there seem to be various forms of prejudice and discrimination which use cultural difference to vilify or marginalize or demand cultural assimilation from groups who also suffer colour racism. (p. 353)

This was confirmed in a study of Muslim women in the workplace, in which it was found that there was clearly a potential for people to suffer double discrimination when religious identity and colour overlap (Parker-Jenkins et al. 1998b).

Significantly, continue Modood et al, (1997), South Asians themselves are 'more likely to identify Muslims, rather than Asians as a whole, as the group against whom there is most hostility' (p. 353). Such anti-Muslim prejudice is seen as 'a white reaction to the revival of Islamic self-confidence and self-assertion in Britain and elsewhere' (ibid.), which was mentioned earlier in Chapter 3. Significantly, communities choose to select a number of ways to respond to racism and xenophobia, and in some cases, notes Werbner (2002b), they may 'naturalise their multiple identities, vesting them with current value in Britain' (p. 14). For others, there is an ongoing struggle to maintain cultural identity despite discrimination in the wider society.

At a legislative level, a new framework making demands on public organizations and employers would extend the grounds for claims of discrimination, and inclusion of religion within such cover would echo that degree of statutory protection which pertains under law in the USA and Northern Ireland. At a community level, if we have protection in one area in the UK, then arguably it could be extended more broadly. This could include introducing measures against both personal prejudice which directly discriminates against minority groups, and public policy which brings about structural exclusion. Although religious bigotry rather than racism may be one label for the discrimination such groups face, their experience could also be subsumed within the category of 'new racism' (Hall 1992; Gilroy 1993; Gillborn 1995). Further, 'cultural xenophobia' and 'the experience of alien citizenship' (Werbner 2002b, p. 14) mean that individuals in some communities may feel disaffected and marginalized, which we have seen manifested in racist riots, such as in the northern towns in England in 2001. More sophisticated analytical models could be developed so that those which apply to 'racial discrimination', could be constructively extended and applied to religion. We could therefore consider 'religious prejudice', 'religious hatred', direct and indirect 'religious discrimination', and 'incitement to religious hatred' as forms of analysis in helping to explain the experiences of minority groups.[11]

In the 1980s there was a belief that, under the umbrella of 'equal opportunities', social inclusion would prevail. This is part of what we now see as a naïve belief in political ideology, which has not been successful in addressing inequality, and in highlighting the interface between race, ethnicity and religion in which cultural identity is a perceived cause of disadvantage. There may be hope in the new Human Rights Act (1998), in which inclusion of the European Convention aims 'to bring human rights back home' (Wadham et al. 2003). As we noted earlier in this chapter, Article 9 of the document refers to 'freedom of thought, conscience and religion' and 'the manifestation of belief', which could provide ample opportunities for use by minority groups. The implications of the Act are that not only followers of the major world religions but also those from new religious movements could look for remedy from discriminatory practices, prejudice and hostility. This kind of approach has support within Muslim communities, notes Hewitt (1998), because for them the issue is about human rights as much as education.

So far we have explored the right to religious freedom, the concept of identity based on cultural heritage, religious adherence and ethnicity, and the way in which racial but not religious discrimination is covered by the law. Next we look at government policy in Britain and elsewhere that has been enacted especially as a result of increased immigration and the inclusion of new communities into the education system, and which has been seen by some groups as undermining cultural heritage and religious identity.

Assimilation and Integration

Immigration after the Second World War called for legal, political and social policy changes, and the education system was not exempt from this process. Post-war immigration led to the increased presence of children from minority groups in the classroom and political ideologies were shaped in response to this reality. In education this took the form of six stages, frequently overlapping, whereby government attempted to respond to the reality of an increasingly multicultural, multilingual and multi-faith Britain.

Massey (1991) provides useful discussion of the key stages of government response to post-war immigration, commencing with one of laissez-faire or inaction:

the assumption was that everyone was equal before the law, and therefore no special policies were necessary. (p. 9)

Accordingly, immigrants were expected to integrate into society after experiencing temporary difficulties. Racial tension in the late 1950s clearly highlighted the inadequacy and naïvety of this ideological position, and a phase of assimilation took place along with greater restriction of immigration to the country. Beginning in 1962 several Immigration Acts were passed limiting right of entry for those born in independent Commonwealth countries or colonies. In educational terms, assimilation via language and numbers took the form of introductory courses in English at infant and junior reception centres. Further, Department of Education and Science Circular 7/65 gave Local Education Authorities permission for the dispersal or 'bussing' of immigrant children where the quota of such pupils exceeded 33 per cent of the school roll: 'justification for such a policy was educational, based on language development and a furtherance of cultural assimilation' (ibid., p. 10). Milner (1983) highlights the fact that children were dispersed regardless of their length of stay in the country or whether language difficulties were experienced, and without parental consent. Assimilation and cultural resocialization were thus the avowed intent of the government, as stated in the Commonwealth Immigrants Advisory Council report:

if their parents were brought up in another culture or another tradition, children should be encouraged to respect it, but a national system [of education] cannot be expected to perpetuate the different values of immigrant groups. (Massey 1991, p. 7)

Moreover, the assimilationist thrust assumed the existence of:

an obvious, definable homogeneous essence (the British culture) into which the hapless migrant might be inducted, given a suitable dose of English and an undiluted diet of the official school curriculum. (Rattansi 1992, p. 15)

An ideological shift to integration as a concept next gained currency, sometimes presented, states Massey (1991), 'as a more sensitive development of assimilation' (p. 11). Social integration was predicated on grounds of linguistic integration, and bilingualism was seen as an impediment to this development. Section 11 funding introduced in 1966 helped support this policy, whereby Local Education Authorities could claim back 50 per cent of the cost of providing English as a second language from the Home Office, and integration through compensation became a feature of this policy. Accordingly:

language tuition itself was mainly confined to Asian pupils, and not extended to Afro-Caribbean children who were seen as speaking a deficient dialect of English which needed correction. (ibid.)

Cultures were thus valued according to how well they measured up to a normative concept, which was white and middle class, and where they failed 'they were seen as deficient and inferior' (ibid., p. 12). As problems of minority ethnic children were perceived as a result of cultural or linguistic deficiencies or family structure, the school was not required to examine its role or teaching methodology of ethnic minority children; rather, policies and practices were presented in a deracialized form, and failure to integrate into British culture could be placed with the minority groups themselves (ibid.). Evidence of racial discrimination and alienation (Daniel 1968) suggested that integration along these lines was unlikely to succeed or be acceptable, and education was seen yet again as an important agent of change in ameliorating the situation.

The development of multiculturalism denotes an important stage in the ideological shift away from the cultural imperatives of assimilation and integration to one of cultural pluralism. Generally acknowledged as originating in 1966 as a result of a speech by the then Home Secretary Roy Jenkins, the Labour government called for an ideology of assimilation through cultural diversity. Multiculturalism was expressed in terms of creating tolerance for minority groups, raising awareness of their religious and cultural practices, celebrating differences, dispelling ignorance and reducing prejudice to create a harmonious society (Lynch 1988; Jeffcoate 1981). This phase can be summed up as one of equal opportunity in an atmosphere of mutual tolerance and cultural pluralism. Educational imperatives stemmed from evidence of underachievement (Rampton Committee 1981); civil disturbances (Scarman 1981); and recommendations that there should be a shift to educating all children about living in multicultural Britain (Swann 1985), thereby providing:

> legitimacy and impetus to local education authorities and schools already tentatively and sometimes vigorously pursuing one or another variety of multicultural and antiracist policy. It is arguable that Swann put multiculturalism and at least weak versions of antiracism on the national educational agenda. (Rattansi 1992, pp. 12–13)

Schools responded by embracing a variety of approaches to teaching policy and practice. For example, in the 1970s Manchester adopted specific policies to tackle underachievement (Massey 1991, p. 14). Likewise, some education authorities, such as Brent, Bradford, Birmingham, East Sussex and the now defunct Inner London Education Authority (ILEA), issued guidelines on how schools could be responsive to the needs of Muslim children through incorporating 'worthwhile initiatives and imaginative developments' (Sarwar 1994, p. 1).

The Select Committee on Race Relations and Immigration (1969) encouraged teaching about countries from which the minority ethnic children originated, including lessons on their art, songs and costume, leading to an approach to multicultural education in the 1970s caricatured as 'the 3 S version – saris, samosas and steel bands' (Massey 1991, p. 13). Asian History and Caribbean Studies as non-examination courses were added to programmes of study, offered predominantly in multiracial schools:

> this kind of approach to multicultural education rested on the assumption that the poor performance and alienation in school of black and Asian children could be remedied by improving their self-images. (ibid.)

Government initiatives and documents endorsed this shift in ideology from assimilation to cultural pluralism thus:

> our society is a multicultural, multiracial one and the curriculum should reflect a sympathetic understanding of the different cultures and races that now make up our society. (Department of Education and Science 1977, paras 10–11)

Adoption of a multiculturalist policy within education in the 1980s was accompanied by a plethora of texts on multicultural education, evidenced by the work of Craft and Bardell (1984); Jeffcoate (1981); Banks and Lynch (1986); and Tomlinson (1984), to name but a few. Critics of multiculturalism focused on the inadequate attempts at addressing cultural diversity through the curriculum; the reinforcing of stereotypes and superficial discussion of culture; the negative assumptions about minority children's sense of self-worth; attempts at social control; and the failure to confront racism both institutionally and personally

(Troyna 1986; Mullard 1981; Troyna and Williams 1986; Troyna and Ball 1987). Furthermore:

> antiracists have pointed out that in privileging prejudice and attitudes the multiculturalists have neglected racism as embedded in structures and institutions. (Rattansi 1992, p. 25)

The models within the umbrella term 'multiculturalism' were doomed to failure since they 'tinker with educational techniques and methods and leave unaltered the racist fabric of the education system' (ibid.).

Beyond 'multiculturalism' lay a phase of anti-racist education in policy, provision and pedagogy (Troyna 1986), aimed at challenging inequalities in society and schools. The two concepts multiculturalism and anti-racism both overlap and coincide within educational policy and practice. Connections were also made with inequality based on class and gender. Whilst there is overlap between the concepts:

> anti-racism was seen as a radical departure from multicultural education, which was attempting to promote racial harmony on the basis of understanding and appreciation of other cultures. (Massey 1991, p. 17)

Moreover, the new model was seen as a radical political movement with an emphasis on inequality, and on understanding of the roots of racism in the economic and political systems. Anti-racism was conceived as being instrumental in acknowledging and focusing on racism in society, and in calling for schools to develop strategies to challenge and remove racist practices. This manifested itself in Local Education Authorities requiring their schools to develop policy opposing racism, and to implement strategies aimed at tackling racist abuse and reviewing curriculum along anti-racist lines. Berkshire and the ILEA, for example, carried this out in 1983, followed by other authorities such as Birmingham and Bradford (Massey 1991).

Combining these two paradigms of multiculturalism and anti-racism is what Massey feels constitutes the sixth stage which has application for all schools. Indeed, Tomlinson (1990) notes the specific need for this type of education in all-white schools, which might be following a predominantly ethnocentric curriculum and assuming that multicultural education is irrelevant to the needs of their pupils. The synthesis of the two paradigms demonstrates a greater awareness of racial injustice, and an implementation of strategies to challenge and combat racism within British schools. Government reports have recently emphasized the need to raise the attainment level of minority ethnic pupils, with particular concern that if ethnic diversity is ignored, and differences in educational achievement, then considerable injustices will be sanctioned (Ofsted 1996, 1999; Department for Education and Skills 2002, 2003a).

There have been similar developments elsewhere. In Sweden, for example, every fourth child has a foreign background, that is, born abroad or with one or more parents born outside Sweden (Hallgren 2002). The main countries of origin are the former Yugoslavia and Bosnia, followed by Iran and Iraq. In the 1980s, there was a heightened visibility of racist groups, for example 'Bevara Sverige Svenskt' ('Keep Sweden Swedish'), a neo-Nazi group which co-ordinated racist activities such as the burning of crosses in different parts of the country (Hallgren and Weiner 2002). Likewise, there have been racist riots in the northern towns in England in 2001, which we will discuss later in Chapter 8. In the face of such racist behaviour European countries have been compelled to consider the efficacy of existing policy and the role of education. For example, researchers in Spain, Sweden and Britain have been developing websites as a pedagogical tool to challenge racism and anti-democratic ideas among young people.[12]

While the concepts of multiculturalism/anti-racism are subjected to continual scrutiny and reappraisal, what multiculturalism has come to mean to many minority groups, however, is that the liberal approach to multicultural education does not adequately address the convictions of the religious adherent: the secular has survived at the expense of the sacred (Qureshi and Khan 1989). For example, among some Muslims, multiculturalism is perceived as an educational philosophy seen as prompting their children to scrutinize and challenge the authority of Islamic texts and authorities (Sarwar 1983). Similarly, for Jewish communities, schools are the place where both assimilation and cultural preservation has taken place. Alderman (1999) argues that, in Britain, 'ethnic separation' has now become respectable and this is demonstrated in what takes place in schools. As such:

> we now live in a time where 'public' displays of Judaism are permitted and this has led to a new lease of life for, and emphasis on, Jewish schooling. (Miller 2001, p. 506)

Interestingly, multicultural/anti-racist teaching has been marginalized in some community schools as the implications of the Education Reform Act (1989) and local school management became apparent in the early 1990s. The publication of the Macdonald Report (Macdonald et al. 1989) into the tragic events at Burnage High School has been widely interpreted as signalling the failure of anti-racism within education (Rattansi 1992). At the same time Weldon (1989) called for a return to an integrationist policy, providing a set of British values to be embraced by everyone living in the country. Added to this, an ideological counter-offensive from the New Right has led to a discernible lobby reacting against a perceived preoccupation with multicultural teaching, and instead invoking a doctrine of a common British citizenship. (We will be exploring how the theme of citizenship has now been incorporated into the school curriculum later in Chapter 6.) It would appear, therefore, that society has come full circle and is again contemplating a notion of assimilation, and the idea of testing for citizenship by the government before citizenship status can be awarded.[13]

It is, however, unlikely that the momentum of multiculturalism can be changed despite the activities of neo-fascist groups in Europe or calls for a return to the concept of assimilation. Some assimilation is bound to take place but there will continue to be binding ties to one's ethnic origins and customs, and the promotion of religious identity, in some cases drawing upon cultural heritage which maintains community cohesion at one level and contributes to the overall reality of a multicultural, multi-faith society. Moreover, it is not acceptable to many groups that integration be a one-way street (Husain and O'Brien 1999). Instead it is argued that:

> individually and collectively, we should be involved in a process of mutual integration shifting away from essentialist definitions of family, culture and belief and towards a recognition of fluid, spatial boundaries and overlapping cultural spaces creating a more hybrid society of re-negotiated non-essentialist identities. (Husain and O'Brien 2001, p. 27)[14]

There have also been calls for a move away from the notion of equality towards a more inclusive concept of social justice. (This point is discussed more fully in Chapter 8.).Recent political change in Britain is also having an impact on the concept of identity. The devolution of the Scottish, Welsh and Northern Ireland parliaments, for example, 'will pose further challenges to the concept of essentialist, ossified cultures' (ibid., p. 26). As such, discussions taking place on what it is to be 'British' or 'English' suggest that:

> it is becoming increasingly apparent in Britain that there is no fixed majority ethnic culture, nor is there a static definition of Britishness. (ibid.)

Conclusion

In this chapter we have explored the key concepts of family, community, culture and overlapping issues of identity based on ethnicity and religion. We have seen that being a minority ethnic group may encourage communities to maintain protective boundaries identified by their religious, ethnic, linguistic and cultural backgrounds. Moreover, the importance of a cohesive extended family unit is embedded within the cultures of many minority ethnic communities, and this is also reflected in their religious practices. Yet both the majority and minority ethnic communities are in the process of change, as are familial structures, whilst identities are being negotiated within a complex and increasingly individualized world. This serves to challenge the fixed and static notion of cultural and religious difference. Cultures, communities and individual families are increasingly subject to societal pressures and influences, resulting in a dynamic and ever-changing perception of the place of religions, and how education should be organized. Tensions between minority communities and majority demands continue unabated as a new social order, characterized by the acceptance of diverse views and beliefs, struggles to emerge. This also impacts on the importance attached to religious values, hence the increased demands for faith-based schooling, the dominant theme of this book.

So far in our discussions we have seen what unites rather than what divides faith-based schools and their communities. They all share a desire to perpetuate faith and this is often associated with cultural tradition. Cultural tradition draws on race and ethnicity, and the importance of the family in securing an appropriate upbringing for the next generation. This is in the face of a perceived increase in secularization in mainstream society, growing support for far-right political parties and increasing racial tensions. Alongside these challenges to diversity and the acceptance of difference are attempts to secure the political and educational rights of religious adherents/groupings. In addition, the patrons of such schools expect the curriculum to reflect and celebrate their cultural heritage, and school to be a place where religious worship can take place. The next three chapters look at the practical aspects of education and the ability of faith-based schools to respond to this need, beginning with discussion of the legal context in which they operate, and issues of accountability to their community and the wider society.

Notes

1   See Robertson and Chirico (1985), Bradney (1993) and Parsons (1993).
2   See Council of Europe (1999) and Kerr (1992).
3   Weller et al. (2000, 2001) explore this in detail.
4   See Brownlie (1981).
5   See Robertson (1982).
6   Boyle and Sheen (1997).
7   This draws on research conducted for the Home Office on the perception of religious discrimination in England and Wales (Weller et al. 2000, 2001).
8   See Weller et al. (2000).
9   See, for example, *Ahmed v ILEA* (1975).
10   Weller et al. (2000).
11   Weller et al. (1999).
12   EUROKID is a European Union-funded project aimed at challenging racism through on-line resources.
13   See *The Guardian Education* (2003).
14   See also Beishon et al. (1998).

Chapter 5

Legal Matters and Accountability

Introduction

Over the last decade there have been a number of educational reforms in terms of redefining and readdressing the nature and purpose of schooling. Organizational and structural changes in education that emphasize accountability, effectiveness, achievement and excellence have been prominent features in many educational systems, nationally and internationally.[1] Faith-based schools are not immune to this development, particularly those in receipt of public funding, and they are required to demonstrate practice that is compatible with current educational perspectives on teaching and learning. Further, state-funded faith-based schools need to be accountable to pupils, their parents and their community, as well as to society at large, as do community schools, and to ensure that their beliefs, culture and practices are inclusive and effective. What makes the situation different, however, is that within faith-based schools the ongoing changes in educational practice have to be reconciled with their own religious principles and commitments.

In this chapter we explore these themes in the light of recent legislative reform and in the context of increasing accountability of schools. To address these issues we will:

- provide a background to the proposed expansion of faith-based schools;
- examine the legal context within which faith-based schools operate;
- discuss the current market forces they are subject to with the ethical and practical implications this raises for supporting diverse learners; and
- explore issues of 'effectiveness' as the emphasis on pupil achievement, especially among minority ethnic pupils, assumes a central place in the government agenda.

We begin by exploring the background to the proposed expansion of this category of school.

The Expansion of Faith-Based Schools

As we noted earlier in Chapter 2, by the 1860s it was clear that faith-based groups alone could not adequately meet the needs of the nation in voluntarily establishing schools. In the debates at the time, arguments were presented for both an expansion of church schools, and the creation of a wholly secular education system. The Elementary School Act (1870), which established an elementary school system for all, was seen as a compromise in that voluntary schools were allowed to continue with state funding, and these were augmented by the establishment of state schools run by local school boards (Lankshear 1996; Locke 2001). In the latter case, Christianity was still taught but schools were forbidden to promote one denomination over another, and parents had the right to withdraw their children from religious instruction. At the end of the 19th century, the voluntary sector had established around fourteen thousand schools representative of, for example, Church of England, Catholic, Methodist and Wesleyan groups (Archbishop's Council Church Schools Review Group 2001, p. 6). Further, categories of denominational schools were designated in the Education Act (1944) with various levels of government control but generally referred to as 'voluntary' schools (Arthur 1995; Francis and Lankshear 2001). Although still in common use, this designation system does not cover all categories of state-funded faith-based schools, as we also discussed in Chapter 2. The different categories used to describe what in general became known as 'voluntary' religious schools were offered the option of either increased funding and control, hence 'voluntary controlled schools', which became common practice among Church of England schools (Arthur 1995; Lankshear 2003), or less support and state interference with greater independence, known as 'voluntary aided', a status assumed by the majority of Catholic schools (Grace 2001a; O'Keefe 1999, 2000).[2]

Importantly, the 1944 Act did not specify religious affiliation. The relevant clauses of the Act provided for different levels of support and state intervention, but they did not specify *which* denominational groups could be included in the scheme. Hence, Jewish schools have received state funding through the procedure of obtaining voluntary aided status (Miller 2001), and more recently so have Muslim, Sikh, Greek Orthodox and Seventh Day Adventist schools (Department for Education and Skills, 2003b), as we discussed earlier in Chapter 3. Other minority groups may also wish to avail themselves of this right in the future, which is consistent with government thinking on the matter. As faith-based communities have initiated schooling and expanded provision, their role has been increasingly underpinned by legislation which has helped reinforce their place in helping to establish a national system of education in England and Wales, beginning in the 19th century, and continuing up until the present time (Cush 2003).

Currently, expansion in the number of faith-based schools can be seen as an attempt by the government to promote diversity, raise standards and develop partnership with the private sector (Schagen et al. 2002). Faith-based schools are said to be popular with parents in that they obtain good results on indicators of academic performance, but as we shall see later there is also some ambiguity about such claims (Marks 2001; Jackson 2001). They are also said to be successful in nurturing a positive school ethos (Judge 2002). Despite this popularity, there is not shared consensus about plans for their future expansion: for example, the British Humanist Association (2002) argues that religious pluralism can be accommodated within the community school.

In order to understand the criticism of developing further faith-based schooling it is also important to place this initiative in the context of the current social and political climate. The White Paper (2001) which announced the government intention to expand these schools was published in the same month as the terrorist attacks in the USA, and, together with the riots in Bradford, hatred and hostility were thought to result from communities being segregated by religion and ethnic divides.[3] Thus, in this context, it is not surprising that making state funding available for faith-based schools steers public debate particularly against those establishments associated with minority ethnic groups, as we discussed earlier in Chapter 3. In a MORI poll of nearly two thousand people, only 25 per cent favoured expansion of faith-based schools, while over 40 per cent were opposed to the policy (Passmore and Barnard 2001). It is interesting to note that the opposition to the expansion particularly targets those schools with less traditional and/or dominant religions, for example Muslim institutions. Yet the Church of England has opened 13 new secondary schools since 2000.[4] There are also plans to expand institutions founded on a Christian ethos in Middlesborough and Doncaster through sponsorship from the Vardy Foundation (*Evangelical Times* 2003). The notion of equality before the law with other religious denominations present in Britain, which we discussed earlier in Chapter 3, has been invoked to support the right of Muslims to establish voluntary aided schools (Mustafa 2001), and in aid of other faith-based groups who wish to have the same opportunities as those available to Christians and Jews (Mansell and Barnard 2001).

On one hand, parents have the right to expect that their children shall be educated in accordance with their own philosophical and religious convictions as countenanced in the European Convention on Human Rights.[5] On the other hand, there is growing opposition towards providing education that is likely to draw on a single religion in that it is perceived as contributing to society becoming divisive and exclusive. The assumption that religion is by its nature divisive, however, needs to be challenged. Jackson (1997), for example, argues that religion is inherently diverse, providing a paradigm to structure the understanding of the world. We found in our research that educational institutions may share a religious belief but have varied cultural, socio-economic or linguistic backgrounds.[6]

There is nonetheless a growing tendency in what might be called 'theologically liberal' faith-based schools to try and be more inclusive by opening up admissions and creating multi-faith schools. Some faith-based schools have changed their admissions policy, reaching out to pupils from different faiths or no faith. For example, the Church of England has devised a new policy aimed at increasing admission to its schools of from 10 per cent to 20 per cent of pupils that are not members of the Church of England.[7] There has also been an attempt to establish a multi-faith school with separate assemblies to accommodate pupils from diverse faith orientations as well as those of no faith.[8]

Despite opposition to the expansion of state-funded faith-based schools from some quarters, their existence is part of the traditional pattern of educational provision in England and Wales, as replicated elsewhere such as in the Netherlands (Walford 2000) and Australia (Donohoue Clyne 2001). Given the reality of religious pluralism in the educational system, therefore, and little likelihood of this changing, it is useful to consider the legal framework within which state-funded faith-based schools operate and the issue of accountability.

The Legal Framework

There have been a number of statutes concerning faith-based schools recently, which are directly relevant to the expansion of this category of school. The Education Act (1996), which has relevance to all independent schools, is a useful starting point to our discussion because new faith-based schools have tended to become independent first and then apply for state funding. This is what has happened in the case of Muslim and Sikh schools, for example, and is likely to be followed by other minority groups (Parker-Jenkins 2004).

The 1996 Act defines a school as one in which there are more than five pupils of compulsory school age, and as such a school can and has been established in a person's sitting room (Hewer 2001b). Fewer than five pupils and the arrangement is seen as constituting the 'education otherwise' category as stipulated in the Education Act (1944), that is, education taking place at home on an individual or small-group basis rather than as a school. If more than five an application has to be made to the Department for Education and Skills (DfES) to be registered as an independent school. In order to do this the institution has to comply under a number of headings. These relate to the suitability of the premises, accommodation regarding the age of the pupils and facilities if boarding children. 'Suitable and efficient' teaching and learning is also required, and the curriculum should be generally broad and balanced. Independent schools do not have to teach the National Curriculum, nor do they have to employ qualified teachers.[9]

Under the Children Act and National Care Standards Commission (2001), issues of health and safety are also considered for boarding schools. Within six months of registering, therefore, there is a visit from Her Majesty's Inspectorate (HMI), the independent sector's equivalent of the Office for Standards in Education (Ofsted). Some faith-based schools offer residency in addition to providing full-time education.[10] When the school meets the minimum required, HMI may recommend it to the Secretary of State for final registration status, and after that the school is visited every five years. The Education Act (2002) looks to modify the existing arrangement and to have a similar cycle of inspections as carried out in community schools. Also, under the new legislation, those wishing to start a new school require documentation pertaining to the state of the premises before a child may start. Likewise, staff require clearance through the Criminal Records Bureau before commencing teaching duties.[11]

In terms of inspection and accountability, state-funded faith-based schools are inspected like all other maintained schools except in terms of religious education, and the social, cultural, spiritual and moral aspects of the school are covered under Section 23 of the 1996 Act, which we will discuss later in this chapter. Also, after September 2003 reports on independent schools will be in the public domain and available on the Ofsted website. Within the new framework, these reports will be shorter and very specific with regard to premises, welfare and arrangements for the school having a complaints procedure. An important change is that independent schools are to be charged for their inspection. Small faith-based schools, such as the majority of Muslim ones, which number over a hundred, may find this difficult. In the consultation paper, it is being suggested that the cost amount to £50 per pupil and on a scale according to the size of the school. This will be an important development for independent faith-based schools, which tend to charge low fees and employ staff on lower salaries than in community schools. Whilst many faith-based schools welcome inspection, charging fees will be a significant issue.

Also relevant in discussing the legal context of faith-based schools is the School Standards and Framework Act (1998), highlighted in Chapter 2. This provides for the creation of 'School Organization Committees' consisting of representatives of the Local Education Authority, governing bodies and the Learning and Skills Council. Importantly, their role is to decide on proposals to establish, close, alter or change the category of a school. In the absence of an agreement, an adjudicator appointed by the Secretary of State takes a decision. A widely based 'Admissions Forum' has also been formed to consider school admissions and the policy governing staff recruitment. In considering candidates for the position of head teacher of a voluntary controlled or voluntary aided school a governing body may 'have regard to the candidate's ability and fitness to preserve and develop the religious character of the school'.[12] More recently, this has been reiterated under the Independent Schools (Employment of Teachers in Schools with a Religious Character) Regulation (2003). Preference may be given in connection with the appointment, promotion or remuneration at a faith-based school of teachers 'whose religious opinions are in accordance with the tenets of the religion or the religious denomination specified in relation to the school' or 'who give, or who are willing to give, religious education at the school in accordance with those tenets' (124A). The Statutory Instrument also allows for the termination of employment for any teacher whose conduct is incompatible with the religious tenets of the school. This means that the governing body may give explicit preference to committed members of the faith-based group in the appointment of head teacher and other teachers, a point we will be returning to later in the chapter. The point to note at this juncture is that the employment, retention and promotion of teachers in faith-based schools, both state-funded and independent, can be conducted with reference to a teacher's adherence to the religious character of the school. Finally, under the 1998 School Standards Act, a governing body can choose to change from 'voluntary controlled' to 'voluntary aided' status without initial financial penalty. As a result of these changes, faith-based groups are more involved in the decision-making at local level, and able to participate in collective agreements.

Currently, there are a wide range of faith-based schools receiving state funding, the majority of which are more correctly described as 'voluntary controlled' and 'voluntary aided', an important distinction, which we discussed earlier. The trust deed determines the basis on which the school should be run, and funding arrangements with the state may cover building works and staff salaries. As of 2003, just under a third of English state-funded schools have a religious foundation, accommodating 23 per cent of pupils, comprising 12 per cent at Church of England schools, 10 per cent at Catholic schools and 1 per cent at schools of other faiths. In terms of the level of control, the majority of Church of England schools are in the 'voluntary controlled' category, whilst the Catholic Church has tended to pursue a policy of 'voluntary aided status' (Department for Education and Skills 2003b). We should also make mention here of 'foundation schools' and City Technology Colleges (CTCs): those owned by trustees, which may or may not have a religious ethos.[13] There is understandable confusion over the status of some CTCs where the sponsor is associated with a religious group. In this case, the institution is not defined as a faith-based school, yet its sponsorship and importantly the composition of the governing body reflects a religious tradition.[14] (We look in more detail at how this impacts on curriculum content in the next chapter.)

The New Labour government's paper 'Schools: Building on Success' (Department of Education and Employment 2001a) is supportive of the Church of England's intention to establish 100 new schools, and encourages state funding of faith-based schools in general. There is an intention to reduce the financial contribution of the faith group 'from 15% to 10% for capital items', and provide for 'faith sponsors' and others taking responsibility for some schools on fixed term renewable contracts (Archbishop's Council Church Schools Review Group 2001). Overall, there is now the opportunity for expansion in these schools and, as in the late 19th century, for developing a partnership between government and various faith-based groups, some of which may be new to the state-funded system, such as Muslim and Sikh institutions.

So far in our discussions we have traced briefly the historical development of faith-based schools, the proposal for their current expansion and the legal framework in which they operate. Recent legislation aims to raise standards by promoting innovation, giving schools more autonomy and removing barriers to new forms of partnership, particularly at secondary school level. Supporters of the new legislation claim that it is not about privileging faith-based schools but about giving opportunities for new providers of education, especially in disadvantaged areas where schools are seen to be 'failing'. Where there are existing independent faith-based schools, the government sees advantages in bringing them into the maintained sector. When considering new applications from faith-based schools for state funding, School Organization Committees are expected to take into account the school's plans to promote inclusion and new partnership arrangements. (We return to the debate over this initiative later in Chapter 8.)

It is timely and of particular relevance to consider issues of effectiveness and accountability regarding these schools, in that, by being publicly funded, they have to reconcile state control and the market forces currently operating on education.

Market Forces and Accountability in Faith-Based Schools

State-funded faith-based schools are expected to 'conform' in terms of adapting to the major forces that shape education nationally and internationally, namely marketization and government-centred policies for the National Curriculum, national standards and national testing. Taking a market-driven approach to education has been justified in terms of increasing efficiency and effectiveness. However, after examining international research, Whitty (1997) argues that market orientation and competition do not necessarily enhance the efficiency and responsiveness of schools, especially in supporting disadvantaged and vulnerable pupils or those from minority ethnic communities.

The increasingly dominant ideology of accountability, management and performance indicators in education is likely to create tensions in faith-based schools in terms of incorporating this thinking into their internal workings and, at the same time, preserving their own identity and ethos. 'Accountability' seems to suggest a move from pupil needs to pupil performance, with the emphasis shifting towards increasing the school status in league tables and competitiveness. Catering for the needs of children with special educational needs (SEN) who may also belong to ethnic and/or religious minority groups places pressures on new faith-based schools particularly, as we will discuss in detail in Chapter 7. Specifically, such schools need to follow and implement new SEN developments (for example, revised Code of Practice, SEN and Disability Act), liaise with the parents and the wider community, and bring together diverse perspectives and needs. Furthermore, the emphasis on standards and increasing freedom of choice and diversity promoted by both the Conservative and New Labour governments (Apple 2001) is likely to put even more pressure on state-funded faith-based schools to become publicly accountable.

A major change likely to occur in faith-based schools is that affecting their admissions policy, to ensure children with diverse needs and profiles will be admitted. Catering for children with diverse needs within this new setting raises important issues on the limits and possibilities for a democratic and inclusive education for these children, and will form part of the agenda of state-funded faith-based schools in their efforts to respond. We found from our research that this issue is particularly significant for faith-based schools which are newly funded and which do not have a history of responding to diverse needs on the basis of, for example, special educational needs or social class.

The professionalization of teachers in faith-based schools is also likely to be a major outcome of publicly funding such institutions. Within the context of managerialism, professional identities are shifted in order to become more responsive to client needs and demands (Menter et al. 1997). Professional control is taken away and a so-called consumer control is established through a market structure (O'Hear 1994). In a study by Gipps and Murphy (1994), the assumptions about teaching and learning that seem to underlie the National Curriculum and the associated national testing are shown to be dominated by traditional models that do not take fully into consideration issues of race, ethnicity, religion and disability. Also, teachers are required to focus more on diversity, and how it occurs in their educational practice and impacts on their world-views, actions and behaviour (Leeman and Volman 2001). By being aware that they do not deal with a homogeneous group, teachers need to create a professional image that can do justice to the complexity of teacher–pupil interactions, as well as the social/cultural characteristics and learning needs of their pupils. For example, financial support allows for the recruitment of fully qualified staff, paid on the nationally agreed pay scales, who are encouraged to engage with the LEA, other schools and inspectors in a way which takes them away from a more insular environment (Hewer 2001b; Osler and Hussain 1995).

Practical and Ethical Dilemmas

Moving on from the legal and theoretical contexts surrounding state funding of faith-based schools, a number of issues emerge about practical implications such as accommodating diversity, carrying out school inspections, the recruitment of staff and enforcing appropriate disciplinary practices.

Many faith-based schools have operated in a market-led economy for many years as independent institutions, and indeed their survival has depended on their ability to respond to both their client base and financial imperatives.[15] One might well ask, therefore, why would they wish to become state-funded? The answer appears to be varied: to perform better academically as a result of financial support; to take away the burden of fees from parents who wish to implement their right to choose the education for their child; to be legitimately recognized as part of the religious landscape; and to enjoy parity of esteem with other faith-based groups (Hewer 2001b; Osler and Hussain 1995; Hewitt 1998; Parker-Jenkins 2002). State funding for faith-based schools has advantages and disadvantages in that it brings state control and regulation over certain aspects such as National Curriculum, testing, admissions criteria, inspection, discipline, and special education policy and practice (Walford 2001b). Schools gain financially from state support; however, we need to ask what 'strings are attached to funding' and 'to what extent the tune played by the piper is modified by the one who pays?' (ibid., p. 360).

Once public funding is forthcoming, schools are required to ensure their policy and practice are consistent with government regulations for maintained schools, with some modification due to the religious character of the institution. For example, they are required to support individual pupils with diverse needs to an extent not required in their independent status. Pupils with diverse needs are likely to pose greater educational challenges than other pupils and, thus, faith-based schools may face a series of dilemmas. An important question to be asked is whether in a market-driven economy children with diverse needs are 'marketable'? Achieving excellence for all as well as accommodating pupils with diverse needs can be particularly demanding, especially in the current climate where parental expectations have been raised by the emphasis on parental rights (Bowers 1996). Again this is an issue which has emerged from our discussions with senior management of newly funded faith-based schools, particularly those institutions that do not have a history of working with such pupils. Through having more open access due to the removal of fees, they find themselves, therefore, responding to a more diverse pupil body, which presents its own set of challenges in terms of resources and staffing.

State-funded faith-based schools are also open to a systematic and formal inspection by Ofsted to establish accountability and raise standards, although on a different basis from that of independent schools. The difference in HMI inspection for faith-based schools as opposed to that of community schools is on the issue of religion. As we have already mentioned, under Section 23 of the 1996 Education Act the religious dimension of the school has to be inspected separately and by a team agreed upon by the school. 'Section 23 inspections' apply to the voluntary aided, voluntary controlled or foundation schools that have 'a religious character'. Section 10 of the Act covers inspection with regard to Religious Education in voluntary and foundation schools, but there is overlap with Section 23 if denominational teaching has been requested by parents and is taking place. Then a 'Section 23' inspector is appointed to inspect this aspect of teaching, who is acceptable to the community. The legal framework for the inspection covers the curriculum and the 'ethos' of the school, namely:

- relationships in the school;
- behaviour/discipline;
- pastoral organization;
- parish/community links;
- chaplaincy/parish support;
- buildings and the school environment;
- special needs/equal opportunities/racism; and
- opportunities for spiritual, moral, social and cultural thought.

Overall, Section 23 inspection involves examining how the school's ethos statement, mission or vision statement is implemented in practice. It is part of a process which aims to encourage the school in its continuing work of self-review through the identification of particular strengths, of areas requiring further improvement and of progress made since the last inspection.

Here we begin to see the distinction between inspection of community schools and that of the different types of state-funded faith-based schools, and the different approaches to the inspection procedure. In the case of those institutions with a long history, such as Church of England schools, the Diocesan Board of Education normally provides help in assisting schools through the process.[16] Likewise, the Catholic Bishops' Conference of England and Wales issues guidelines for inspection of Catholic schools, and the Association of Muslim Schools provides support for Muslim schools.[17] In the case of newly funded faith-based schools, this level of assistance has not traditionally been available and we found from our research that in establishing support these schools look beyond as well as within their own community.[18] Another important issue is the relationship with the Local Education Authority. In the absence of support from a body such as the Diocesan Board of Education, newly funded faith-based schools are particularly reliant on the head teacher, the chair of the governing body, and those in the community responsible for the school premises and finances. In dealing with the wider community, there also needs to be a member of the staff or governing body to maintain links with the local media on behalf of the school, through whom communication about inspection results can be channelled. It is likely that some faith-based schools may not have experience of 'managing' the media prior to funding being awarded, and they may have had little contact with the press.

Further, the provision made by schools for SEN pupils is inspected to ensure that practice is consistent with the Code of Practice (Department for Education and Skills 2001). According to the framework for inspection, there are a number of criteria set for standards of achievement and the quality of teaching and learning. Several issues may arise when applying the inspection criteria to pupils with diverse needs. In practice, standards in special schools are not assessed in relation to national norms; instead, notes Sebba (1993), they are graded in accordance with the pupils' ability and previous achievement. (We will be discussing this issue in more depth in Chapter 7.)

The recruitment of staff in faith-based schools is another area which can generate controversy and raise issues with regard to employment practice. Faith-based schools cannot employ anyone on 'List 99', that is, those who have been found to be unfit to teach, more recently extended to include those debarred under the Criminal Records Bureau, as we noted earlier. But there is some protection for individual teachers whose behaviour does not fall foul of criminal law. For example, 'the right to a private life' is stipulated in the European Convention on Human Rights (Article 8), which is now part of domestic law by virtue of the Human Rights Act (1998).[19] Criticism of a teacher's behaviour in their private life, on the part of a school, might be seen to be a breach of the individual's human rights.[20] Under current law, education staff must be, as we have highlighted, 'fit and proper persons'.[21]

However, what constitutes a 'fit and proper person' may be perceived differently within some faith-based school communities.

In the UK and abroad, there have been cases when faith-based schools have failed to offer continuation of employment to those staff members who are not seen as adhering to the tenets of the faith in their private lives, for example in the case of marrying divorcees (Parker-Jenkins 1985). Recruitment, retention and promotion of staff whose manifestation of their convictions and beliefs/values are not compatible with the faith orientation and belief systems of a particular faith-based school may be particularly challenging. For example, a teacher in a Catholic school who demonstrates religious and sexual orientations that are not compatible with the Catholic Church may lose employment and/or be subjected to discriminatory practices, breaching his/her right to a private life.[22] The Canadian judiciary has tested the extent of individual teachers' rights versus the collective rights of the faith-school community and there has been a tendency for decisions to be made in favour of the school.[23] There is less case-law in the UK which has examined the extent of school rights in this area, but now that the European Convention on Human Rights has been enshrined in domestic legislation and individuals do not have to take their cases to the European Court of Human Rights in Strasbourg, there is greater opportunity for individual teachers to seek redress against schools which they feel have breached their rights, especially with regard to their private lives.

Recruitment of suitably qualified staff can be a general problem for faith-based schools. The Muslim, Sikh and Hindu schools we researched for this study all employed staff from a variety of faith backgrounds, but difficulties emerge over leadership of the institution. Recently, Catholic schools have been reported as experiencing problems in the recruitment of practising Catholics for senior management positions (*Times Educational Supplement* 2003a). Similarly, as we saw earlier in Chapter 2, Jewish communities have been attempting to provide teacher training for Jewish teachers due to the absence of suitably qualified staff in some locations. The King David School in Liverpool, for example, has appointed its first non-Jewish head teacher, although in this case it should be noted that the student body is no longer predominantly Jewish.[24]

Disagreement or controversy over employment practice raises the question, to whom are state-funded faith-based schools accountable? Are they accountable to parents, pupils, LEAs, DfES, and/or society in general? When we asked this question of senior management in our research study the unanimous answer was 'everyone'! There are various levels of accountability that impact at the school, community, local and central government levels, for example academic performance in league tables. Similarly, in terms of pupil discipline, schools are required to ensure that sanctions lie within what is legally permissible. Under the Education (No. 2) Act (1986), corporal punishment was outlawed in all community schools and this was extended to protect children in all schools in 1998. Therefore, regardless of a school community's belief with regard to the appropriateness of physical chastisement the ban covers all schools in England and Wales, as it does throughout Western Europe. This can potentially create friction and disagreement – for example in new independent Christian schools, as we saw earlier in Chapter 2, where there is support for the use of physical chastisement in some of these schools. However, in this case the courts have continued to uphold the rights of the child in faith-based schools, whether independent or not, as they have in community schools.[25]

Overall, as Walford (2001b) suggests, with money comes control, and some faith-based schools may choose not to receive state funding if it is seen to interfere with the running of their school in areas like selection of staff or in attempting to respond to issues of diversity.

Accommodating Diversity

The tension between the individual needs of pupils and curricular requirements, as well as the market forces placed on schools, is an area of concern when discussing standards, effectiveness and school accountability. Teachers are expected to plan their teaching in ways that encourage participation, understanding, and effective teaching and learning. To ensure that they are accountable for meeting the needs of diverse pupils in faith-based schools, teachers should be aware of and incorporate the requirements of the equal opportunity legislation that refers to race, disability and gender (Race Relations Act 1976; Disability Discrimination Act 2001).

Cummins (1986) identifies four characteristics crucial for schools, including faith-based schools, to ensure that they will accommodate diversity in an inclusive educational setting. These are:

- *cultural/linguistic incorporation* – in terms of incorporating the language and culture of minority pupils into the curriculum;
- *community participation* – the extent to which the surrounding community is involved via parental involvement or participation in cultural events;
- *pedagogy* in terms of models of knowledge construction, transmission vs constructivist models; and
- *assessment* the extent to which assessment refers to within-the-child deficit or takes an interactionist approach.

With regard to the first characteristic, that is, cultural/linguistic incorporation, it is arguable that including minority languages into the curriculum may not be adequate if they are not clearly valued and accepted by the culture and ethos of the school (Frederickson and Cline 2002). Teachers need to be aware that minority ethnic pupils bring to school not just a different language but also different experiences, expectations, modes of learning, beliefs, and values that are likely to influence the way they learn and interact. Likewise, community participation can be achieved by openness, acceptance, and a genuine interest in involving parents, families and community representatives in decision-making, planning, and implementation of educational and social activities. Extending educational activities to working with local communities may be seen as overcoming historical or cultural barriers, leading to an educational environment that is both dynamic and outward looking (Connell 1993).

With respect to the third characteristic, several pedagogical issues emerge in terms of whose knowledge is conveyed and what the methods are to educate all pupils successfully. Grimmitt (2000) argues that the pedagogy for diverse learners should draw upon theories of teaching and learning, school ethos and aims, curriculum content and methodology. (We will be providing a detailed discussion of curriculum issues next in Chapter 6.) Finally, assessment is another area that can prove to be particularly problematic for pupils with diverse needs who may or may not experience special educational needs. Culturally sensitive and linguistically fair tests are needed to ensure that individual difference is not perceived and understood as deficit, and that the interaction between the learner and the learning situation is taken into consideration when evaluating pupils' learning and social/emotional development (Frederickson and Cline 2002).

Cummins (1986) concludes that these four characteristics should be examined along a continuum extending from a school that takes an intercultural and multi-faith orientation to one that takes single perspectives on children's educational and social development. This is particularly relevant and timely with the introduction of citizenship education, which requires that all children should have knowledge and understanding of religious diversity in the country, making it more difficult for schools to countenance a single-faith/monocultural perspective within teaching and learning. This is also apposite for faith-based schools, which are perceived as being insular in their promotion of a single faith, but the issue is equally important for community schools in areas around the country which are predominantly monocultural (We shall be looking at citizenship education in more detail in the next chapter.)[26]

Issues of fairness and accountability are also linked to providing effective education, which increasingly is evidence-based. Next we explore what effective education means within the context of faith-based schools and we suggest a framework for achieving best practice, which incorporates collaborative working relations and the concept of 'inclusive beliefs'.

Effectiveness in Faith-Based Schools

The concept of school effectiveness has occupied a major part of school agendas in the last decade (Hopkins and Reynolds 2001; Harris 2001) and is unlikely to diminish in importance in light of the government effort to raise standards, particularly of minority ethnic pupils. There is particular concern to raise the attainment levels of Black-Caribbean, Pakistani and Bangladeshi pupils who are underperforming in terms of the government's national testing system (Department for Education and Skills 2003a). Effective provision for pupils in faith-based schools, as in any other educational institution, is linked with an understanding of fairness, social justice and human rights; respect for diversity and difference at school and in the community; encouragement of cultural and religious pluralism; construction of an individual and social identity; and participation in community activities.

As we have already mentioned, existing and new faith-based schools in receipt of public funding have to cope with multiple facets of diversity with various levels of accountability. To ensure that good quality of services are provided for pupils with diverse needs four criteria have been identified (Clerkin 1996). These are:

- equity in terms of treating fairly diverse groups of individuals as well as acknowledging and accommodating their differences;
- economy in terms of providing cost-effective services for pupils, including human resources, equipment, expert services and premises;
- efficiency in terms of improving the ratio between services provided and student outcomes; and
- effectiveness conceptualized as a direct relationship between educational policy aims and learning outcomes.

Understanding and managing change in faith-based schools in an effective and efficient way can prove challenging. Researchers in many countries have studied the factors that seem to make schools effective in their practice. For example, in a survey by the Organization for Economic Cooperation and Development, Kelley-Laine (1998) argues that school effectiveness, accountability and standards should be conceptualized in terms of making the schools responsive to the society's requirements; addressing social problems through tackling disadvantage and improving equity; and accessing available resources. The 'effective school movement' incorporates a belief that all pupils can be educated, places an emphasis on individual outcomes and stresses the responsibility for educating all pupils (Murphy 1992). Moreover, Rouse and Florian (1996) raise the question as to how a school can become both 'equitable and inclusive' as well as being 'excellent'. They argue that achieving equity and excellence requires the development of shared values and beliefs, in terms of celebrating diversity and valuing all pupils, respecting cultural, religious and linguistic diversity, and supporting a culture of collaboration. The importance of giving a 'voice' to pupils and involving their parents and the community in the school's decision-making is also stressed. For example, it has been argued that the establishment of faith-based schools, especially Muslim schools, is in part a result of the community wanting to have a 'voice' (Gundara 2000).

Of particular importance regarding faith-based schools is the ability to evidence academic success, especially when public funding has been allocated.

Evidence-Based Performance?

The appeal of faith-based schools is complex. It may be explained by considering the strong system of values and clarity in the moral purpose present in faith-based schools, as it is encouraged in community schools (Crick 2002). However, although faith-based schools have existed for many years there is limited research on their impact on pupils' academic performance, as we noted in Chapter 1 (Grace 2002b). Factors likely to explain their success have been explored in a study by Schagen and colleagues published by the National Foundation for Educational Research (NFER) (Schagen et al. 2002). This study looked at the performance of faith-based schools at Key Stage 3 and GCSE. Four categories of faith-based schools were considered, namely Roman Catholic, Church of England, 'other Christian', and Jewish. As we noted earlier, the vast majority of state-funded faith-based schools are Roman Catholic and Church of England, with schools from other faiths (Muslim, Sikh, Seventh Day Adventist and Greek Orthodox) being relatively few in number.[27]

Findings from the NFER study suggest that faith-based schools vary considerably in their performance in different subjects at different stages. More specifically, Jewish schools obtained the best overall results, scoring above the norm (as represented by both religious and non-religious schools) across the board except for Key Stage 3 science. Roman Catholic schools were above the norm at GCSE and below the Key Stage 3 level. The Church of England schools scored above average in terms of GCSE and Key Stage 3 except for maths. The performance of faith-based schools compared to community schools was also analysed. At GCSE level, faith-based schools performed above the norm, but at Key Stage 3 the picture was unclear. This challenges an overall perception that faith-based schools are universally successful, as evidenced in political statements by politicians who wish to 'bottle their success' and replicate it elsewhere through an expansion programme.[28]

There is also very limited research on the effectiveness of faith-based schools, state-funded or independent, for specific religious groups, such as Muslims and Sikhs. Even though faith-based schools have existed for many years, there appears to be little evidence of their impact on raising academic standards. One study by Mortimore et al. (1988) found that 'voluntary schools' (mostly faith-based institutions) demonstrated effectiveness in almost all areas except for oracy. That was explained by the differences in teaching strategies and styles. It was acknowledged that the measures for pupils' background were not adequate. This is an important factor when evaluating school effectiveness and needs to be taken into consideration, especially now that faith-based schools are expected to widen access to pupils from diverse backgrounds and a multitude of needs. Presently, what we have in the public domain are inspection reports, which signify some measure of success in terms of school effectiveness and performance in league tables.[29]

It is important to note that lack of baseline assessment regarding factors at an individual pupil level, which are likely to explain effectiveness in faith-based schools, would make any future evaluations particularly difficult. Is high academic attainment in faith-based schools explained by the characteristics and attributes of their pupils, which are in some cases the result of a highly selective admissions procedure? How does the inclusion of SEN pupils impact on the academic standards of a state-funded faith-based school as a whole? These are some of the issues that all schools face but which are particularly relevant to newly funded faith-based schools that wish not only to be accountable but also to establish their credibility in the maintained school sector.

A Framework for Achieving Best Practice

State-funded faith-based schools need to continually review their existing policies for developing good practice, as do community schools. If there are elements that are exclusionary or not effective in meeting diverse needs then a thorough examination of the curriculum, teaching methods and styles, classroom arrangements, assessment procedures and home–school relationships is required.

Tooley and Howes (1999) looked at performance in specialist schools, not faith-based necessarily, and found evidence of good practice conceptualized in terms of:

- focus on school ethos;
- good leadership and management;
- focus on students' learning and meeting individual pupil needs;
- innovation to promote school goals;
- quality control;
- organizations and structures consistent with the school ethos and culture; and
- parental and community links.

In effective state-funded faith-based schools all these elements of good practice should be evident. Because of the nature and ethos of faith-based schools, additional elements such as pupils' family background, culture and religion-specific values contribute to good practice (Schagen et al. 2002). The distinctive and positive ethos of faith-based schools is likely to be shaped by both extraneous factors – for example, family/community values and beliefs, parental involvement, a strong sense of community, religious orientation, and pupils' motivation and ability – and internal factors such as school leadership, innovation and quality control. Also, the ability to engage in collaborative problem solving, display inclusive beliefs and plan teaching for diverse learners all contribute to good leadership, management and innovation (Carrington and Elkins 2002). The success of faith-based schools, both funded and non-funded, is very much dependent on the quality of school leadership, and its ability to 'manage' the external environment and liaise with other schools to share good practice. This needs to go beyond the level of 'twinning schools' (Parker-Jenkins 1995), and to provide opportunities for collaboration at a number of levels for pupils, staff, school management, governors and parents.

Collaborative Problem Solving

Existing and new state-funded faith-based schools will have to respond to the changes occasioned by the responsibilities and challenges that public money and scrutiny bring. Organizational and cultural changes in their internal workings are expected to generate solutions to problems encountered in teaching students with diverse profiles and needs. Opportunities to discuss assessment and diagnostic procedures and programmes, as well as allocation of resources and co-ordination of activities, are likely to contribute to inter-professional collaboration. As in community schools, there has been an increasing emphasis on collaboration. For example, teacher and speech and language therapist collaboration is gaining ground rapidly to support children with language and communication difficulties to access the curriculum successfully (McCartney 1999; Law et al. 2000). Newly funded faith-based schools particularly will look at different types of collaborative links, at school, community and LEA levels, as well as new ways of setting up collaborative arrangements. From our research we found that partnerships already exist between different faith-based schools at a number of levels, for example sporting activities and special events, and that during the process of applying for state funding and obtaining 'voluntary aided' or 'voluntary controlled' status, these links become stronger in terms of support for the senior management and school governors.

Inclusive Beliefs

It has been suggested that teachers' world-views and beliefs provide a strong value base for inclusive practices (Carrington 1999), but how does this operate in the context of schools that have been established to promote a particular faith? Teaching pupils in a faith-based setting will require teachers to examine their own views and teaching principles, especially in a society that is increasingly culturally and linguistically diverse. This examination includes a close look at the values and the assumptions that teachers make about pupils' motivation, learning, behaviour and the pedagogies that are thought to be appropriate for learning. Shulman's (1987) work mentions the importance of both pupils' learning and the characteristics of the educational context, for example teachers' expectations and attitudes, suggesting a new theoretical framework to address teachers' world-views and roles. There is increasing empirical evidence to suggest that a democratic classroom climate, one that is led by teachers' democratic enquiry and discussion, underlies the development of political attitudes for participatory democracy and dialogue among pupils (Hahn 1999; Ipgrave 2001). We will be looking at the rights of the child, as opposed to those of the parent, in faith-based schools later in Chapter 8, but it is worth considering the extent to which faith-based schools which have a strong emphasis on respect for adult authority, as for example in Muslim and Sikh schools, are able to accommodate this view of a democratic school. Also, to what extent does the concept of 'inclusive beliefs' conflict with a single-faith school? This is particularly important in terms of access to knowledge other than that pertaining to the school's faith tradition, and the selection of curriculum material, which we will be exploring in the next chapter.

Teachers' views on issues of inclusion and cultural/religious diversity are of paramount importance. There is evidence to suggest that teachers' beliefs and orientations can impact on how and what they teach (Calderhead 1992; Wilson and Wineburg 1988). More specifically, teachers' knowledge of the subject matter has been found to be 'as much a product of their beliefs as it was an accumulation of facts and interpretation' (Wilson and Wineburg 1988, p. 557). The teachers' perspective is expected to shape the principles and strategies of classroom management and organization, and the discourse on subject matter. It is also expected to shape teachers' personal reflection on their own practice. There is, therefore, a need to support teachers in exploring their world-views (for example ideological, philosophical, political) and constructions on cultural and religious pluralism, through investment in teacher training and professional development. Independent faith-based schools are not required to engage in this level of professionalization, but this is a particular issue for faith-based schools which have newly moved from independent to state-funded status and for whom the opportunity to engage in dialogue beyond the school community may be a relatively new experience.

Children's values are expected to be influenced by the examples that are set by the teachers in their relationships, attitudes and teaching styles (Halstead and Taylor 2000). Developing a political/ideological understanding, showing tolerance and respect for others' culture, religion and language, and displaying an active interest in community affairs are likely to be encouraged by teachers who are committed to reflection and change. Dyson (1992) described a teacher as being an 'organisational inquirer' engaging in self-questioning of new and existing practices, and reflecting on issues of diversity and refining responses to meet challenges. What this suggests, therefore, is that staff in faith-based schools need to ensure that they resist being insular and inward looking, and instead engage at a wider level with educationalists for themselves, their pupils and the wider school community.

Conclusion

Faith-based schools are said to be popular with parents in that they obtain good examination results, although the evidence for this is far from clear-cut. The government has expressed its commitment to expanding such institutions in order to promote diversity, raise standards and develop new partnerships with the private sector. It is apparent that faith-based schools, especially those newly in receipt of public funding, are required to adapt to the current climate in education with greater levels of accountability than they assumed in their 'independent' status. They are governed by a legal context which is more demanding in terms of inspection, and, whilst they still need to remain secure in the market, issues in their selection of teachers and the professionalization of their staff are open to outside scrutiny. The tension between the pupils' diverse needs and market forces impacting on schools need to be considered when discussing issues of accountability, standards and school effectiveness. This is particularly evident in the need to respond to pupils with special educational needs and to raise the standard of pupils from culturally diverse backgrounds. Principles that underlie good practice, such as inclusive beliefs, collaborative problem solving, and the capacity to plan teaching and learning for a diverse student body, need to be adopted and further shaped by the distinctive ethos and culture of faith-based schools. Another area of accountability derives from the statutory requirements of the National Curriculum and choice of teaching material, which are the foci of the next chapter.

Notes

1   See, for example, Fullan (1992, 2000).
2   See also Lankshear (1996), and Francis and Lankshear (2001).
3   This has been expressed, for example, in The Cantle Report (2001).
4   As cited by The National Society (2003b), 'Latest News', http://new.churchschools. co.uk/schools/the way ahead, 06/06/03
5   The European Convention on Human Rights, First Protocol, Article 1.
6   For example the Islamia Primary School in Brent. The Catholic Education Service (2003) also document the diverse ethnic composition of their schools.
7   Mansell and Slater (2002).
8   Brown (1997).
9   The Education Reform Act (1988) and the Education Act (1996).
10 *Times Educational Supplement* (2003m). See also 'Boys lag behind', *Al-Madaris* (1998), no. 7, Winter, p. 7, and 'A Muslim Boys' Secondary School', *Islamia* (1994), March, pp. 6–7.
11 Teacher Training Agency (2002).
12 Ibid.
13 See, for example, Vardy Foundation (2003).
14 See also The Kings' Academy: Latest News (2003) http://www.thekings'academy. org.uk/latestnews/vardyfoundation
15 This is evident in the survival of over a hundred Muslim schools; see Association of Muslim Schools (2003).
16 www.churchschools.co.uk
17 Association of Muslim Schools (2003).
18 For example, the Guru Nanak Sikh Schools, Hayes, Middlesex.
19 The Human Rights Act (1998).

20   The European Convention on Human Rights, Article 8; and the Human Rights Act (1998).

21   Teacher Training Agency (2002).

22   See, for example, Canadian Catholic schools: the British Columbia Court of Appeal in *Margaret Caldwell v Ian Charles Stuart, Principal, St. Thomas Aquinas High School and the Catholic Public Schools of Vancouver Archdiocese*, May 1979, Official Court Reporters, Box 34, Courthouse, 800 Hornby St., Vancouver BC V8Z 2C5.

23   See Friedenberg (1980) and Berger (1982).

24   Inspection Report (2003b).

25   See Parker-Jenkins (1999a, 1999b) and *Times Educational Supplement*, 10 September 1999.

26   See Department for Education and Skills (2003b) website for statistical data on this issue.

27   See http://www.churchschools.co.uk and Department for Education and Skills (2003b).

28   See speech of David Blunkett , *The Guardian* (2001c).

29   See, for example, Inspection Report (2003a), Guru Nanak Sikh Voluntary Aided School; Inspection Report (2003d), The Swaminarayan Independent Day School; Inspection Report (2002b), Leicester Islamic Academy; and report of the independent Nottingham Islamia School, *Nottingham Evening Post* (2003).

Chapter 6

Curriculum Issues

Introduction

All curricula are potentially controversial but for faith-based schools there are particular aspects of teaching which require careful consideration to avoid conflict with the schools' own religious principles. When thinking about curriculum development and implementation there are three integrated educative functions of key importance: cognitive in terms of constructing knowledge; social in terms of sharing knowledge and understanding social situations; and pedagogical in terms of actively engaging in making sense and facilitating the construction of knowledge (Mercer, Wegeriff and Dawes 1999). It is also important to consider ways in which knowledge is socially constructed, and who makes decisions as to what has value and what is to be taught. These concerns are raised by Apple (2000) in his explanation of the ways in which *official* or *state-sanctioned* knowledge is promoted through the curriculum.

In this chapter we look at practical issues involved in teaching and learning, especially those aspects of the National Curriculum which may present particular challenges in faith-based schools. All faith-based schools which are state-funded are legally obliged to teach the National Curriculum. Those which are independent are not required to do so, as we have noted earlier; however, from our research we found the majority opt to follow the National Curriculum, whilst adjusting the content to reflect religious ethos and convictions. The objectives of this chapter, therefore, are to:

- examine what constitutes 'knowledge', particularly within the context of faith-based schools;
- discuss teaching and learning in general, and assessment of pupils' learning, within the National Curriculum framework;
- explore areas of the timetable which can be particularly problematic or controversial, namely religious education, literacy, the teaching of science, sex education and citizenship; and
- consider the need for an intercultural curriculum, which better reflects the reality of a multi-faith society and the needs of religious communities.

We turn first to discussion of what we mean by 'knowledge', a fundamental issue in terms of transmitting culture and values in school.

The Nature of Knowledge

The acquisition of knowledge depends not only upon mastering academic content or subject matter but also upon developing social knowledge, communication skills and meta-cognitive skills. It is important to note that the value placed on knowledge can be influenced by the cultural, religious and social experiences of pupils and their families. Delivering the curriculum in a faith-based school requires incorporation of all of these aspects, taking into account other factors, such as pupils' interpersonal and communicative skills, socio-economic class, the ethnic/cultural diversity of their environments, and teachers' world-views and values. Over the years, education has been expanding to include many viewpoints, and an understanding of people's ethnic/cultural backgrounds and the latter's influence on their religion. In faith-based schools, education needs to be conceptualized not only as a curriculum aspect but, most importantly, as a set of ideas, activities and behaviours likely to define and be defined by the ethos and culture of the school. Thus, an important question which emerges concerns the nature of knowledge being promoted, especially if the school is supported by public money.

We begin by looking at what we mean by 'knowledge'. One definition of the curriculum is 'the transmission of culture' (Lawton 1980), but whose knowledge are we selecting and from which cultural base? Incompatibility between educational philosophies is particularly apparent in aspects of the curriculum where content and values cannot be separated, and this has implications for all faith-based groups:

> Western attitudes are criticised, not only regarding Islam but regarding revealed religion in general. It may be asked if the pre-suppositions of Western education place Christians, Jews and others, as well as Muslims, at a disadvantage in schools dedicated to the pursuit of pluralist ideologies. (Hulmes 1989, p. 37)

If we take Islam as an example, essential knowledge or information which a Muslim is encouraged to seek before everything else is a correct understanding of reality and the precepts of Islam in religious texts. So in the Qur'an, for example, key points in the characterization of knowledge are:

(i)   the concept of absolute knowledge, which is God Himself and is not fully manifest in temporal life but will be so in the Akhira or Afterlife and

(ii) the concept of functional knowledge, an evolutionary process embracing intelligence and experience obtained in all sub-systems (Choudhury 1993, paraphrased).

As such the primacy of Divine Law establishes the epistemological foundation of knowledge. Epistemological study of Qur'anic verses has, in contemporary times, been used to justify and support the Islamic perspective on knowledge: indeed, debate is advocated to revitalize Islamic instruction, and move beyond recital and quotation of sayings (Raza 1993). Knowledge is thus conceived within the context of religion and Qur'anic interpretations, whereas in the Western model of education, religious knowledge is constructed as a discipline in its own right rather than as a subject which permeates the curriculum and establishes the school ethos. Similarly, the Islamic Educational Trust (1991) summarizes the key features of Islamic education as being:

- acquisition of knowledge;
- imparting of knowledge;
- inculcating moral values;
- consideration of public good; and
- development of personality and emphasis on actions and responsibilities. (Islamic Educational Trust 1991, paraphrased)

At face value, such an educational framework would not appear to be inconsistent with other educational philosophies, except that 'inculcating moral values' would presumably rest on some religious or ideological base. For example, within one state-funded school, the aim is:

> to provide opportunities to practise the Sikh religion and to ensure that this faith is central to the work of the School.[1]

Ideally, secular and religious knowledge should complement each other rather than conflict, but some types of knowledge may be considered unacceptable or offensive. For example, knowledge of technology from non-Muslim sources is permitted but not 'the values and behaviour of people or societies which are not ruled by a strict sense of accountability to God' (Haneef 1979). Raza (1993) states that Islam does not put any bar on the acquisition of knowledge but suggests: that it be planned in a balanced and interdisciplinary way; that the spiritual, moral, intellectual, imaginative, physical and emotional development of the individual are kept in view; and that the development of personality is seen in the context of the individual's relationship with God, and nature. Similarly, Husain and Ashraf (1979) maintain that Muslim scholars do not see knowledge by itself as being harmful or damaging but that 'the extraneous values and assumptions which man imparts into it cause it to produce a spiritually harmful fall-out' (p. 40). The selection of knowledge should accordingly be scrutinized to 're-examine the commonly accepted Western classifications of knowledge in the light of Islamic fundamentals' (ibid.).

In order to accept modern knowledge but reject the secular philosophy which is seen to accompany it, Muslims have been encouraged to establish Muslim schools, along the lines of other faith-based groups. The characteristics of Islamic education centre on the acquisition of knowledge, developing moral values, and nurturing an

Islamic identity whereby moral and social responsibility is fostered. Definition is provided by Ashraf (1994) as follows:

> education is ... defined as the process through which the balanced growth of the total personality of a human being is achieved ... Education is not an end in itself. (p. 4)

This destinction between the appropriateness or inappropriateness of knowledge is shared by other faiths. The Brethren, for example, a 'fundamentalist' Christian group, has in the past actively protested to the government, expressing the view that information technology courses, made obligatory by the National Curriculum, conflict with their religious beliefs, and that the use of computers, television and video is strictly forbidden in the New Testament (National Curriculum Council 1989). In the case of this group no exemption was permitted and schools have been left to deal with the problem themselves, sometimes allowing Brethren children to sit at the back of the class and not participate, but not necessarily providing alternative arrangements. Nor is the principle of the parental right of withdrawal from unacceptable curricula being addressed in this instance. Religious groups are thus left to try and correct what they feel is the damage through their own religious arrangements, either in the form of supplementary education, or by means of full-time faith-based schools which are responsive to their needs.

'Education' signifies the transmission of culture from one generation to another, as we discussed earlier in Chapter 4, that is, the cumulative experience of past generations enshrined in folklore, customs and poetry, crystallizing around the basic concept of the place of the individual in society. It is important to highlight what may appear to be inconsistency in the arguments presented about the value of knowledge, for there is a view that the aims of religious education are about obtaining blind obedience, fostering ritualistic pursuit of religious duties, and showing unquestioning deference to authority. (We return to look at children's rights in this matter later in Chapter 8.) Children's relation to adults in some religious communities has been described as one in which deference is expected to be shown to authority figures such as parents and teachers, as we highlight in the next chapter, and indeed such behaviour is highly regarded (Haneef 1979). To seek knowledge may require pupils to question teachers, and Muslim scholars, for example, reject the notion that there is no room for this within the Islamic concept of knowledge.

State-funded faith-based schools aim to develop educational policy along religious guidelines, and at the same time provide flexibility in that they incorporate the National Curriculum within the school's religious framework. It would be a mistake, however, to suggest that there is consensus among religious groups about this issue of selection of knowledge for children. As we have said earlier in Chapters 2 and 3, a variety of philosophies of education may exist within faith-based schools, such as within 'Orthodox' and 'Liberal' Jewish schools. As such, whilst there is no consensus among and within faith-based schools about content and methodology, the pivotal place of religion is the constant and agreed objective. This contrasts with what these school communities see as the conflict between secularist and religious perspectives on education.

The National Curriculum implemented as a result of the Education Reform Act (1988) has been seen as a major challenge to some Muslims, and other religious groups, since:

> the curriculum used in state maintained schools is based on a secularist approach to education which claims to take a neutral stand on the question of religious values, [but] a secularist approach is, however, far from being neutral. As with all faiths or world-views, secularism is based on, and promotes, a certain philosophy of life. The secularist philosophy is based on the supremacy of 'reason' and a secular religion is supposed to 'rescue' human beings from the 'shackles' of religion and religious beliefs and practices, often viewed as 'irrational'. The absolute and immutable norms and values, which for all major religions are God-given, are denied. (Mabud 1992, p. 89)

Many community schools have worked hard to try and accommodate the needs of Muslim pupils and other pupils who find subject matter unacceptable with sensitive handling of controversial issues, and the use of withdrawal from what might be considered unacceptable curricula in, for example, sex education. However, as we saw earlier in Chapters 2 and 3, some Muslim and Jewish communities are dissatisfied with aspects of the curriculum, which they see as inappropriate, offensive or in conflict with the school's values. Hulmes (1989) posits:

> can the western world's scientific and technological knowledge be imparted without the secularism which is so closely associated with it?. (p. 35)

Much of Western culture is considered by many Muslims and other groups to be based on materialistic, non-religious values. For them, the conflict in values as espoused by the family community and as reflected in the school curriculum, both formal and informal respectively, can cause difficulties. This tension, it is argued:

> is often overlooked or disregarded, even by teachers who are genuinely trying to understand what it is like to be a Muslim in Britain today. (ibid., p. 37)

Yusuf Islam argues that beyond numeracy and literacy in the British school system:

> there is a complete culturalisation process which underlies the whole system. Every school has a cultural base, from which it derives its goals, objectives and ultimate character, and this is where the process of indoctrination ... overtly and covertly begins.[2]

(Interestingly, the term 'indoctrination' is also applied to the teaching that takes place within some faith-based schools, a point we shall return to later.) What Muslims and other groups see happening, he continues, is that the entire philosophy of state schools is built on 'the rejection of God and his authority.'[3] Community schools are seen as institutions intent on providing only a secular interpretation of reality and providing an education which 'prepares the individual for a society free from religion' (Raza 1993, p. 42). There is significant value placed on knowledge within Islam and other faiths, and a belief that knowledge should be beneficial in helping individuals understand both this life and the Hereafter,[4] and the attendant obligations for adherents to the faith. Hence the imparting of knowledge within a secularist framework devoid of religious values is seen as in conflict with the overall aim of raising children within a religious context. (We examine secular and humanist perspectives on these issues later in Chapter 8.) It is partly because of this claim of increasing secularization in education that some Muslim and Jewish communities, for example, choose to establish their own schools to ensure the delivery of a curriculum which is reflective of their religious principles, both formally and informally.

To summarize this section on types of knowledge or information valued, the overall view of faith-based communities is that children be exposed to such knowledge as will assist them in understanding their religion, religious obligations and identity. Whilst disagreement can exist among and within religious communities over what may or may not be acceptable, the overall governing factor is, first, that knowledge should be seen within the context of a religious and moral framework; and secondly, that it has a part to play in helping the individual seek religious understanding. Knowledge within a religious framework places emphasis on belief in a spiritual being and morality, in addition to intellectual development. Together these two premises provide for the education of the whole person within a religious context. Such a view of the nature of knowledge, however, may present faith-based schools with significant challenges in the case of an open enrolment system through which pupils who are 'non-believers' could potentially be accepted.

Interestingly the Education Reform Act (1988), which introduced the National Curriculum, conceived of education as a balance in which the spiritual as well as the religious growth of the child should be fostered. The place and quantity of religion in this instance, however, is somewhat different in that a religious dimension does not permeate community schools in the way advocated by religious groups. Furthermore, the potential for conflict exists within the state school system where the compulsory nature of the National Curriculum is seen by such groups as providing little room for exemption from unacceptable curricula. As such some parents look to faith-based schools for supporting and maintaining religious belief and identity.

We look now in more detail at the nature of the National Curriculum, and the issue of assessment of learning, before exploring potential areas of controversy in the school timetable.

The National Curriculum

Learning at school requires children to master several curricula both formal and informal. They can be characterized as follows:

- the *official curriculum*, which exists based on the textbook choices made by schools, mostly referring to facts;
- the *social/cultural curriculum*, which is the knowledge that pupils are expected to acquire if they are to become literate and educated members of their communities;
- the *classroom curriculum*, which consists of sets of explicit or implicit rules and social skills that pupils need to acquire in order to function properly; and
- the *hidden curriculum*, which consists of teacher expectations and beliefs and unspoken rules for social interaction likely to determine peer attitudes and acceptance (Nelson 1992).

The National Curriculum (National Curriculum Council 2000) provides a framework to assess pupils' learning as well as to evaluate schools' performance with respect to academic attainment. It incorporates a statement on inclusion to ensure that effective opportunities are provided for all children. This states that in planning and teaching the National Curriculum, teachers have responsibility for setting suitable learning challenges; responding to pupils' diverse learning needs; and overcoming potential barriers to learning and assessment for individuals and groups of pupils.

Schools have to meet their statutory responsibility to provide a broad and balanced curriculum for all pupils. The nationally prescribed curriculum allows scope for the individual school and the individual teacher to develop knowledge, skills and competences that reflect the ethos and the priorities of the particular school. Nevertheless, HMI inspectors expect to see a broad and balanced curriculum, and some faith-based schools have been criticized in that their range of curriculum subjects has not been sufficiently broad.[5] It is interesting to note the links between curriculum scope and content and faith orientations in faith-based schools. Sometimes these are due to financial restraints. For example, it can be particularly challenging for independent faith-based schools to accommodate diversity of needs, for instance in terms of enhanced provision for pupils with English as an Additional Language.[6] In other instances, there may be a narrowness of choice in the curriculum due to religious or ideological reasons.[7]

The general and subject guidelines on planning, teaching and assessing the curriculum, produced by the Qualifications and Curriculum Authority (QCA), help schools and others differentiate the curriculum. In the process of differentiation, emphasis is placed on strategies to support pupils with diverse needs that may relate to gender, social and cultural/ethnic background (including Travellers, refugees and asylum seekers) and special educational needs (Frederickson and Cline 2002).

Although there is scope for individual teachers to adapt the National Curriculum, it is legitimate to ask whether teaching pupils with diverse needs can be effective with the constraints within the current National Curriculum. Schools are advised to take a wide range of actions to ensure that teachers will respond to pupils' needs, whether due to disability or different social, linguistic and cultural experiences. Changes in our understanding of what the notion of 'diverse needs' entails, and the conceptual difference between SEN and special needs, are reflected in the National Curriculum handbooks for primary and secondary teachers (Department for Education and Employment and Qualifications and Curriculum Authority, 1999a, 1999b). (A detailed discussion of this theme is provided in Chapter 7.) Diversity can exist even in what appears to be a monocultural, mono-faith or mono-ethnic context, suggesting that diversity is a wider concept, with many facets likely to exist in educational settings that, traditionally, would not have been seen as being diverse. As such, schools have to respond to differentiated needs in the broadest sense, and here we begin to see some of the challenges facing all schools, but particularly new faith-based schools which are financed by the state.

Differentiation in the National Curriculum

Ideas about what constitutes diverse needs have changed, and so has thinking about the aims of education. Inclusive educational practices are more widely implemented, and differentiation has become an important aspect of the National Curriculum. Differentiation can be achieved by teaching the same curriculum to all pupils through tailoring their needs, setting different goals, modifying teaching practices and styles, and removing barriers to learning, for example use of information technology. Differentiation of tasks and materials is expected to facilitate access to learning by supporting children to develop the necessary language and communication skills, making equipment and special aids available, encouraging collaborative workings with peers and adults, and supporting social/emotional development.

In order for differentiation to be effective in pupils' learning, it is necessary to analyse pupils' needs and requirements, and take into consideration both the learners' profiles and the learning context, including their linguistic and social/cultural background. Access to curriculum can be facilitated if differentiation is manifested, according to King (1989, p. 2), in:

- general aspects, including aims, content, language used and subject matter coverage;
- requirements for social interaction, referring to systems likely to support teacher–pupil and peer interactions. For example, teaching communication skills that are required for social problem solving, negotiation, conflict resolution, group entry and participation to group activities;

- teaching and learning strategies, in terms of teaching styles, classroom set up, rewards systems and behaviour management; and
- assessment strategies to support pupils with revision and self-study, and facilitate access to appropriate resources and materials.

In the context of faith-based schools this process of differentiation may need to go further in terms of differentiating for many facets of diversity including SEN, linguistic, cultural and religious differences. Differentiating for religious diversity can be particularly challenging in that it involves the establishment of what Simpson (1997) calls 'partnership between teachers, pupils and their families'. This involves a 'major change in the relationship between teacher and pupil, from one where the teacher controls what is taught, what is learned and how that learning is judged, into one where learning goals are agreed between teachers and pupils and assessment is both shared and normative' (ibid., p. 100). In the context of faith-based schooling there is a view that there is little scope for this to take place due to a prescribed curriculum by the community or parish, an issue we will discuss later in Chapter 8 within the context of 'pupils' rights'.

We look next at assessment issues in the curriculum and how faith-based schools assess success beyond a narrow, academic definition of achievement.

Assessment Issues in the Curriculum

As we noted earlier, faith-based schools with independent status do not have to follow the National Curriculum (Walford 2001a, 2001b). However, those being publicly funded are required to deliver the National Curriculum and engage in national testing, to create markers and 'comparative bases of information for choice' (Apple 2001: p. 112). In this context, faith-based schools have to consider certain curriculum issues, such as teaching sex education and exploring issues of human sexuality, as well as issues concerning the values, beliefs and behaviour of the teachers employed in faith-based schools. Regarding the latter point, the European Convention on Human Rights and the new UK Human Rights Act forbid schools from discriminating against employees on the basis of their religious and philosophical convictions. Yet, as we saw in the previous chapter, there is an expectation that teachers who opt to work in faith-based schools will be supportive of the school ethos.

The National Curriculum handbook for primary and secondary teachers sets out in general terms how learning can be promoted across curriculum subject areas such as spiritual, moral, social and cultural development:

- *spiritual development* through fostering pupils' understanding of values in society and the purpose of life;
- *moral development* by helping children to develop an appreciation of right and wrong, fairness, social justice, rights and obligations in society;

- *social development* by helping pupils to understand how they would be able to contribute to the society effectively; and
- *cultural development* through fostering an appreciation of different cultures and the capacity to celebrate difference and see it as a source of inspiration (paraphrased, Cairns and Gardner 2002).

It is of particular relevance for faith-based schools to expand conventional understandings of religion and culture to include a critical thinking and exploration of cultural contexts and social/moral responsibilities, as well as to address issues of teachers' views and values along with pupils' learning and development. (We will be looking further at understandings of religious education later in this chapter.) Due to their nature, faith-based schools are in a position to show the relevance of religion to the whole of the human experience, as well as to draw upon a specific faith on which to base discussion of ethics and other moral issues of contemporary 'secular' societies. For example, in our research we observed that practitioners in faith-based schools look for opportunities to connect aspects of the National Curriculum with knowledge as understood in their own community. It is also possible to draw links and highlight the commonalities across different faiths. We found evidence of this in faith-based schools which are representative of minority ethnic groups, such as Jewish and Sikh schools, which seek the chance to highlight the contribution of Judaism and Sikhism, but also demonstrate a willingness to incorporate an appropriate religious dimension to the curriculum drawing from other faith traditions. They also use the opportunity to tackle what might be perceived as a monocultural, non-inclusive curriculum.

Positive ways of using the curriculum, therefore, involve looking at sections of the National Curriculum and using them as a springboard to engender those experiences that children bring to the school. For example, study of Ancient Greece can be incorporated into the history curriculum, as we saw practised in our discussion of St Cyprian's Greek Orthodox School earlier in Chapter 3, and is a topic with which parents can identify. So although the opportunities to use the personal experience of the pupils within teaching is seen to have diminished substantially since enactment of the Education Reform Act, schools continue to use individual experience and the community as a resource.

In looking at the content and the purpose of the curriculum and its use for transmitting values of particular religions, such as Christian, Jewish or Muslim, we need to consider whether some bodies of knowledge are valued more than others and how this relates to the issue of assessment. It should be said, however, that the situation is complex as there is no uniform set of values across any of these religions, and within different religious traditions there are very different moral viewpoints.

Faith-based schools are expected to incorporate new national assessments to evaluate whether pupils achieve certain criteria set for their age and the National Curriculum objectives they need to achieve in order to reach the criteria. For all curriculum subjects there are attainment targets and a statutory programme of study that needs to be delineated clearly. State-funded faith-based schools have to cater for the needs of pupils with diverse profiles, for example linguistic, ethnic and religious, and thus assessment is expected to identify pupils' educational needs in relation to the curriculum. The level of educational need is understood as an interaction between the learner, for example pupils' strengths and weaknesses, and the learning environment, for example educational support and teacher–pupil interactions. Thus, the assessment should have close links with the curriculum offered (Frederickson and Cline 2002).

According to Gipps (1994, p. 25) the purpose of assessment is:

- *administrative and managerial* – in all schools there is a need to collect data on pupils' performance to monitor standards, to diagnose needs and to provide a basis for selection and progression; and
- *educational* – whereby assessment is seen as a mechanism to support pupils' academic achievement.

Elsewhere, assessment has been defined as incorporating a number of principles. For example, the Western Australian Curriculum Framework (Western Australian Curriculum Council 1988) sets the following principles as essential for assessment. These are:

- *validity* – assessment should provide information that is valid and meaningful;
- *education* – assessment should be formative in terms of giving thorough and relevant feedback to pupils and helping them to learn and apply that learning across different contexts;
- *clarity in purpose* – assessment criteria should be clear and explicit;
- *equity* – assessment should be fair to all pupils and not discriminate on grounds that have to do with diversity in pupils' backgrounds, differences in systems of beliefs and religious orientations; and
- *comprehensiveness* – an evidence-based approach towards collecting information from multiple sources (Western Australian Curriculum Framework 1988, paraphrased)

For children who come from diverse backgrounds with a multitude of needs and educational requirements, differentiation of the curriculum is necessary to match their existing skills with the entry requirements of the curriculum. Assessment criteria that focus on norm-referenced tests may need to be reconsidered in that they may be affected by cultural and social bias. Thus, in faith-based schools that have a large proportion of students from diverse ethnic backgrounds, norm-referenced tests need to be used with caution (Frederickson and Cline 2002).

Added to this are the issues of achievement and the underperformance of pupils from culturally diverse backgrounds (Gillborn and Mirza 2000; Wright and Weekes 1999; Brown 1996; West and Pennell 2003). Such is the concern over the underachievement of particular groups, such as Bangladeshi, Pakistani and Black Caribbean pupils, that the issue remains high on the political agenda (Department for Education and Skills 2003b). So as well as questioning the validity and legitimacy of knowledge, we need also to ask what counts as 'achievement'?

The government's agenda is concerned with achievement in terms of the academic acquisition of knowledge as measured in academic environments. Within educational circles this is evidenced by performance in formal testing such as the Statutory Framework (SATs) or GCSEs, measured against the National Curriculum (Department for Education and Employment and Qualifications and Curriculum Authority 1999b). Pupils are expected to reach certain attainment levels throughout their school careers: for example, Year 2, level 2; Year 6, level 4; Year 9, level 4/5; and at GCSE a grade C or above for the majority of pupils (QCA 2000). As such, specific criterion-referenced levels of the curriculum at specific ages form a substantial part of the monitoring and assessment of pupil progress. Importantly, these types of results are how a school is judged, and are made public in league tables. This therefore makes schools more accountable, especially when state funding is awarded, as we noted earlier in Chapter 5. Yet for many religious communities achievement is defined in other terms, such as the ability to recite prayers, undertake fasting and to demonstrate adherence to the faith. As such, some communities may wish to celebrate pupil achievement of a broader nature. For faith-based schools the measure of success is more clearly drawn in that nurturing children into the faith is part of the measure of the school's success. Therefore, it is not just a matter of 'whose knowledge' are we transmitting in schools, but also, what constitutes validity in terms of 'success' and how is that measured beyond academic attainment to personal and spiritual achievement? These are the challenges facing teachers in faith-based schools who are required to teach and assess different types of performance among pupils, yet who wish to acknowledge achievement as understood within the faith community.

Teachers in faith-based schools can be supported in the process of curriculum planning, teaching methods and assessment of pupils' progress through the curriculum management model developed by the Educational Psychology Group at the University of Southampton (Cameron et al. 1986). According to this model, the first stage of curriculum planning involves the setting of teacher management objectives. Pupil objectives and curriculum content refers to the next stage of curriculum planning, where emphasis is given to the content of the National Curriculum that is relevant and appropriate for pupils' age range and educational needs. The final three levels of this model, namely task analysis, behavioural objectives and attribute analysis, are particularly suitable for pupils who experience special educational needs.

Thus, according to this curriculum management model, assessment is curriculum-related in that its aim is to describe what pupils know and can do in relation to the curriculum objectives. Bernstein (1990) has provided a useful framework to understand the interplay between knowledge construction, curriculum and assessment especially during educational reforms. This framework may be particularly relevant to faith-based schools undergoing change in their status from independent to that of state-funded. According to this framework, there are three fields that characterize an educational change: (a) the field of 'production' where new knowledge is constructed; (b) the field of 'reproduction' where pedagogy and curriculum are actually enacted at schools; and (c) the 'recontextualizing' field where discourses from the field of production are conceptualized in such a way as to be transformed into policy. Within the context of a faith-based school, the assessment of certain subjects, such as religion and citizenship, can focus mainly on the ability to engage in classroom discussions and debates and undertake practical assignments that may need to be completed not necessarily in the classroom but in the wider community. The forms of thought that characterize discussions about citizenship, religion, culture, human rights and civic/moral responsibilities can be contentious in that they can be interpreted differently by different people in different situations (Huddleston and Rowe 2002). However, one of the main challenges that faith-based schools face is to raise awareness of the contested nature of these issues and put in place evaluation procedures capable of assessing pupils' attainment in relation to these fields.

From the point of view of faith-based schools with large numbers of minority ethnic pupils, examinations determined by the National Curriculum may have a limited view of academic assessment. For example, the emphasis on such areas as literacy and numeracy may mean there is little in the mainstream system that acknowledges alternative achievement which faith-based schools and communities value. A further issue concerning assessment is that the National Curriculum prescribes certain standard assessments, and there are accordingly implications for pupils in all schools whose background is disregarded. This may involve having lessons which incorporate questions on what the family consider are unacceptable curricula. For example, aspects of music education are forbidden by some religious groups, and yet pupils may be expected not only to undertake examinations in this area, but also to take those based on culturally biased testing (Scarfe 2001). This leads us on to explore other areas of the curriculum which may be problematic in faith-based schools.

Curriculum Issues in Faith-Based Schools

For the purpose of this discussion we will provide a brief overview of the National Curriculum statutory requirements concerning core and foundation subjects, before focusing on particular aspects of teaching and learning that are potentially controversial, in particular: religious education, literacy, science education, sex education, and citizenship will be considered.

The National Curriculum identifies core and foundation subjects which should form part of a balanced curriculum. Core subjects are English, Mathematics and Science from Key Stages 1–4, that is, for pupils aged 5–16, and in Wales, Welsh as an additional subject (QCA 2003). Foundation subjects provide a broadening of the curriculum and are: Information and Communication Technology, Geography, History, Art, Design and Technology, Music, Physical Education and Languages, which are optional at Key Stage 2 but obligatory at Key Stage 3, and Citizenship, which has been compulsory at secondary level since August 2002.

Religious Education

Beyond core and foundation subjects is the area of 'Religious Education', which is not governed by a national syllabus but instead is approved at local/regional level. Under legislation, 'religious education is part of the basic curriculum in maintained schools' and must be taught to all pupils registered in a school (QCA 2003, p. 6). Religious Education is particularly significant in this discussion because it relates to both the substance of faith-based schools and the manner in which the subject is dealt with in these institutions. It is particularly important to try and separate out the overlapping issues of 'collective acts of worship', 'the religious character of a school', and 'religious education', to help explicate religious education in the context of state-funded schooling.

The practice of having *'collective acts of worship'* has been a feature of faith-based schools since their inception, and many would argue that these observances lie at the heart of school activities; the coming together of the community to share religious belief. In England and Wales the legal requirement that schools shall provide 'collective acts of worship' was first stipulated in the Education Act (1944), and reaffirmed in subsequent legislation, most recently in the School Standards and Framework Act (1998):

> each pupil in attendance at a community, foundation or voluntary school shall on each school day take part in an act of collective worship. (section 70)

This requirement is subject, however, to the parental right of withdrawal from these activities. The legislation also notes the different practical arrangements for the ways in which activities may be conducted, and for that reason 'collective acts of worship' are provided in a variety of ways by schools.

For community and foundation schools which do not have 'a religious character', a distinction we noted earlier in Chapter 2, the collective worship provision is the responsibility of the head teacher in consultation with the school governors. The activities in this case should be 'wholly or mainly of a broadly Christian character', subject to the age and aptitude of the pupils. Consideration should also be given to the family backgrounds of pupils which are relevant in determining the nature of 'collective acts of worship' in different educational settings. Therefore those community schools with predominantly Muslim pupils, for example, can attempt to accommodate their needs within the daily event. Conversely, for schools with 'a religious character', arrangements are made by the governors, after consulting with the head teacher, and 'collective acts of worship' are in accordance with the trust deed relating to the school, a point we shall return to later in relation to 'religious education'. Further, in faith-based schools 'collective acts of worship' may, for example, take the form of daily prayers, and often involve attendance during the term at a synagogue, church, mosque or temple in or close to the school.

The British Humanist Association (1998) maintains that the term 'collective worship' is a contradiction in terms, that is, 'collective' suggests a collection of different individuals, and beliefs and 'worship' denote 'reverence for a divine being', thus excluding humanists and other non-religious pupils and teachers (p. 1). Further, the concept of 'corporate worship', it is argued, better describes activity when everyone is committed to a particular faith, as in the context of a synagogue, temple, mosque, church or other religious setting. The Association, which ideally would prefer no faith-based schools, suggests instead the use of 'assemblies'. This is because assemblies would, arguably, have educational value in developing both shared beliefs and the notion of a whole school community, inclusive of everyone. Further, such an arrangement, it is suggested, would remove the need for the right of parental withdrawal from what might be deemed unacceptable 'collective acts of worship'. (The British Humanist Association's vision of 'the inclusive school', which has gained support from parents of both religious and non-religious backgrounds, will be discussed later in Chapter 9.) Strictly speaking, 'collective acts of worship' are not the same thing as 'religious education' and it is unlikely that religious education teachers would be content with the fusion of these terms. In some school settings, however, the lines may be blurred. For example, a school may seize the opportunity to invite different religious leaders to lead or participate in the 'collective act of worship' who may in turn draw heavily on their own faith and what it means to them.

The '*religious character*' of a school is determined by the school governors, not the Local Education Authority, and this does not change if government funding is awarded. It is interesting to note, however, that 43 per cent of the 7 000 faith-based schools in Britain funded by the state are voluntary controlled (Department for Education and Skills 2003b). This contrasts with the situation of voluntary aided or foundation status schools, which may have 'a religious character' that 'reflects the school's trust deeds or, if there is no trust deed, the traditional practice of the school' (Jackson 2003b; Lankshear 2002). So in government figures, for example, we see schools categorized as 'schools with a religious character' which are inclusive of those having the different status of voluntary aided, controlled or foundation. This, as we stated at the outset of the book, demonstrates the complexity of the situation, and the oversimplification in applying the term 'faith school' to all groups and attempting to subsume them into one broad category. The distinction between these different categories of schools also has a direct bearing on the nature of the religious education being taught.

The Education Reform Act (1988) is an important starting point on the issue of '*religious education*'. Pupils in schools other than voluntary aided should be taught religious education according to the Local Education Authority Agreed Syllabus for Religious Education, and the Standing Advisory Council for Religious Education (SACRE) which reviews this part of the curriculum every five years (section 8 (c)). Although LEAs interpret this provision differently, notes Brown (2003):

> there is the legal requirement that pupils will learn about Christianity and the other principal religions in Great Britain, the implication being that more time will be spent on Christianity than any other religion. (p. 109)

It is not uncommon, therefore, to see a variety of religious symbols being displayed in community and voluntary controlled schools, and arrangements for religious leaders from other groups to visit and lead 'collective acts of worship' – that is, to participate in group or school gatherings of a religious nature but not to specifically provide religious education, as we stated above. Whether a faith-based school is classified as 'voluntary aided' or 'voluntary controlled' has a direct bearing on the nature of religious education practised in the school. For example, a voluntary controlled school like the White Waltham Church of England has to follow the LEA syllabus unless parents ask for faith teaching.[8] Similarly, the voluntary controlled Hartshorne Church of England Primary School 'aims to promote Christian values'[9] and its school syllabus is taken from the Derby City LEA *All Our Worlds* document. The curriculum in this case:

> is based largely on Christian history and beliefs but also draws upon stories and figures from other cultures and creeds in order to reinforce concepts which span many religions.[10]

To summarize so far, most voluntary aided, voluntary controlled and some foundation schools have a religious character, and therefore may conduct collective worship which is distinctive of the religious group concerned. Only voluntary aided schools, however, can have 'denominational' religious education. As such, voluntary controlled and foundation schools with a religious character are required to use the local Agreed Syllabus for Religious Education, except in the case of children whose parents have specifically requested 'denominational' religious education. A few Church of England dioceses expect even their voluntary aided as well as their voluntary controlled schools to use the Agreed Syllabus, for example in Coventry (Jackson 2003b).

In terms of whose faith is being taught in state-funded faith-based schools, which lie outside of this 'voluntary controlled' classification, the religious education syllabus, notes Brown (2003), is the responsibility of the governing body:

they have the power to decide that the content of the subject will reflect only the religious foundation of the school or that other religions or denominations will only receive a cursory amount of time and resources. (p. 109)

He notes the importance of this at a number of levels. First of all there is 'the implicit assumption that religious education is not an academic subject' but instead is 'one largely concerned with nurture, and moral and social behaviour (ibid.). As such it may be felt that religious education may only have relevance when taught within the context of a religious community. But there are obvious implications here for other children:

why should pupils who attend voluntary controlled and community schools acquire a knowledge and understanding of a range of faiths with particular emphasis on Christianity yet pupils at the increasing number of voluntary aided schools learn of nothing but their own religion or denomination or sect at the wish of the governing body? (ibid., p. 110)

The British Humanist Association (2002), for example, is concerned that this may be particularly true of the new state-funded faith-based schools. Brown (2003) continues that if parents are presented with a genuine choice, faith-based schools could get on with their own agenda, and:

the community and remaining voluntary controlled schools would carry the torch for the academic study of religion and philosophy or worldviews. (ibid.)

We will be looking more closely at alternative models in schooling later in chapter 9, but at this juncture it is useful to illustrate the legal situation concerning religious education with examples of practice.

From our research a range of approaches were found to be used in state- funded faith-based schools. Some voluntary aided schools had adopted a multi-faith approach, that is, the inclusion of Sikhism, Buddhism, Islam, Judaism and Christianity but with a particular emphasis on the faith tradition of the school. This also includes the more recent minority faith-based schools. In the case of Church of England schools, a combined course which is developed at national level forms the basis of 'Religious Education' with a predominant focus on Christianity. Likewise, on an individual basis, Muslim and Sikh schools we visited included scope for looking at alternative faith traditions, whilst having a very clear emphasis on Islam and Sikhism respectively.

As we noted earlier, the question has been raised as to whether a faith-based school in receipt of government funding may teach its own faith alone and disregard all others. The potential for this is clearly provided for under the trust deeds of the school although the reality is likely to be that some reference to other faiths is made. The head teacher of the Islamia Primary School, for example, one of the first Muslim schools to be granted voluntary aided status, stated:

we can practise any religion we like. We pray five times a day, we learn the Koran [*sic*] in the traditional manner – but with translation, explanation and discussion. One thing we never do is celebrate Christmas.[11]

He added, however,

the school looks at other religions, but we examine the historical aspects quite critically. Was Jesus really born on December 25?[12]

Overall, the majority of state-funded faith-based schools in our study were comfortable with giving space to the discussion of other faiths, whilst focusing on religious education reflective of their own religious community.

We should also note that some commentators argue that it is important to distinguish between 'religious education' or 'religious instruction', and 'religious nurture' (Smart 1999). In keeping with the belief that God is the source of all knowledge that is of value, religious instruction may form a significant part of a child's education in a faith-based school yet this may be seen to conflict with the desire to provide 'religious nurture'. One of the conflicts is that of relativism as opposed to absolute values, and whether Muslim, Sikh or Catholic children can become spiritually, morally and intellectually confused by the aims of multicultural education and the concept of pluralism. The teaching of religion in faith-based schools through the Religious Education curriculum can, in a broad sense, make a significant contribution to the understanding and commitment of historical circumstances and issues of inclusion, equal opportunities and anti-racism which all groups share.[13] However, some commentators feel that such an approach may also present challenges to teachers, especially those of religious studies, if courses not only include knowledge of a variety of religions but also involve the scrutiny of what some would see as fundamental beliefs and the undermining of religious nurture. Further:

one consequence of this style of educational approach, therefore, is a deep unease about the nature of teaching especially as it relates to the home and the community. This concern is shared by many parents within Islam, Judaism, Christianity and other groups. (Falaturi and Tworuschka 1991, p. 64)

It is for this reason that religious communities such as Muslim and Jewish have developed their own forms of independent and/or supplementary schools, where they have the scope to determine for themselves what constitutes knowledge and what should form curriculum content and methodology in religious education. In some cases, as we saw in Chapters 2 and 3, they have sought state funding to support their schools.

In practice we found in our study an overlap in the use of the terms 'religious education' and 'religious instruction', and differences in the approach to the religious nurturing taking place in faith-based schools. For example, in the Guru

Nanak Sikh Secondary School, 'Religious Instruction' and collective worship take place daily alongside Sikh studies which are taught in all classes.[14] This, however, is an individual case of one type of faith-based school operating in isolation of any other Sikh schools. The opposite is true of Catholic schools, which tend to be voluntary aided and for which there is a national policy governing religious education that will help support parental wishes to raise children as Catholics (Francis and Egan 1993; O'Keefe 2000). For example, this is expressed by the Nottingham Diocese as follows:

> at the heart of the Catholic education lies the Christian vision of the human person. This vision is expressed and explored in Religious Education. Therefore, Religious Education is never simply one subject among many, but the foundation of the entire educational process ... Religious Education is, then, the core subject in a Catholic school.[15]

Further, the outcome of Catholic Religious Education is intended to produce:

> religiously literate young people who have the knowledge, understanding and skills to think spiritually, ethically and theologically, and who are aware of the demands of religious commitment in everyday life.[16]

This translates into practical activities so that pupils can have 'genuine opportunities for spiritual experience on a daily basis' and 'understand the place of the Mass and the Sacraments in the living tradition of the Church'.[17] As such the school timetables in faith-based schools may accommodate the need to nurture religious identity and obligations through the vehicle of religious education, as well as through the informal curriculum. This is seen as important as children prepare for particular stages of adherence to the faith or rites of passage, such as the 'first holy communion', or in demonstrating religious practice, such as fasting during Ramadan. For example, the Clore Shalom School invites parents into the school on Fridays for 'kabbalat shabbat' to celebrate individual achievement, such as those who have performed 'mitzvot'.[18] Indeed, it is the school's ability to accommodate, support and help nurture these religious traditions and values which provides its distinctive character and normally accounts for the establishment of the institution in the first place. From the community, priests, ministers, rabbis and imams, for example, are brought in to assist in this endeavour. Many of these religious leaders also visit community schools, but their role in faith-based schools is different for they become involved in activities aimed specifically at religious nurture. Overall, therefore, there are a variety of responses to what 'religious education' means in practice in state-funded faith-based schools, and we found this ranged from a formalizing of religious instruction in a manner to convey what the school described as 'orthodoxy' to one where there was not a strong denominational feature but rather a spiritual dimension to the school.

One final point worth highlighting is the issue of 'spirituality' (Ericker and Ericker 2000). Brown (2003) asks whether the failure of community schools to take religion seriously is a contributing factor in the desire to increase the number of faith-based schools. He argues that whilst Ofsted reports suggest an increase in provision for religious education (Ofsted 2002c, 2002d):

> there is still a substantial number of religious education lessons taught by non-specialists in secondary schools. (Brown 2003, p. 111)

This is due to what he sees as inadequacy in provision in the community school sector and some faith-based schools. He raises the question whether 'schools with a religious character might major in spirituality' since 'all the religions wrestle with spirituality in some form or another' (ibid.). Faith-based schools, he continues, could be encouraged to put aside set 'spiritual development' targets and instead take a long-term view of spiritual development. Set within a secure religious framework, he suggests they could challenge the values of British society in a positive and creative way: 'perhaps these schools will feel empowered to explore the spiritual and what belief means in terms of faith and practice' (ibid.).

Some schools would argue that they are already doing this, moving beyond rote learning of scriptures to an approach of exploring what it means to have a spiritual dimension to life. Interestingly, religious education will continue to remain left to interpretation by schools, determined at local level in consultation with the Local Education Authority, a diocesan board of education or its equivalent in faith-based communities, and school governing bodies. For whilst the expansion of faith-based schooling is proposed by the government no change in the legislation which underpins religious education is planned and 'none is likely in the foreseeable future' (QCA 2003, p. 6).

Having looked at the place of religious education in schools, the subject can also be reflected in other ways, such as in the selection of appropriate material for teaching purposes in the formal and subscribed curriculum, for example within Literacy.

Literacy

One of the basic features of the curriculum is that of literacy and its pivotal place in learning and teaching. The National Literacy Strategy (NLS) is a national initiative that requires teachers to teach reading directly to the whole class and to groups, and covers the statutory requirements for reading and writing in the National Curriculum. State-funded faith-based schools are required to implement this initiative and incorporate a range of strategies to support reading development in particular, namely knowledge of context, knowledge of grammar, word recognition and phonological development (Frederickson and Cline 2002). Having to cater for children from diverse linguistic environments, some faith-based schools need to adapt the NLS for those pupils whose first language is not English, as do some community schools. The need varies, however, as the large number of rural Church of England primary schools, for example, do not have to respond to such a diverse spectrum of languages in the classroom (Department for Education and Skills 2003b; National Society 2003a). The National Literacy Strategy framework document (Department for Education and Employment, 1998) focuses on the features of Literacy Hour that are likely to support multi- or bilingual pupils. These are:

- *content features*: emphasis on listening skills, clarifying/explaining vocabulary, making use of pupils' home language to illustrate certain points and using it for examples; and
- *process features*: whole-group discussions, participation in hands-on activities, individual support.

There are some helpful suggestions brought forward by the NALDIC Working Group (1998) as to how children's linguistic needs can be identified and supported during the Literacy Hour. These include:

- building on previous experience within and beyond school (understanding and incorporating family perspectives and educational experiences);
- positive teacher and peer role models for language development;
- encouragement of communication and social interaction with plenty of opportunities to practise the target language;
- matching cognitive demands according to pupils' strengths; and
- making connections between the native language and the new one.

Within Literacy the main features are reading, writing, speech and listening, and the National Literacy Strategy promotes a certain genre of writing, such as instruction, explanation, recounting, persuasive writing and narrative.

Most of this theory is unproblematic and is practised by community and faith-based schools, both state-funded and independent. However, whilst a variety of different writing genres are used for such classes in Western societies, in other communities – for example those of Pakistan – the religious text is regarded as the most important genre. This cultural difference is reflected in the fact that in some faith-based schools religious texts such as the Qur'an and the Torah are used in Literacy, whereas in community schools religious texts are not widely used as a source of knowledge or for teaching purposes. Likewise, in new independent Christian schools in this country and schools in the southern states of America, the Bible is also used as an important text within the curriculum, as a form of reading as well as providing moral authority.[19]

Another potentially controversial issue within Literacy is the selection of reading material. Plays, novels and poetry are chosen for each key stage of the National Curriculum which are acceptable to the school community and which avoid what might be deemed offensive or inappropriate curricula. So, for example, faith-based schools may omit potentially controversial plays or novels to avoid having to tackle sensitive issues in the classroom, or the criticism of parents. There are similar potential problems in the National Numeracy Strategy, for whilst 'number' is seen as culturally neutral, the choice of mathematical questions may draw on monocultural examples (Virani-Roper 2001) and the opportunity to celebrate the contribution of other societies may be lost.[20] Again, faith-based schools may attempt to select material reflective of their group: for example, from our research we noted some Muslim schools incorporate into their teaching the Islamic contribution to mathematics.

Overall, in teaching the National Curriculum, existing and new faith-based schools look for opportunities to select options within the National Curriculum which provide the opportunities for development along, for example, Islamic, Jewish and Sikh lines, trying to avoid unacceptable curricula. There are also possibilities for the curriculum to be used to: challenge negative stereotypes and racism (Brown 1996; Nehaul 1996; Sewell 1996; Gaine 1996); explore the media portrayal of religious communities (Wrigley 2000); and examine what we mean by responsible citizenship (Osler 2002), which we discuss later in the chapter. The question of possible 'imbalance' in the curriculum, from the point of view of the religious community, may also be an area of concern. Independent faith-based schools find this less problematic since their private status gives them freedom to develop curriculum according to their needs. Many independent schools, however, maintain that their curriculum offering is still balanced and appropriate; for example, the Swaminarayan School states that the school was founded:

> to provide the best elements of state and independent education, cradled in the supportive atmosphere of the Hindu ethos [and it] follows a curriculum which superimposes independent school expectations onto the National Curriculum.[21]

Conversely, state-funded faith-based schools seek to work to the National Curriculum but avoid compromising their religious convictions, for example in the teaching of science.

Science Education

Science education has been described as developing an empirical approach to learning: to hypothesize, to demolish argument that does not stand up to scrutiny, and to abandon the proposition (Popper 1945). Likewise, the Science National Curriculum is a part of the curriculum that involves challenging ways of doing things and ways of thinking. Within the National Curriculum, Science is classified as a core subject and obligatory at Key Stage 1, 2 and 3; and at Key Stages 4, there are single and double Science awards for GCSE level (Department for Education and Employment and Qualification and Curriculum Authority 1999a).

With regard to Islam, for example, Husain and Ashraf (1979) state that according to Sharia (Islamic law), all sciences are capable of being considered Islamic sciences as long as they operate within the framework of Islam and are not inconsistent with Islamic concepts and attitudes. However, argues Mabud (1992), in science education in some schools the concept of God is challenged and found unscientific and irrelevant:

> values are disassociated from religion, values change along with external change. In this scheme of things human beings are but the end product of evolution, mere earthly creatures, temporal beings possessed of mind and body but not soul or spirit, (p. 89)

Moreover, it is contended that all school subjects are taught from this philosophical framework and provide the prevailing ethos for the entire school (ibid.). This contrasts markedly with the Islamic perspective, and that of other religious groups, of an unequivocal belief in God attendant with concerns over moral codes and moral responsibility detailed earlier. There are, however, community schools which would reject this view and instead argue that they do explore the relationship between science and religion, a point we return to later in this chapter.

Specific areas of the Science curriculum present the possibility for conflict in values and beliefs, such as in the teaching of sex education.

Sex Education

It is not uncommon for parents of both religious and non-religious backgrounds to question the content and delivery of sex education lessons. The Education (No. 2) Act (1986) gave governors the option of deciding whether sex education should be offered in school or not.[22] Added to this the Education Reform Act (1988), as we stated earlier, sets the National Curriculum within a framework of a balanced and broadly based curriculum which 'promotes the spiritual, moral, cultural, mental and physical development of pupils … and prepares them for the opportunities, responsibilities and experiences of adult life' (section 2 (a)(b)). Sex education is clearly an important part of this broad educational aim of preparing children for responsible and informed adulthood.

More recently, the Education Act (1993) removes the governors' option clause and sex education is compulsory for children. Within the Science National Curriculum, sex education is obligatory at Key Stage 2 as follows:

> pupils should be taught that the life processes common to humans include … growth and reproduction. (Sc.2)

Also included within the subject of sex education is Acquired Immune Deficiency Syndrome (AIDS), Human Immune-deficiency Virus (HIV) and any other sexually transmitted disease (section 241(2)). National Curriculum Science is the only place in which sex education is mandatory in the curriculum, and only 'biological facts' should be incorporated within sex education as a compulsory section: the other issues remain outside the National Curriculum and therefore provide the possibility of avoiding what might be considered unacceptable or offensive curricula (section 242(2)). For example, in the Guru Nanak Sikh Secondary School 'sex education is taught to all pupils as a natural part of the curriculum' and 'facts are presented in an objective and balanced manner, set within a clear framework of values and with an awareness of the law on sexual behaviour'.[23] In this case the lessons take place in part within the 'Personal, Social and Health Education' programme in the school, but, in keeping with practice elsewhere, 'pupils may be withdrawn from part or all of the sex education programme by parents'.[24]

As noted earlier in Chapters 3 and 4, Muslim and Jewish schools include in their teachings certain obligations on pupils such as modesty and decency, and sexuality is countenanced only within lawful marriage. The sexual etiquettes of Islam, notes Sarwar (1989), stress modesty and a sense of morality, and exclude extra-marital sex and homosexuality. A difficulty arises, therefore, when sex education is seen to move from factual knowledge on human development to sexual activity outside religious boundaries. For example, as Islam does not contemplate sexual activity outside of marriage, the issue of contraception is not considered an area of concern, except on the grounds of the mother's health. Similarly, abortion is only permitted when continuation with the pregnancy might also endanger the mother's health. It is within this moral framework, therefore, that sex education should ideally be set for Muslim children. For example, in *Sex Education: The Muslim Perspective*, Sarwar (1989) states that:

> the need for sex education is not in doubt. The debate is concerned with where, how and by whom this education should be given. (p. 6)

The teaching of sex education can also present problems for other religious groups who feel the need to carefully negotiate this aspect of the Science curriculum. For example, the head teacher of the Ultra-Orthodox Jewish School, the Hasmonean High School in North London, states:

> in biology, we tell students that, in true Judaism, reproduction takes place only within marriage. If a biology book shows the nude female form that is one reason why a page might be removed. We would rather use line drawings.[25]

The controversial nature of this part of the curriculum may, however, leave educators in faith-based schools walking a tight-rope between providing explicit material, or leaving pupils ignorant and ill-informed. Another aspect of the Science curriculum that presents challenges in faith-based schools is that concerning the different explanations for the beginnings of the universe.

Creationism versus Evolution

All curriculum is potentially controversial, as we have said throughout this chapter, and within the context of some faith-based schools this is particularly true in the teaching of Science and the origins of the universe. Differing and conflicting accounts are put forward about 'creationism' and 'evolution', and there are a number of places in the Science National Curriculum where it is expected that schools will provide education on these issues. For example, in the National Curriculum at Key Stage 3 it is compulsory for pupils to be taught issues concerning inheritance and evolution (Sc.2, 4c), and at Key Stage 4, 'pupils should be taught how scientific controversies can arise from different ways of interpreting empirical evidence, for example Darwin's theory of evolution' (Sc.1b). Likewise, trainee teachers have to demonstrate, in their preparation for teaching Science, that they know and understand life processes including 'continuity and change'. Further, they are advised (Teacher Training Agency 1998) that

> most biologists believe that variation caused by genetic mutation and re-combination, coupled with interaction between organisms and their environment, leads to natural selection and evolutionary change. (circular 4/98, 13f)

This view conflicts with that held by some faith-based schools that believe exclusively in the 'creationist' view, that is, that God is at the heart of the beginning of the universe, and that alternative explanations, such as that the earth is an inevitable consequence of matter, are not true. These schools constitute a tiny minority of state-funded faith-based institutions, and the vast majority of Church of England and Catholic schools, for example, do not experience major difficulties in terms of science education and provide science teaching which engages with a variety of perspectives. Reports by sections of the media and some religious commentators on this controversial issue, however, tend to obscure the balance. A polarization is presented of faith-based schools being theologically conservative *vis-à-vis* a highly secular community school system in which there is little sensitivity to religion. This is far from the truth: there are many community schools which make great efforts to provide an inclusive curriculum in terms of theology and science, and which are sensitive to religious groups. Conversely, many state-funded faith-based schools have negotiated the curriculum in a manner which does not compromise their religious convictions. Difficulties with science subjects tend to be expressed by a tiny minority within this category of schools, namely some Jewish and Muslim schools. However, as it is the latter group which has established the largest number of new schools, as we saw in Chapter 3, and which have further applications pending for state funding, it is important to recognize that for some communities it is an issue.

As we said earlier, what the Science National Curriculum is trying to achieve here is encourage pupils to be aware of the world and their place in it and to test hypotheses. That is:

scientific method is about developing and evaluating explanations through experimental evidence and modelling. This is a spur to critical and creative thought. (Department for Education and Employment and Qualifications and Curriculum Authority 1999, p. 13)

As inheritance and evolution are stipulated as part of the National Curriculum there could be a potential problem here in science teaching, if schools prohibit teaching which provides critical and creative thought on such issues as the evolution process and instead perpetuate a single view, such as 'creationism'.

This is the criticism levelled at some faith-based schools in their teaching of this aspect of the curriculum. As we noted earlier in Chapter 2, there are a number of new independent Christian schools which wish to teach a biblical view in explaining the origin of the world (Walford 1995a). For example, the Emmanuel City Technology College in Gateshead has presented creationist theories to pupils as part of its Science Curriculum. This was defended by the school which counter-argued that a variety of approaches can be used and that both creationism and evolution are 'faith positions'.[26] Legally this is an interesting situation because the Emmanuel City Technology College is designated as an independent institution funded by the government and 'it has to teach the subjects but not necessarily the content' of the National Curriculum prospectus.[27] As such it has chosen to teach creationism as part of the content of this aspect of the curriculum. Similarly, the state-funded Seventh Day Adventist school, John Loughborough in North London, takes a biblical line, which appears to be in conflict with the National Curriculum.[28] Whilst founded by private benefactors, the school is funded by the state, but it reserves the right to determine its own ethos, and this, it argues, extends to the selection of subject matter in the curriculum.

These schools are not alone on this issue of teaching creationism. Some Muslim schools use a religious view in opposition to that of Darwinism, as do some Jewish schools such as the ultra-Orthodox Hasmonean High School cited earlier.[29] In the latter case:

> we teach creationism and evolution as part of the science syllabus. But a lot of Jewish scientific thinking sees no contradiction between the two. When the Old Testament talks about an event happening in a day, that day is understood to be an era of time.[30]

Likewise, the Islamia School in Brent argues that :

> we approach Darwinism theory in a phenomenological way. We say, 'there is a theory, believed by some, that we are descended from apes'. It's just one idea among many.[31]

The teaching of 'creationism' alongside or instead of Darwinism is not problematic for independent faith-based schools for, as we noted earlier, they are not obliged to follow the National Curriculum. However, for those in receipt of government funding there is a difficulty here as critics from the scientific community demand open-minded education be a condition of funding.[32] The British Humanist Association, for example, has called for the National Curriculum to be rewritten to avoid creationism being taught as an alternative to Darwinism.[33] Similarly, the National Secular Society has forcefully warned:

> Mr Blair's enthusiasm for faith schools will give the green light to every crackpot religious group to start peddling their own mad fantasies in schools that are paid for by the taxpayer.[34]

As we noted earlier in the chapter, in the southern United States, the Bible is used as a central text in teaching, and there is an overt 'Christian fundamentalist' presence which has been very influential in the teaching of creationism.[35]

From a legal point of view, if a state-funded school is alleged to be failing to teach the obligatory sections of the National Curriculum, such as in this instance Science Education, an inspection can be called for with the school being given the opportunity to correct the omission. If there is a continued failure to do so, ultimately funding may be withdrawn.[36] Thus far there has not been a case to test out this area of the curriculum, and in the meantime faith-based schools deliver this aspect of science education in a manner which they feel reconciles the requirements of the National Curriculum with their own religious convictions.

Citizenship Education

The final area of the curriculum for discussion with regard to faith-based schooling is the newest addition to the National Curriculum, that of 'citizenship education' at secondary school level.[37] Citizenship education is potentially much broader than other areas of the curriculum, including the hidden curriculum, pupils' social experiences and moral understandings, participation in community affairs and other extra-curricular activities (Kerr 2003). Developing effective citizenship education is a multifaceted process (Klein 2001; Osler and Vincent 2002; Crick 2000a; Hall 2000; Starkey 2000). It involves the developing of knowledge, skills, attitudes, world-views, participation and engagement. Thus, citizenship education cannot be contained within the school context; it permeates family and community, and it is influenced by the political culture in society.

The introduction of 'Citizenship' into the National Curriculum in the academic year 2002–2003, at Key Stages 3 and 4, provides a powerful opportunity for all schools to enrich teaching with a subject directly related to the future lives of young people. This formed part of the revised National Curriculum with new frameworks for Personal, Social and Health Education and Citizenship (QCA 1999, 2000). Nowhere is the new addition more evident than in the teaching offered by faith-based schools, which have often been the target for accusations of segregation and isolationism, and which have also been accused of delivering a curriculum inappropriate for the preparation for life.

In accordance with the European Charter on the Rights of the Child (1979),[38] there is a consensus to promote children's participation in decision-making that affects them. This right should also be exercised at school where there is an expectation that children will develop respect for human rights and for different cultures, religions and people's philosophical convictions. Kerr (2003) argues that schools that model democratic practices are effective with respect to teaching and learning citizenship that goes beyond the subject matter, involving an understanding of moral and civic responsibilities. This is particularly important for faith-based schools, requiring them to model democratic processes, discuss and debate different systems of beliefs and values, and encourage pupils from diverse backgrounds to bring into the classroom different views and experiences. A significant dimension of teaching and learning citizenship is that of critical thinking and values development, and not a mere transmission of factual knowledge. This suggests that the schools themselves should function as an example of civic engagement and democratic participation.

All schools have the potential to influence and encourage what Kerr calls 'civic preparation of young people' (ibid., p. 21). Pupils who feel they belong in school and that their culture is being valued are more likely to develop a sense of community and trust, and thereby to become active members. However, there are many challenges that schools, and faith-based institutions in particular, are likely to face. These include:

- consensus on what citizenship entails – this has curricular implications in terms of locating citizenship in a specific curriculum area or taking a cross-subject approach and seeing it as being a part of History or Personal and Social Education teaching; and
- modes of teaching and learning citizenship – does it focus on factual information or involvement in specific activities that take place in the community, or strike a balance between knowledge and practical activities?

Shifting views and attitudes in faith-based schools in terms of seeing the teaching of citizenship as a significant way of promoting social and moral development in their pupils, and developing healthy home–community relationships, can be challenging especially in the current climate of divisions among communities across religious, social and ethnic lines. Rioting in Oldham and other northern towns in England in 2001 is evidence of this tension.[39]

Faith-based schools that cater for pupils from minority ethnic backgrounds may encounter a paradox in terms of teaching these pupils citizenship and principles of democracy while, at the same time, they and their families' citizenship rights may be restricted or undermined due to racism and xenophobia. The 1998 Crick report, 'Education for Citizenship and the Teaching of Democracy in Schools, concluded that citizenship education should be able to 'promote a vision of a multicultural society founded on principles of human rights, and of schools where children are able to realise their rights on the basis of equality' (Osler 2002, p. 43). We should note, however, that the committee which produced this document was itself allegedly not equally representative of a variety of different faith groups in its membership.[40]

As the British government has now made citizenship education part of the compulsory curriculum of secondary schools and a recommended element for primary schools, both of which are subject to inspection, the issue has direct implications for faith-based schools in receipt of public funding. If we take the Citizenship Framework (2002), we find it provides a number of key areas which can be easily used by faith-based schools, and which can support the crucial role they can play in promoting social harmony and social justice. These are as follows:

- *Human rights* – faith-based schools have, along with other schools, provided a place to pray, and a right to physical safety.

- *Social justice and inclusion* – many faith-based schools have provided opportunities for dialogue with other religious and community schools. As such, teachers in a variety of schools can and do learn from each other.

- *Sustainability* is a concept very much understood by faith-based schools, especially those based on Islam, Judaism and Hinduism which mostly do not enjoy financial support from the government. The lessons learnt have application beyond the confines of their school walls, to the wider society and the need to maintain the resources we have.

- *Interdependence* – educational organizations of different faith groups already work in trust with each other and with the secular community. At school level this has been in the sharing of resources, and at local government level there has been meaningful co-operation between parents, schools and governors, as we noted earlier in Chapter 3.

- *Conflict resolution* – faith-based schools are no different from community schools in having had experience of conflict resolution. In terms of dealings with the local community and challenging negative stereotyping, they have had, and continue to have, an important role to play. A major example of this would be the number of Islamic organizations who publically condemned the terrorist attacks on September 11, and gave concrete offers of help in this country and in the United States.[41]

- *Values and perceptions* – faith-based schools are permeated by a religious ethos based on values. Tolerance, for example, is one such value, and such schools have worked hard producing materials to communicate their beliefs in a secular society and to challenge prejudice.[42]

- *Diversity* – our society is multicultural, multilingual and multi-faith, and this diversity is representative of many faith-based schools. There are many different ways of having faith, of which Judaism, Hinduism and Catholicism are some. Indeed, apart from religious pluralism in society, there is a huge amount of diversity within religious groups, as we saw in earlier chapters, and they are as communities excellent examples of diversity within themselves.

As we can see, therefore, the Citizenship Framework offers faith-based schools the opportunity to explore wider issues and to encourage pupils to see themselves not just as members of their own religious community but also as citizens of the world, aware of the wider issues and challenges of global interdependence and responsibility. For example, the Guru Nanak Sikh Secondary School has within its mission statement a commitment to 'providing a preparation for each student's entry into the wider community',[43] and its recent inspection report noted that 'citizenship had been introduced very successfully [and] students progress very well in developing skills of inquiry, participation and responsibility'.[44]

Notions of citizenship can still be problematical, however, for communities who feel marginalized or alienated from wider society. For example, it has been said that the creation of Muslim schools is evidence that people are desperate not only to maintain their cultural identity but to have a 'voice', and to articulate it within an understanding of what 'citizenship' means to different communities (Gundara 2000). The religious dimension of identity, discussed earlier in Chapter 4, can be explored within the concept of citizenship and the different levels at which this concept can operate. Also very useful for new faith-based schools is the opportunity to study media literacy and to encourage the critical analysis of images of racism, Islamophobia and homophobia, exploring their construction and their often misleading representation. This is an approach used effectively in community schools with large numbers of pupils from diverse cultural backgrounds (Wrigley 2000). To do this successfully, all pupils need to be encouraged to make sound critical judgements based on appropriate and relevant curriculum material, for religions themselves can reinforce and confirm negative images of different groups. As Young (1990) highlights:

> groups have distinct cultures, experiences and perceptions on social life with humanly positive meaning, some of which may even be superior to the culture and perspectives of mainstream society. (p. 166)

Research on independent faith-based schools, such as those of an Islamic ethos, has demonstrated that their curriculum offerings may be very narrow, due to financial restraints and ideological choice in the selection of curricula (Hewer 2001b; Walford 2001b). Once state funding is made available the inclusion of Citizenship as a subject in the curriculum cannot be avoided, and indeed provides an excellent opportunity for pupils to explore their identity, and how this fits with the notion of citizenship, through the creation of a learning environment in which *all* pupils experience a sense of belonging, feel truly valued and are able to participate fully (Irving et al. 2003).

Within citizenship education the development of attitudes and skills is not the sole responsibility of the classroom teacher. Theoretical knowledge by itself is insufficient: schools need to provide opportunities for their pupils to engage in activities beyond their own community and avoid being inward-looking, insular and concerned with the minutiae of the rituals of daily life, important though they may be. From our research on Muslim and Sikh schools, for example, we saw evidence of the beginnings of this engagement with the wider level of social responsibility, and the nurturing of pupils as global citizens, and in fact many schools we visited rejected the idea that they were not interacting with groups externally and instead reported that they felt themselves to be part of the wider community. This is in keeping with what Osler and Starkey (2003) refer to as 'education for cosmopolitan citizenship'. This theory locates the subject in the context of globalization, in which citizenship addresses local, national, regional and global issues in order that pupils are better prepared to live together in increasingly diverse local communities and an interdependent world. The approach also encompasses different understandings of 'community', which we raised earlier in chapter 4, and different levels of civic engagement, as well as exploring multiple identities and loyalties as understood in different sites of learning, for example school, home and community.

So far we have been looking at the challenges and opportunities that aspects of the National Curriculum present to faith-based schools, but we should go further and question whether present provision measures up to the reality of a multi-faith society.

Changing the National Curriculum

A curriculum, national or otherwise, needs to reflect a balance of perspectives, incorporating the achievements and contributions of cultural groups. Reviewing the National Curriculum documents implemented since the Educational Reform Act (1988), these appear at best Eurocentric and at worst Britocentric, but rarely multicentric. A movement away from what Leicester (1989) describes as seeing education 'through ethnocentric spectacles' (p. 42) requires a deliberate shift from this bias. Notwithstanding the perceived strait-jacket of the National Curriculum when it was first introduced, there have been possibilities to acknowledge the contributions to knowledge by Islam and from other groups, and to broaden the received canon of knowledge.

Finding the right balance between the indigenous and minority cultures as expressed in the curriculum continues to be an area of concern. It is not possible to make the curriculum responsive to Islam, Sikhism or Judaism in state-funded schools without simultaneously negotiating the National Curriculum. The Dearing

Report (Dearing 1994) recommended that the British National Curriculum be reduced by about a third, which provided the scope for curriculum innovation in some subject areas. By attempting to seize the initiative and use space to develop an appropriate religious dimension to subject areas at relevant Key Stages, schools can compensate for previous omissions. Without commitment to do this, this aspect of multicultural teaching is jeopardized or sacrificed for the dictates of a homogenized, ethnocentric curriculum.[45]

Whilst Britain is in reality a multicultural and multi-faith society, critics argue that a secular monocultural perspective predominates within the schools, aimed at achieving social harmony and marginalizing all religions. Mabud (1992) argues:

> Muslims do not expect the curriculum in state schools to be Islamic. What they do expect, however, is that the multicultural, multifaith character of Britain, will be reflected in the curriculum and in the school ethos. (p. 91)

There is also dissatisfaction with the notion of 'multi-faith' education which we discussed earlier:

> even at the best of times 'faith' is presented as a narrow, spiritualistic and rather confusing concept. 'Religions' are grouped together and offered as a hotch-potch optional subject. (Hulmes 1989, p. 31)

Some Muslims, for example, are suspicious of the inclusion of Islam within a multi-faith curriculum and the ability of community schools to adequately convey the religion's features and dimensions.

Overall, therefore, there is dissatisfaction with and a lack of confidence in the ability of the National Curriculum as it stands to adequately provide teaching experiences for the next generation of citizens. Gundara (2000) argues against a National Curriculum:

> a fundamental issue is the need for an intercultural curriculum. Nation-centred or European-centred curricula can only reinforce the sense of exclusion and disadvantage and, as in Britain, lead to a demand for separate schools, to the 'politics of recognition' with its own 'curriculum of recognition'. (p. 127)

Others share the view that if schools respond sensitively in providing a balanced curriculum, there are benefits to be gained for children in all schools:

> the achievement of respect for others lies in knowledge – the concept of respect for self is achieved in a similar way. (McGee 1992, p. 18)

As such all schools need to build in sensitivity to the religious and cultural norms by which children are being raised, for example a sensitivity in teaching to Judaism, Islam, Hinduism and Sikhism.

It is arguable, however, that schools do not have sufficient opportunity to develop an intercultural curriculum as the law stands. In the case of state-funded schools, agendas are not set by schools; they are set nationally and managed locally and within the institutions. Faith-based schools have to respond to the National Curriculum in a creative way which optimizes pupil outcomes within what is seen as a changing context, and also must develop curriculum which is consistent with the community's religious principles. A school's ability to change the curriculum is affected by the fact that it is centrally driven. Muslim schools, for example, wish to develop an Islamic orientation to their curriculum, and they try to seize opportunities to provide innovative ways in the National Curriculum to do this. For example, in History, the subject can be taken from the child and traced back through parents and grandparents, as we noted with reference to schools in our study.

Other examples of how faith-based schools can be affected by the National Curriculum are in the matter of pupil absence. For example, families may return to Bangladesh or Pakistan for periods of time. In the past this may have been viewed as a positive experience and children could return and share these experiences and knowledge gained. Now, children may miss large chunks of the National Curriculum through being back in their parents' own countries and this can present a challenge especially when pupil assessment is taking place. A similar difficulty may be experienced in community schools in accommodating these visits. Overall, the issue concerns the ability of the curriculum to accommodate children from diverse backgrounds with family traditions and expectations.

A further issue which is particularly important in the context of faith-based schools, and which was highlighted earlier, is that of 'indoctrination'. As we have noted throughout this chapter, education without an awareness of God or a spiritual Being is meaningless to faith-based schools. Mabud (1992) maintains that without the religious dimension 'it is not education at all but indoctrination into a particular world view' (p. 90). The word 'indoctrination' is particularly apposite here since that is precisely what sceptics and non-believers contend is happening within faith-based schools in general. The clash between religious and secular educational philosophies is complex. In countries such as the United States and Turkey, for example, which claim to operate only secular curricula, the issue is no less contentious, since it is arguable that no education is ever value or culture free. Interestingly, the principles which underline the major religions are consistent with producing good people with high personal values within a community of believers. Community schools would likewise maintain that they are aiming to produce individuals of impeccable character and that faith-based schools do not have the monopoly on wanting to encourage high moral values among their pupils.

Some writers also take issue with the view that religious models of education require blind obedience with no room for critical enquiry.[46] The problem is twofold: religious communities may see community school education in a predominantly negative light, as unable to satisfy the needs of religious adherents; school educators may perceive religious education in terms of narrow and restricted provision based on ritualistic following of religious belief. Fortunately the picture is not all bleak: all faith-based schools are not theologically conservative and nor are community schools completely secular. There are many examples of community and faith-based schools twinning together and forming partnerships, and through a variety of activities breaking down barriers and challenging negative stereotyping of each other. This type of initiative is also evident among schools in Northern Ireland where religious sectarianism has generated hostility and dislike between Catholics and Protestants.[47] Modifying the National Curriculum to open up greater possibility of dialogue between different groups would help break down the stereotypical assumptions between different faith-based schools, and community schools.

Conclusion

Faith-based groups place great value and significance on the acquisition of knowledge, and see it as part of an individual's development and journey in discovering God or a Divine Being. Knowledge is not divorced from religion; rather the two complement each other as part of a wide-ranging educational experience. The pivotal importance of religion and religious values is reflected in particular aspects of the curriculum such as science education, religious education, and, in some cases, social and health education. Conflict is perceived between Western-secular and religious philosophies of education in which different emphasis and interpretation are placed on concepts such as critical enquiry. Furthermore, it is suggested that secular modes of thinking and conceptualization are inadequate to explain religious concepts of educational issues. Finally, some groups see multi-faith education at best as an inadequate, ill-informed attempt to explain tokenistically different religions operating within a pluralistic society; and at worst as an imposed ideology with a dominant slant on non-religion aimed at undermining belief in religion. For this reason the National Curriculum is challenged as being too ethnocentric in its approach and in its failure to adequately recognize the contribution of diverse groups. Faith-based schools, therefore, face challenges on two diverse and potentially competing fronts. On the one hand, the development of a curriculum that is not only sensitive to, but actually incorporates, religious views and values is seen to be of extreme importance. On the other, there is a fine line to be trod between this and the implementation of a curriculum that is founded on a particular faith to the exclusion of other perspectives, and alternative ways of living. If faith-based schools are to develop a curriculum model that is inclusive, open and socially just they will be required to think carefully about how this polarization can be avoided. Moreover, as pupils, families and communities operate within a wider pluralist society, attempts to voluntarily exclude themselves from this 'lived reality' may lead to further mistrust, prejudice and social division.

Having looked at the nature of the National Curriculum, the area of assessment and potential areas of controversy in the timetable, we move next to explore how special educational needs can be accommodated in faith-based schools. This is a particular issue for those institutions which, through recent access to state funding or changes in their admissions policy, have for the first time to respond significantly to special educational needs in the classroom, and a more diverse pupil body.

Notes

1 Guru Nanak Sikh Secondary Voluntary Aided School, School *Prospectus (2001–2002)*, p. 5.
2 As cited in Raza (1993), p. 42.
3 Ibid.
4 Ashraf (1994).
5 See Rendle (1997).
6 See Hewer (2001b) and Walford (2001b).
7 See Keiner (1996), for example, with reference to Jewish schools.
8 Inspection Report (2000b).
9 Inspection Report (2001b).
10 Derby City LEA (2003), pp. 5–6.
11 *The Sunday Telegraph* (2002).
12 Ibid.
13 See Broadbent and Brown (2003).
14 Guru Nanak Sikh Secondary Voluntary Aided School, *School Prospectus (2001–2002)*.
15 Nottingham Diocese (2002), p. 4.
16 Ibid., p. 5.
17 Ibid., p. 18.
18 Clore Shalom School, *Brochure (2002–2003)*.
19 See Francis and Lankshear (1993).
20 Wrigley (2000).
21 The Swaminarayan Secondary School, *School Prospectus(2002–2003)*, p. 2.
22 The Education (No. 2) Act (1986), London: HMSO.
23 Guru Nanak Sikh Secondary Voluntary Aided School, *School Prospectus(2002–2003)*, p. 9.
24 Ibid.
25 *The Sunday Telegraph* (2002).
26 Inspection Report (2001a), and 'Press Release from Emmanuel College' (11 March 2002) at http://www.christianpublications.co.uk/emmanuel11march02.htm
27 *Times Educational Supplement* (2003f), and *The Independent* (2002) See also http://www.church.org.uk, http://www.evangelical-times.org. and http://christian publications. co.uk/emanuel11march02.hrm
28 *The Guardian* (2002a). See also Inspection Report (2001c).
29 *The Guardian* (2002a).
30 Ibid.
31 Ibid. See also Inspection Report (2000a).
32 Stephen Dawkins in *The Sunday Telegraph* (2002).
33 British Humanist Association (2002).
34 *The Independent* (2002).
35 Francis and Lankshear (1993).

36 The Education (No. 2) Act (1986).
37 The Education Act (2002).
38 The European Charter on the Rights of the Child (1979).
39 See, for example, The Cantle Report (2001).
40 See Advisory Group membership for *The Crick Report* (Crick 2000a), p. 5.
41 Yusuf Islam's immediate visit to New York in the aftermath of the September 11 attacks.
42 See Virtual Classroom project website, www.virtualclassroom.co.uk
43 Guru Nanak Sikh Secondary Voluntary Aided School, *School Prospectus (2002–2003)*, p. 5.
44 Inspection Report (2003a).
45 See also Leicester (1989), Eggleston (1990) and Troyna (1986).
46 See, for example, British Humanist Association (2002) .
47 See Gallagher (2002), McGlynn (2003) and Smith (2001).

Chapter 7

Special Educational Needs Practice in Faith-Based Schools

As society becomes more heterogeneous the terms used to describe diversity can themselves become the focus of debates and extend to incorporate difference on the basis of special educational needs. Accommodating pupils categorized as Special Educational Needs (SEN) forms an important aspect in all state-funded schools. As we noted earlier in previous chapters, independent schools are not required to follow the National Curriculum, nor are they obliged to enrol pupils with SEN. Indeed, league tables and fee structures may prevent independent schools from responding to a wide range of pupils. By contrast, the expansion of faith-based schools with government funding requires those schools to be responsive to SEN pupils officially, and provide resources, staffing, facilities and expertise which before lay outside their legal remit. In this changing climate, understanding SEN in faith-based schools requires us to place the issue in the context of diversity and inclusion, and to discuss potential challenges to religious and cultural identity. There is also a need to consider SEN policy and practice as it relates to human rights issues and the guiding principles for providing 'education for all'.

Dimensions of diversity, that is, ethnicity and SEN, raise issues related to newly funded faith-based schools and their obligation to respond to multiple facets of differentiation. As we saw earlier in Chapter 4, ethnicity and religion are associated with visible markers of diversity, but there are also important issues regarding disability and special educational needs (Corbett 1998). One reason for discussing dimensions of diversity when exploring SEN issues in faith-based schools is that there is strong evidence to suggest that, in many Western societies, children with SEN have been discriminated against (Tomlinson 1984; Tucker 1980). Thus, an important question is how faith-based schools with public funding deal with multiple dimensions of diversity, and acknowledge and celebrate differences in pupils' profiles and needs. To explore these issues this chapter will:

- examine the broad area of diversity and inclusion;
- explore the concept of special educational needs as an aspect of diversity;
- investigate the challenges SEN policy poses to cultural and religious identity;
- relate special educational needs to faith-based schools in terms of policy, practice and parental involvement;

- distinguish between language difference and SEN; and
- locate the issue of SEN within a human rights context.

Diversity and Inclusion

Society is rapidly changing and becoming increasingly diverse. Societal aspects that affect education – namely the cultural, ethnic and religious profile of the population, patterns of family organization, human rights and social/moral responsibilities – all change and continue to evolve (Frederickson and Cline 2002). The role of education in promoting cultural pluralism and social cohesion is seen as an important instrument of multicultural societies, with learning being conceptualized as a process of constructing cultural meanings and identities. It is argued that this type of learning is more likely to take place in an inclusive setting, that is, a place where children can be educated together even though they are different in terms of ethnicity, religion, socio-economic background and ability (Wang and Reynolds 1995).

A worldwide movement towards inclusive education has been supported by many international developments over recent years, including the Salamanca Statement and Framework for Action (UNESCO 1994), the European Convention on Human Rights, and the UK Human Rights Act (1998). Notions of inclusion are embodied in the Salamanca Statement, in which it is noted that:

> inclusion and participation are essential to human dignity and to the enjoyment and exercise of human rights. Within the field of education this is reflected in the development of strategies that seek to bring about a genuine equalisation of opportunity.[1]

In the UK, the Special Educational Needs and Disability Act (2001) strengthens the right to a mainstream education for children with special educational needs. The Act has amended the Education Act (1996) and transformed the statutory framework for inclusion into a positive endorsement of inclusion. The legislation seeks to enable more pupils who have special educational needs to be included successfully within mainstream education. Inclusive educational policies are expected to support and protect the rights of citizenship for all pupils – for example ethnic-religious minorities, SEN and disadvantaged pupils – extending the idea of inclusion from a concept relevant to special education to one that permeates all educational experiences in schools. According to the Department for Education and Skills (2001), inclusion is conceptualized as a process by which schools, Local Education Authorities and others develop their cultures, policies and practices to include pupils from all backgrounds. With the right training, strategies and support nearly all children with special educational needs can be successfully included in mainstream education. The rationale for supporting inclusive practices is as follows:

- an inclusive education service offers excellence and choice, and incorporates the views of parents and children;
- the interests of all pupils must be safeguarded;
- schools, Local Education Authorities and others should actively seek to remove barriers to learning and participation; and
- all children should have access to an appropriate education that affords them the opportunity to achieve their personal potential (ibid., paraphrased).

Achieving inclusive education has become increasingly important for faith-based schools in that, by law, they are required to accommodate their pupils' diverse profiles in terms of religion, ethnicity and SEN. With their own distinctive ethos and character, faith-based schools are well placed to support diversity and strive for inclusion by making their services accessible to the wider community, and engaging in dialogue with parents and pupils regarding learning and behavioural support of students with diverse learning and developmental needs.

As Slee (2001) argues, inclusive education is 'a project of educational reconceptualisation and radical reconstruction' given that some current school practices are likely to 'deny human rights and exclude students on the basis of race, ethnicity, disability and class' (p. 174). Thus, as part of an educational reconceptualization, faith-based schools, like other schools, are expected to engage in an exploration of what disability means and its social outcomes – for example exclusion and marginalization, particularly for ethnic and/or religious minority pupils. Such schools need to take into account historic inequities in education. The reasons behind social inequality are complex; however, limited access to resources and support systems are likely to contribute to poor education especially for minority ethnic children and their families, and this has been the situation for some new faith-based schools, as we discussed earlier in Chapter 3. Cross-cultural and religious differences in child-rearing and parental values and practices shape views on individual and collective rights and responsibilities. For example, parents from certain cultures may believe that it is the teacher's sole responsibility to teach their child without seeing themselves being involved in the education process. The teacher may perceive that as a sign of parental indifference and a lack of home–school communication. Moreover, some parents may question single-religion perspectives and practices, whereas others may see them as a way of supporting religious identity and cultural heritage. And finally, differences in culture, religion and socio-economic background shape parents' views and children's behaviour, social/emotional development and attitudes towards learning.[2]

Having placed SEN in the context of diversity and inclusion we will look next at issues of SEN and their relevance to faith-based schools.

SEN: Another Aspect of Diversity

Special Educational Needs is an all-encompassing category that reflects diversity in children's learning and developmental profiles. Specifically, this category refers to characteristics that can be grouped into the following four domains: cognitive and learning difficulties; emotional, behavioural and social difficulties; communication and interaction difficulties; and sensory and/or physical difficulties (Department for Education and Skills 2001). These subcategories do not form homogeneous groups in that there is a great deal of diversity within each domain. There is also a great deal of overlapping, with boundaries that are 'cross-cutting, fluid and shifting' (Thomas 1997, p. 103).

Traditionally, the field of special education has lacked critical and rigorous examination of the links between notions of disability, and social justice and equality (Apple 2001). The political and ideological nature of the mechanisms that are there to support individuals with disabilities is rarely debated. There is, however, an ongoing debate about competition, markets and choice on the one hand and accountability, performance objectives and delivery of the National Curriculum on the other, leaving special education hanging somewhere in between. Further, current conceptions of social justice developed by the Commission on Social Justice (1994) lack cohesion and clarity, especially when applied to those with special educational needs. The four key principles that underlie the Commission's findings, note Riddell, Baron and Wilson (2001), 'leave a number of questions unanswered, in particular, what criteria to be used to decide what counts as a just and unjust society' (p. 42). According to Rizvi and Christensen (1996), those who argue for social justice in education for children with disabilities should engage in an 'explicit and sustained analysis' (p. 25).

There is a tension between the 'inclusion agenda and the education reform agenda', and thus National Curriculum testing, inspection, competition and pressure to raise the standards are likely to impact on inclusive education negatively (Frederickson and Cline 2002, p. 36). State-funded faith-based schools may experience these tensions, providing the ground where issues regarding disability, ethnicity and religion will be debated. It is thus timely and of particular importance to understand the challenge of providing for pupils with disabilities from ethnic minority and religious groups, and to take into account the interplay between cultural and religious differences and academic achievement. Accumulating empirical research points to both an over- or under-representation in special education among ethnic/religious minority students.[3] Differences in cultural values and norms, and potential conflict with the school culture and ethos, make ethnic minority pupils more susceptible to disability categorization (Jacobs 1987; Wright 1996). Socio-cultural and linguistic factors also affect the academic achievement of minority ethnic children (Hartman and Fay 1996; Hudley 1997). As some of the new faith-based schools are highly representative of pupils of ethnic minorities as well as second- and third-generation children of immigrant parents, this point is particularly important in terms of the school response.

The educational attainment of minority ethnic pupils with special educational needs is sometimes connected to the issue of 'bilingualism'. Underachievement due to English being an additional language is often taken to be caused by language difficulties rather than language differences but this may not be the case. Most research has adopted a colour-blind approach to ethnic minority pupils with SEN, providing a limited insight into how certain cultural/social and religious aspects may be linked to special educational needs.[4] Bilingualism and biculturalism alone cannot provide adequate explanations for over/under-representation of ethnic minority pupils in SEN registers; religion may also be a contributing factor by having a differential impact on particular ethnic minority groups. For example, in a study conducted by Diniz (1997, 1999) with predominantly Asian and Chinese parents in Edinburgh, it was found that service providers often overlook the diversity within Asian and Chinese groups – for example in religion and/or parental beliefs – and often 'treat them all the same'. There are many factors, such as religion, history of settlement, social class and language, that affect parents' understanding of SEN, provision and access to resources.

Due to the multiplicity of factors that are likely to have a differential impact on minority ethnic groups, Tomlinson (2000) argues that minority issues should be taken into consideration when conceptualizing new frameworks in education. Ainscow (1995a, 1997) adds that providing high-quality education for all students, including minority ethnic pupils with SEN, requires schools to develop certain qualities. The same qualities are relevant to faith-based schools, and include:

- *leadership* in terms of establishing a clear vision for the school that emphasizes individuality, and a strong ethos/identity without sacrificing critical and innovative thinking;
- *involvement of parents* and other members of the community in decision-making through the creation of an open climate and a school ethos that is supportive of diversity and pluralism;
- *planning and discussions* about teaching and learning and curriculum development; and
- *reflection and debate* on issues of disability, religion and ethnicity, as well as pedagogy and inclusive education.

Added to this, there is the issue of identity based on culture and religion. In Chapter 4 we provided discussions on the importance of religion and cultural heritage in people's lives, and in this chapter we look at the relationship between these issues and those of inclusion and SEN.

Challenges to Cultural and Religious Identity

So far in this chapter we have seen how the concept of diversity can be defined broadly to include not just issues of religion and ethnic background but also those of disability and special educational needs. We have also seen how the accommodation of special educational needs relates to faith-based schools, especially those in receipt of state funding which are legally obliged to respond to this level of diversity in the classroom. Next we look at the challenges policy on special educational needs makes to schools predicated principally on religious ethos, in terms of the shifting nature of the establishment, the pursuit of academic excellence and the notion of social inclusion.

Historically, acknowledging and accommodating diversity and pluralism have been constrained within mono-faith schools, partly attributed in some cases to the conservative/orthodox element within some religious groups which avoid 'outreach'. Clearly, this is a paradox if we consider that diversity is inherent in the teaching and learning of religion. There is a great deal of variation found within religions characterized by fluid boundaries in terms of religious expression and cultural manifestations (Jackson and Nesbitt 1993). Thus, taking a single-religion perspective on issues of SEN and ethnicity may result in adopting the notion of 'otherness' and developing divisive rather than inclusive educational practices.

Keogh et al. (1997) highlight the dilemmas involved in accommodating ethnic, cultural and religious diversity in schools. Specifically, by accommodating the needs of minority ethnic students there is a danger of stereotyping them by assuming that they share the same traits as others from similar ethnic backgrounds. It is an oversimplification to use ethnic differences as a yardstick of cultural differences in that cultural and religious differences may exist within groups that share similar ethnic backgrounds. Faith-based and community schools need to be aware of this and acknowledge variation and diversity at many levels: between ethnically defined groups, within ethnically defined groups, and between individuals within ethnically, culturally or religiously defined groups.

With access to public funding, the expectation is that faith-based schools will take an approach that emphasizes not only cultural diversity and academic excellence but also equity (Gundara 2000). One criticism in the 'equity versus excellence' debate is that equity usually involves accommodating 'otherness' and promoting 'sameness' by taking a colour- blind approach to difference. This can be alleviated by teaching about various cultures and religions, and promoting a positive self-image and tolerance. Academic excellence, on the other hand, should not be seen in a vacuum but as an outcome from equal access to good-quality inclusive education that caters for diverse learners, includes parents, values community languages and incorporates them into the curriculum (Rouse and Florian 1996). Some would argue that academic excellence is also about introducing different religions on an equal basis, and monitoring policies to ensure a balanced multi-faith perspective, a point we shall return to later in Chapter 9.[5]

Moreover, faith-based schools are required to take on board notions of equality of opportunity and access to education, inclusion of pupils with diverse learning needs and religious profiles, and, if funded, to be publicly accountable. The challenge that faith-based schools face is to reconcile a single-religion perspective with the principles that underlie inclusive education, social justice and human rights. The link between the right to inclusion and social justice is not always straightforward. Social justice is not a universally shared concept (Christensen and Dorn 1997), and thus, culture- and religion-specific views on what social justice entails may highlight apparent contradictions in the ethos and policies of faith-based schools. Furthermore, the teaching of a diverse subject such as religion challenges faith-based schools further by 'making explicit the crucial role of shared human experience and personal search' (Blaylock 1999, p. 22), and encouraging an 'impartial investigation and personal engagement with the material' (Bigger 2000). We look in more detail at the issue of encouraging independent thought in the context of children's rights in the next chapter. Next we look at the challenges faced by faith-based schools in responding to a broad understanding of inclusion.

In a market-driven educational system, the ideal of inclusive education is to ensure that all children succeed academically. However, there may be less emphasis placed on the social-cultural and personal development of pupils. If we consider Bruner's (1987) perspective of a school as a place where pupils develop social identities and socio-cultural meanings then inclusive education cannot be defined in terms of academic success only. According to this analysis, education becomes truly inclusive when it contributes to the development of pupils who can act and behave as citizens in a pluralistic society. In the current climate where state-funded faith-based schools are being encouraged to accept pupils of diverse religions, cultures and developmental/learning profiles, Bruner's views on inclusive education are meaningful and relevant. However, acceptance of such broad interpretations of inclusive education is likely to present challenges to faith-based schools, particularly those without government funding or those with little experience of responding to this level of need. Based on our research, we note that it is in the area of SEN that newly funded faith-based schools experience the greatest change as their pupil profile is altered and new policy and practice need to be developed.

SEN Policy and Practice in Faith-Based Schools

Governmental thinking and policy on SEN places an emphasis on the school ethos in terms of playing a crucial role in alleviating the impact of learning and other developmental difficulties, and promoting inclusive education. According to Halstead and Taylor (2000), school ethos refers to the nature and intensity of social relationships, the attitudes and expectation of teachers, the physical environment, links with parents and community, the nature of pupil participation, discipline and anti-bullying procedures, and, ultimately, the school's underlying philosophy and policy. Furthermore, in the SEN Code of Practice, it is clearly stated that 'effective management', school ethos, and the learning-environment, curricular, pastoral and discipline arrangements can help to prevent some SEN problems arising and minimize others.

A school's own practices make a difference in responding to SEN pupils (Department for Education and Skills 2001, p. 53, para. 5:18). Thus, if we are to take an interactional approach on SEN issues then we need to consider and assess not just the characteristics of the individual learner but also the learning environment. In other words, 'the assessment should always be fourfold: It should focus on the child's learning characteristics, the learning environment that the school is providing for the child, the task and the teaching style' (ibid., p. 24, para. 5:6). The emphasis on the learning environment raises important issues about the need to create a school environment that is supportive of all learners including those who present learning difficulties for a variety of reasons, for example SEN, social disadvantage and language differences (Ball and Harry 1993). In this context, inclusive education is successful only if educational provision is structured in a way that meets diverse needs.

Reynolds (1989) argues that inclusion is a process of extending responsibility to educate groups that have previously been excluded from the mainstream society. Moreover, understandings of race, religion, language and disability play an important role in influencing exclusion from mainstream education. Intolerance to difference can be a major obstacle to inclusion. Thus, it is important that when dealing with minority ethnic pupils with SEN (actual or perceived), teachers and other child professionals take into consideration the following:

- their own biases towards respective minority groups;
- the impact of social exclusion on the minority ethnic pupils and their families;
- the meaning of group identity;
- stereotypical views about the respective culture; and
- assessment issues (how valid tests are) (Booth et al. 2000, paraphrased).

Faith-based schools are expected to respond to such principles as well as take reasonable steps to ensure that the needs of all children are met in the mainstream. At a practical level they may, for example, choose to:

- use flexible grouping arrangements including ones where SEN pupils can work with more able peers;
- provide for all pupils experiences which are of benefit to most pupils but particularly to those with learning difficulties;
- use appropriate language in the classroom and incorporate strategies to promote the learning of vocabulary and the rules of classroom discussions;
- set appropriate targets so that personal progress as well as progress towards externally determined goals can be tracked; and
- consider carefully the pupils' learning styles and cultural/religious values and ensure that these are reflected in the styles of teaching.

There are clearly resource implications here in terms of staffing and facilities which again may add to the challenges faced by newly funded faith-based schools.

The Disability Act (2001) strengthens the right to a mainstream education and delivers comprehensive enforceable civil rights for disabled pupils. It also gives the Disability Rights Commission the power to issue a Code of Practice in relation to duties imposed on schools. Schools and Local Education Authorities have new duties to prevent discrimination, which will help facilitate inclusion, and are expected to build inter-agency partnerships – for example between LEAs and health authorities – to support children with complex developmental needs, in cases where there is a need for both medical and educational intervention.

Since September 2002, schools and Local Education Authorities must also:

- not treat disabled pupils less favourably, without justification, for reasons that relate to their disability;
- make reasonable steps to ensure that disabled pupils are not placed at a substantial disadvantage compared to other pupils who are not disabled; and
- plan strategically for and make progress in improving the physical environment of schools for disabled children, increasing disabled pupils' participation in the curriculum and improving the ways in which written information which is provided to pupils who are not disabled is also provided to disabled pupils (Department for Education and Skills 2001).

Ofsted monitors effective schools in terms of their capability in applying inclusive policies and practices. Specifically, they look at how well a school reaches out to all its learners and the practical steps that it takes to consider pupils' varied lives and experiences. This raises important issues for new faith-based schools where pupils are likely to constitute a diverse body in terms of religion, ethnicity, socio-economic background and SEN.

The SEN Code of Practice includes rights and responsibilities as introduced by the Disability Act (2001), and the United Nations Convention on the Rights of the Child, and places an emphasis on including parents in decision-making regarding provision of services, for example statutory assessment, classroom support and encouraging pupil participation. With respect to the latter, the Code of Practice highlights the importance of children and young people participating in all the decisions about their education. It makes clear that schools, Local Education Authorities and others should seek to ascertain the views of pupils regarding their needs and aspirations, and their thoughts on how they might like their needs to be met. Again this may present a challenge to some new faith-based schools in which culturally there is not an expectation that the child will consult with teachers, but rather an assumption that he or she will defer to adult authority.

Parents of Children with SEN

The emphasis on involving parents of children with SEN is expected to have particular implications for faith-based schools. In many cases parents have been instrumental in the success of the school and, as we saw earlier, parents have very actively helped support the establishment of new faith-based schools. Parental involvement is seen as a means of making school more accountable to the community it serves. Parents also choose the education they want for their child and thus they have the right to articulate their expectations and be part of the school's decision-making. However, as we noted in the case of children, there may be a cultural tradition in some faith-based schools that questions of pedagogy and decisions about classroom management are left to the authority of the teacher.

There are many reasons why schools and public authorities endorse effective home–school partnerships, but the main one is supporting children's learning. In a study by Okagaki and Frensch (1998) the need to be sensitive to religious and ethnic differences among parents from diverse backgrounds was stressed. Diversity in parents' beliefs and values has particular implications for children's education. Also, cultural differences are likely to shape parental involvement and expectations, as well as the quality of patterns of home–school interactions.

Traditionally, faith-based schools have been characterized by good home–school partnerships (Schagen et al. 2002), and this is seen as having a positive impact on achieving high standards. With state funding, faith-based schools are encouraged to interact with and facilitate participation of, parents from diverse cultures and religions. There is research to suggest that parents and professionals from different ethnic/cultural backgrounds are likely to misunderstand each other (Grugeon 1992) when discussing SEN matters. State-funded faith-based schools, as well as community schools, will have to follow the official guideline that formal notification to parents about SEN issues regarding their children has to be in the language the parents speak or, alternatively, schools need to obtain an interpreter (Department for Education and Skills 2001).

In addition, parents of children with SEN have the right to be actively involved in any decision and procedure relating to their children's needs. Cunningham and Davis (1985) conceptualize parent–professional relationships in terms of three models:

- an *expert model* where professionals are perceived as being the source of knowledge and expertise and the parents passive recipients of it;
- a *transplant model* in which professionals are considered as the main source of expertise and parents as a valuable resource able to deliver an intervention and ensure its continuity; and
- a *consumer model* in which parents are the key decision-makers and active in terms of exercising their choice and selecting the services they deem necessary.

Thus, in faith-based schools, the role and responsibilities of parents need to be negotiated and perhaps redefined by taking into consideration multiple aspects of diversity, current SEN legislative frameworks and new trends in a market-driven education.

Areas of Need: Language Difference or SEN?

According to the Qualifications and Curriculum Authority, teachers must take into account the educational requirements of pupils with SEN by becoming aware of the nature and extent of the difficulty experienced by the pupils. An important challenge that faith-based schools, as any other state educational institution, face is to understand the differences between special educational needs and special needs. A child has special educational needs if she or he has a learning difficulty that requires special educational provision. Frederickson and Cline (2002) assert that a child may present special needs if they come from a linguistic, social and cultural background that is different, and perhaps not represented in the school setting. Taking this further, Robson (1989) discusses four areas within which special needs are likely to be triggered, namely language, culture, overt racism and socio-economic disadvantage. As a result of widening participation, new faith-based schools are likely to deal with these phenomena and need to differentiate between SEN and other types of needs by taking into consideration children's diverse social and cultural experiences.

The current literacy movement in cognitive and educational research points to interrelationships among language, culture and value systems in that cognitive functioning and social/cultural understanding are normally externalized via language (Westby 1996). Specifically, Westby states that children's communicative competence includes organizational and pragmatic competence. Organizational competence refers to how children use vocabulary, syntax and grammar to produce coherent statements. Pragmatic competence refers to the ability to use language for different functions and purposes – for example requesting, protesting, greeting, negotiating, generating solutions – and to display social-linguistic ability in terms of being sensitive to and aware of the social parameters of an interaction – for example the listener's background knowledge of the conversational topic, social setting and social/cultural conversational norms.

Regarding language and social/emotional development, a child who has grown up in different linguistic environments with social conventions and belief systems that are different from those that he or she encounters at school may present special needs. Thus, there is a particular need for the school curriculum to provide support with English and, if possible, to maintain the child's first language, and to show respect to a wide range of cultures. It is also expected that the school be proactive in tackling racist behaviour by promoting a positive image of different ethnic groups and cultures. Finally, schools should acknowledge the impact of socio-economic deprivation on academic achievement and ensure that there are policies in place to ameliorate it (Frederickson and Cline 2002). Again, as a result of state funding, new faith-based schools can find themselves open to pupils who may share the same religious identity but who are from a wide range of backgrounds and have a diverse range of learning needs.

The process of language acquisition is long, complex and developmental. It is well documented that language proficiency in reading, writing and speaking is crucial for academic achievement. The use of language as a 'thought-supporting mechanism' has been found to encourage learners' use of self-monitoring strategies, for example planning, revising, cross-examining information and making links with background knowledge (Fitzgerald 1995). Working with bi- or multilingual children can be particularly challenging for some faith-based schools in that they may enrol large numbers of minority ethnic children from diverse linguistic backgrounds and thus English as an Additional Language (EAL) may form an important aspect of the learning environment.

In the context of a conversation, states Westby (1996), pragmatics refer to functional aspects of language use (requesting, informing, commenting); description of speech events (greetings, apologies, arguments, negotiations); and analysis of how people engage in everyday conversation (turn-taking, repair of a conversational breakdown, changing a topic). Competent communication involves the intention to communicate some information to another person, an understanding of what successful communication entails, and a recognition that the other person may have goals and beliefs that are different from those of the listener/talker. Cultural and ethnic differences are reflected in the way language is used, and thus, it is important to establish whether children's diverse linguistic profiles are simply different or in need of special educational arrangements.

Due to the multicultural and multi-ethnic nature of some faith-based schools, teachers have to deal with a large number of pupils for whom English is an additional language. These pupils have diverse needs given that language permeates every aspect of the curriculum and plays a crucial role in engaging in classroom discussions and peer collaborative learning. Planning and instruction should take into account many factors, such as the pupil's age, language(s) spoken at home, interactions with an extended family and the community, previous educational experience and parental support with the acquisition of English (Frederickson and Cline 2002).

The ability of pupils for whom English is an additional language may be far ahead of their communication skills. A discrepancy may be evident suggesting the need for developing spoken and written English and facilitating access to curriculum. Good language skills are crucial for academic achievement in that they are central in teaching and learning knowledge and skills, and this may carry resource implications for faith-based schools, as it does for some community schools.

Finally in this chapter, we will look at SEN issues within the context of human rights.

Human Rights Issues

The government's decision to grant public funds to a wider range of faith-based schools, the new enactment of the Human Rights Act and the introduction of citizenship education in the National Curriculum are all likely to impact on the socio-political and legal landscape within which notions of ethnicity, religion and disability are situated. As we have seen from discussions so far, within faith-based schools issues regarding race/ethnicity, social justice, cultural heritage, language, socio-economic background, curriculum and special educational needs have constantly to be reassessed. In some cases these issues have been the focus of continual development; for others, the issues may be new and challenging to a school's status quo and practices.

Article 9 of the new Human Rights Act (1998) specifically refers to 'freedom of thought, conscience and religion' and 'the manifestation of belief', entitlements which could provide ample opportunities for use by ethnic minority and religious groups. The implications of the Act are that not only followers of the world's major religions but also those from new religious movements could look for remedy from discriminatory practices, prejudice and hostility, a point we will return to in Chapter 9.

According to Article 29 (Convention on the Rights of the Child, 44/25, annex, 44 UN GAOR) the education of the child shall be directed to the development of respect for the child's parents, his or her own cultural identity, language and values, the national values of the country in which the child is living, the country from which he or she may originate, and civilizations different from his or her own. The Article also stresses the preparation of the child for responsible life in a free society, in the spirit of understanding, peace, tolerance, equality of sexes, and friendship among all peoples, ethnic, national and religious groups and persons of indigenous origin.

Both Articles 9 and 29 take a holistic and inclusive approach to child development in that children are expected to develop social and moral responsibility in terms of tolerance and understanding of others regardless of religion and ethnicity but also to be reared in accordance with their parents' cultural identity and values. For children who belong to ethnic, religious or linguistic minorities, 'they shall not be denied the right, in community with other members of his or her group, to enjoy his or her own culture, to profess and practise his or her own religion, or to use his or her own language'. Children should be fully prepared to live an individual life in society, and be brought up in the spirit of the ideals proclaimed in the Charter of the United Nations, in particular in the spirit of peace, dignity, tolerance, freedom, equality and solidarity.

The Human Rights Act makes it 'unlawful for a public authority to act in a way that is incompatible with a Convention right'. Faith-based schools entering the maintained sector will find that there is likely to be local agreement on this matter. The Guidance to School Organization Committees are expected to give proposals from faith communities to establish academic institutions the same consideration which they give to those from other groups, including LEAs. However, faith-based schools are expected to adhere to these legal requirements and ensure that cultural and religious pluralism is promoted.

When discussing the granting of public funding to faith-based schools from a 'rights perspective' important questions are raised. For example, is it sufficient to develop educational legislation and policies based on 'rights' arguments? Mithaug (1998) has offered a comprehensive review on disability rights as they relate to ethnicity and race. Different conceptualizations of rights, religious pluralism and inclusion are likely to lead to different and even conflicting educational policies. Muslim organizations in particular have been voicing concerns about the moral and spiritual development of children in community schools. Mukadam (1998) describes the present multi-faith approach to religious education as inadequate in that it does not provide for the spiritual and moral development of children. Khan-Cheema (1996) also states that 'the demise of multifaith schools is not in the interest of any faith community'.[6]

In the light of these concerns, it is important to consider the key distinctions between rights and accountability/effectiveness in educational policy and practice which we raised earlier in Chapter 5. In the field of SEN, for example, there has been an ongoing debate over whether there is a need for evidence to support the effectiveness of inclusive education, with some theorists arguing that inclusion is an issue of rights not evidence (Gallagher 2001). A similar argument may also apply towards responding to religious diversity and accommodating the learning needs of children with diverse ethnic/religious profiles, rendering the need for evidence unimportant.

Conclusion

Faith-based schools have a significant history as a part of the state education system, and they play an important role in contributing to its diversity. Recently, the government has increased the range of faith schools in the maintained sector, including the first Muslim, Sikh and Greek Orthodox schools, as we discussed earlier. The understanding is that faith-based schools will enter the maintained sector, adding to the inclusiveness and diversity of the school system, and hopefully develop collaborative links with non-denominational schools and those of other faiths.[7] Currently, the expansion and funding of faith-based schools have caused a great deal of controversy, with an argument that decisions to establish these schools should take into account the interests of all sections of the community. The guiding principles should be inclusion, diversity and human rights, as well as the commitment to providing a socially just education for all children in an inclusive setting, regardless of their linguistic, ethnic, religious, intellectual or physical condition. To achieve this, faith-based schools may need to adopt new thinking about faith orientation and religious schooling for children with diverse needs, and support diversity as it is manifested at various fronts – for example religious, socio-economic, intellectual and special needs – within the context of inclusion. Such schools are encouraged to take a child-centred approach and listen to the voices of minority ethnic students with disabilities and their families, and respect other perspectives by supporting inter-agency collaboration, involvement of voluntary organizations and generally by being open to the wider community. Finally, they need to raise awareness among teachers and other child professionals about the culturally and linguistically diverse children that they encounter and will continue to encounter in their classrooms, and encourage teachers with disabilities from diverse ethnic/religious backgrounds to function as role models. Some of these issues may challenge conventional thinking in some faith-based schools, as they may do in some community schools. For those schools which have recently received public funding, the development of policy and practice in these areas may be at an early stage.

The last three chapters concerning legal issues, the curriculum and, here, special educational needs have all demonstrated that the allocation of state funding brings with it additional responsibilities and accountability, as well as benefits. State funding brings control, which some independent faith-based schools resist, and instead provide education based on their religious convictions without these constraints. This raises philosophical issues about the expansion of faith-based schools and if, in practice, such a development can be regarded as socially just. The exploration of these issues within a wider political context forms the basis of the penultimate chapter.

Notes

1   UNESCO (1994), Salamanca Statement and Framework for Action, p. 34.
2   See, for example, Diniz (1997, 1999).
3   Ibid.
4   See Ainscow (1995a, 1995b) and Ball and Harry (1993).
5   See British Humanist Association (2002).
6   See Mustafa (2001).
7   Judge (2002).

Chapter 8

Social Justice or Social Division?

A number of issues emerge from the discussions so far concerning the construction of identity, securing social cohesion and accommodating freedom of religion within an educational setting. We noted earlier that new faith-based schools, such as Sikh, Muslim and other minority faith institutions, and their communities do not fit easily into existing theoretical, social or educational models. Issues of culture and identity are fluid and subject to continuing change in both their construction and their internal behaviours. Moreover, how such communities are viewed by the majority society within Britain is also subject to change as a result of events that occur both locally and globally. Examples of this at a local level have been particularly evident as a result of the so-called 'race riots' during 2001 in Bradford and Oldham. Overlapping with the international scene, there has been heightened concern about the alleged role of Muslim clerics and mosques in promoting Islamic 'fundamentalism' and acting as recruitment grounds for al-Qaida (Burke et al. 2002). Moreover, in Europe, Australia, New Zealand and the United States, it is evident that concern with illegal (and in some cases legal) immigration is impacting on negative public attitudes toward those who are culturally different (Aaronovitch 2003; Talcott 2000). The emergence of new faith-based schools, therefore, must be seen within this wider socio-political context. The development of these schools, and especially of those based on Islam, which represents a significant sociological development in England and Wales, has also raised questions concerning the nature and extent of equal opportunities today.

This chapter seeks to examine broader philosophical concerns about the expansion of faith-based schools, such as the threat they may be perceived to pose to social harmony and a 'British way of life'. The extent to which faith-based schools can be regarded as socially just within a secular society is critically explored, thereby exposing arguments that suggest such schools will serve to contribute to further social division, lead to religious indoctrination and aggravate racial disharmony. We also consider the argument that, whilst faith-based schools may be a victory for parental choice, they may not necessarily be a good thing for children. To explore these issues the discussion is arranged around three main themes, and we will:

- consider the adequacy of 'equal opportunities', as presently understood, to accommodate the development of faith-based schools;
- examine the argument that these schools may be perceived as socially just and/or socially divisive; and

- consider the argument that, whilst the expansion of faith-based schools may be important for parental choice, they may not necessarily be a good thing for children.

We begin by examining the concept of 'equal opportunities' and whether the achievement of 'equality', as aspirational language, adequately covers issues of social justice in a broader sense.

Equal Opportunities Revisited

When exploring the current debate about the place of faith schools in society, it is important to locate this within a broader context that is concerned with issues of 'race', power and cultural dominance. Moreover, for people of colour and/or members of religions that are outside of the Judaeo-Christian tradition, issues of identity and a sense of belonging are crucial (Modood et al. 1997). Modernist standpoints on religion, 'race' and ethnicity have proved to be unstable in a shifting terrain of social relations and the development of multiple senses of identity, as we discussed in Chapter 4. Giroux (1992) notes that:

> caught within the limiting narratives of European culture as the model of civilization and progress, liberal and radical theorists have never been able to break away from Western models of authority that placed either the individual white male at the center of history and rationality or viewed history as the unproblematic progressive unfolding of science, reason and technology. (p. 113)

Clearly Giroux identifies a number of fundamental issues that will need to be addressed in a world characterized by increasing difference, diversity and change. Established practices and an unquestioning acceptance of how things should be, and who 'we' are, are and should be exposed to continual and critical scrutiny.

Modood et al. suggest that anti-racist approaches of the 1980s had a tendency to categorize groups into either 'black' or 'white', essentialize difference and polarize the causes of racism. Further to this, Sivananden notes that:

> such an analysis of racism is at best superficial and at worst counterproductive since it ignores the material, social and political conditions which help to reproduce discrimination and racist ideas.[1]

Support for this is found in the writings of Hall (1992), Gillborn (1996b) and Siraj-Blatchford and Siraj-Blatchford (1999) about the relationship between culture, colour and social identity. Similarly, Wilson (2000) observes that culture and identity are inextricably intertwined and that therefore, if culture is discussed in such oppositional terms, it inevitably leads to a simplistic definition of cultures in terms of dominator and dominated. Discrimination may not only occur on the basis of a person's 'race', cultural or religious affiliation, but may be further exacerbated due to their gender and/or social class (Weiner 1994). Therefore the impact of multi-layered social identities requires consideration in the exploration of these wider issues (Mirza 1998).

Issues of domination and subordination, cultural hegemony, and the imposition of majority rules, laws and practices add to the complexity associated with any discussion concerning ideas of equality or equitable treatment, or the developing nature of equal opportunities. Clearly, what is being argued for here is a right for *all* ethnic groups to be equal *and* different, to participate in the majority world but not at the expense of their own collective sense of being, as reflected in their cultural and/or religious affiliations. As Parekh (2000) asserts:

> the good society does not commit itself to a particular political doctrine or version of the good life and ask how much diversity to tolerate within the limits set by it … Instead it begins by accepting the reality and desirability of cultural diversity and structures its political life accordingly. (p. 340)

The observations of Irving et al. (2000) are also helpful here. They advise that political acknowledgement and recognition of cultural difference and diversity be regarded as a legitimate component of a 'British way of life', agreeing with Swann (1985) that a fundamental reappraisal of values and attitudes in education is required. Making a break with the conservatism of the past, and accepting the need for a radical culture shift that more appropriately represents changing times, will result in overall gains for all. Such a move will serve to contribute to the (re)creation of a multicultural society that goes beyond the moral relativism associated with simplistic pluralist forms that have tended to exoticize minority cultures (Troyna and Carrington 1990; Blair and Cole 2000); failed to engage with the uneven distribution of power and privilege (Kincheloe and Steinberg 1997; Irving et al. 2000); and in many respects further marginalized minority groups by positioning them as the 'other' (Said 1993).

The achievement of simple equality, therefore, whereby each *individual* citizen is regarded as having the same needs, values and desires in relation to access to goods, services and opportunities, is not altogether helpful. We would suggest that the notion of 'equality of opportunity' be overtly replaced with the language and goals associated with the pursuit of equity and social justice. This is a more holistic concept in that it incorporates all aspects of socio-political organization and accommodates scope for individual agency, thereby providing a much broader framework through which to determine fairness (Irving et al. 2000). Whilst the term 'social justice' itself is open to multiple interpretations,[2] the recognitive form developed by Gale and Densmore (2000) is particularly helpful within the context of faith-based schools. Recognitive justice starts from the standpoint of the least advantaged and:

advocates three necessary conditions for social justice: the fostering of respect for different social groups through their self-identification; opportunities for their self-development and self-expression; and the participation of groups in making decisions that directly concern them, through their representation on determining bodies. (p. 19)

However, as Bradley (1996) points out, if there is a persistent stress on difference, 'this may entail the setting up of uncrossable boundaries between "them" and "us"'. She writes further that there could also be 'a spiral into individualism, an infinite process of fragmentation, in which we lose all sight of the commonality of ... experience' (p. 102). Concern that the imposition of a multicultural state will impact upon the culture and identity of indigenous peoples has shown itself to be a reality and should not be taken lightly. This has been particularly evident in Fiji in recent years where the success in elections of an Indian-Fijian-led government resulted in a military coup by the native Fijian army (Vakatale 2000). Similarly, as the Cantle Report (2001) into the rioting in English northern towns demonstrated, there is 'community envy' from indigenous groups over what they see as the privileging of minority ethnic groups within the same locality. If suspicions that the development of a multi-ethnic, multi-faith community will result in some form of cultural genocide for indigenous peoples are to be allayed, effective and ongoing communication between various cultural and/or religious groupings must be regarded as an essential component.

This fits comfortably within a critical social justice approach which extends the recognitive form advocated by Gale (2000). Critical social justice seeks to ensure that a relationship is created through which a dialogue is established that facilitates a lively interplay between cultures (Freire 1999; Apple 2001), with *all* cultures subject to both internal and external critique. The development of critical multiculturalism in the United States (Kincheloe and Steinberg 1997; Mahalingham and McCarthy 2000; Apple 2000) and of critical anti-racism in the United Kingdom (Cole 1998; Gillborn 1998) encompasses wider dimensions of power, social class, patriarchy and inequality, seeking to expose the ways in which these aspects are interconnected. This is particularly true with regard to the allocation of state funding for minority groups, and the extent to which the goal of cultural diversity goes beyond the celebration of difference.

It appears evident, therefore, that the development of a critical version of social justice could create a climate for change that will prove to be beneficial for all. Whilst respect for a community's right to its culture and self-determination is paramount, that does not mean that those on the 'outside' are not able to be critical of beliefs and practices that are felt to be unjust, and to advocate for change. This can lead to a constructive tension, whereby differences are aired and debated, rather than hidden or restricted to ill-informed information. Such intercultural dialogue should take place on equal terms, however, with all parties being given equal standing. Ultimately, unless the beliefs and practices of diverse cultures present a physical, psychological or social danger to any of its members, the autonomy of distinct communities, which we noted earlier in Chapter 4, should generally be respected. As Levin (2002) states: 'a world that has no room for difference has no room for humanity' (p. 7). What is of key importance here is the gaining of consensus around a basic set of principles and human rights founded on inclusive approaches that allow all voices to be heard when concerns arise, and which serve to guide all members and groups within the wider society. Parekh (2000) sees the success of this as resting on the acceptance of:

> mutual respect and concern, tolerance, self-restraint, willingness to enter into unfamiliar worlds of thought, love of diversity, a mind given to new ideas and a heart open to others' needs, and the ability to persuade and live with unresolved differences. (p. 340)

By removing the privileged status of dominance and subordination, 'a community of citizens and a community of communities' (ibid., p. 140) could thus be established, which share a commonality of goals and desires. Whilst the importance of critical dialogue and constructive tension cannot be understated, there is also a need to guard against a dominant group simply imposing its will *without* clear justification and legitimacy. Moreover, such decisions should remain open to public scrutiny and challenge, when engaging with issues of concern to minority cultures in particular.[3]

We focus next on whether faith-based schools specifically can be perceived as socially just or socially divisive.

Faith-Based Schools: Socially Just or Socially Divisive?

Theoretical perspectives underpinning the issue of faith-based schools in England and Wales can be located in a shifting economic, social and cultural terrain, as we noted earlier in Chapter 4. Such understandings draw on 'race', culture and difference (Solomos and Back 1996); the politics of difference (Young 1990), and the acceptance of the dominant group (Modood 1992) in the schools' seeking to secure their cultural identity and gain equitable access to resources. Wilson (2000) adds a salutary note to this discussion. Contributing a New Zealand perspective, she comments that 'unless the dominant culture engages with the issue of cultural rights … we are likely to experience increasing conflict as various "minority cultures" compete for recognition and dominance' (pp. 14–15). This also has a profound resonance in relation to the British situation at this moment in time. If faith-based schools outside of the Christian tradition grow in number, will this lead to a ghettoization of educational provision for ethnic communities, the promotion of culturally restricted knowledge, and a deepening social divide? These are the key questions that need to be explored if we are to gain a full understanding of cultural identity, and to judge whether faith-based schools can ever be considered as socially just within a secular nation.

Currently, under the Race Relations Amendment Act (2000) it is not illegal to discriminate on the basis of religion *per se*. Yet it is clear that, for some within British society, the construction of personal identity is intertwined with their socio-cultural location, which in turn cannot be divorced from their religious beliefs. Further, when we attempt to decide upon majority and minority rights, especially in the allocation of funding and privileges such as support for significant numbers of Christian schools at both primary and secondary level, the accommodation of diversity and difference begins to take on a complex form. A more sophisticated analysis is required, therefore, that adequately addresses the multi-faceted factors involved in discrimination, particularly at an institutional level (Gillborn 1995). To use the language of the Lawrence Inquiry (Macpherson 1999), we need to consider the impact of 'unwitting discrimination' on the grounds of religion. The new wave of faith-based schools are, as we discussed in Chapter 3, often representative of minority ethnic groups, and race and ethnicity overlap with issues of religious identity. The expansion of these schools is less acceptable to some sections of society when they are established and supported by black ethnic rather than white ethnic communities.

Throughout the 1970s and 1980s there was a belief that, under the 'equal opportunities' umbrella, fairness would be achieved for all members of society by the removal of unfair barriers, enforced through administrative controls and formalized systems, such as legislative procedures and policies (Riley 1994). The ultimate goal was the creation of a 'level playing field' by which individuals, irrespective of their gender or 'race', would have equality of access to compete for goods and opportunities. Whilst well meaning in nature, it is now recognized that this ideology was based upon a political naïvety which has had limited success in addressing issues of inequality within British society. As Irving and Marris (2002) observe:

> too often the decision to promote 'equal access' has resulted in an attempt to 'treat everyone the same' … individualistic constructions about the nature and cause of disadvantage, when allied to well intentioned approaches towards promotion of equality of opportunity, may become a perverse form of tyranny. (p. 139)

There is some hope that the new Human Rights Act (1998) will be more dynamic in addressing inequalities and discriminatory practices, particularly with regards to religious freedom. It is important to acknowledge, however, that the concept of 'human rights' must itself be subject to cultural interpretation if it is to have meaning and resonance for all (Wickliffe 2000). As noted in earlier chapters, Article 9 of the Act refers to freedom of thought, conscience and religion, and the manifestation of belief. This could provide ample opportunities for ethnic-religious minorities in Britain to advocate further the introduction of faith-based schools that adequately reflect their own beliefs, and recognize their own sense of being as distinct ethnic groups. Muslim schools, for example, might cater for many different ethnic groups, and we have seen this reflected in some of those in our study. Such a move might also illustrate one way in which the pursuit of human rights can be located within a cultural context. In relation to Islam, Hewitt (1998) maintains that for Muslim communities the issue is about human rights as much as it is about educational provision, as we noted earlier in Chapter 3.

In recent years government policy has shifted noticeably in favour of the provision of funding for the establishment of minority faith schools. Yet this does also raise issues concerning state intervention, future funding and the categorization of such 'new' institutions. The old maxim that 'with money comes control' prompts us to ask: to what extent will financial support of such institutions impact upon curriculum development, staffing and school ethos – and will this have positive or negative outcomes for both pupils and school? Will it simply be a matter of accommodating difference, or is the end-game conformity over time as new faith-based schools are brought into the mainstream? These issues were highlighted earlier, when we noted that only time will tell whether the potential for conformity will begin to override the accommodation of difference.

Certainly we know that Muslim and Sikh schools will not wish to undermine their religious ethos, decisions concerning curricular choice and disciplinary practices. Yet this will have to take place within the context of the National Curriculum which, notes Tomlinson (2001), offers 'little change or guidance to the next generation of young people, on how to live together in conditions of mutual respect and equity' (p. 148). It is also evident in Crick's (1998) development of the citizenship framework, which we discussed in Chapter 6, that there was an absence of minority faith representation on the Curriculum's working group, with only the General Synod of the Church of England in membership.[4] Other directives from the Department for Education and Skills (DfES), such as those related to attendance, school management, organization and academic achievement, are also likely to impact on state-funded faith-based schools, as we discussed earlier in Chapter 5 – unlike for schools in the independent sector, that have traditionally received little state interference, as noted earlier in Chapter 2. The new funding arrangements will see not only greater accountability to predominantly externally set outcomes, but also increased likelihood of greater government inspection.

The government's initial decision to award state funding to Muslim primary schools neatly avoided the issue of single-sex schooling, which in the past has been criticized for providing 'a narrow curriculum for domesticity' (Rendell 1997). This has subsequently changed, as we noted in Chapter 3, and now a girls' secondary school has received government funding.[5] It is also important to note that both Muslim and non-Muslim writers have expressed concern about the position of women in 'orthodox' communities (Hussain 1984; Weldon 1989), although strong feminist positions have also been identified (Haw 1998). As Deen (1998) observed from her visit to Bangladesh and Pakistan, whilst those societies are still primarily organized on patriarchal lines, there are women who do resist, and a feminist movement is evident *within* Islam rather than in opposition to it. However, many of those liberal principles and attitudes that are regarded as a central aspect of British life, such as individual freedoms in relation to employment, gender identity and choice, may not fit comfortably within all cultures.

Clearly this presents challenges to those who see only one culture, that is, a dominant Western-inspired culture, as having the desired ethical values and moral practices necessary to sustain a 'civilized' society. It is also clear that these values and morals are culturally derived, and have a tendency to reflect the competitive capitalist nature of the West both existing in tension with, yet also continuing to draw from, a traditionally conservative Christian ethos (Apple 2001). Moreover, many writers have observed that Christian 'fundamentalism', perceived liberal freedoms and pseudo-democratic assertions (Young 1990; Apple 1996, 2001; Franklin 1998; Goodin et al. 1999) have served to hide or disguise many other forms of social division, inequity and injustice (Tomlinson 2001). When considered alongside freedom within Islam, for example, the differences become more apparent. Islam is premised upon the development of a confident sense of self yet within a supportive collective culture, built upon religious tenets. Perhaps, in response to pressures for change in Britain, it is clear that Muslims, Sikhs, Jews and others are beginning to be more strident in affirming who 'they' are, explaining why their culture should be recognized and respected, and openly talking about the injustices they feel they have been subject to. Bradley (1996) highlights this changing consciousness and sense of self-esteem in relation to Muslim women. She writes:

> the international revival of Islam has opened up a positive identity and source of pride for Muslim women, as opposed to the experience of being the stigmatized 'Other' in the playground. Thus many women willingly embrace Islamic dress styles, such as wearing of headscarf or veil. (p. 108)

The view that minority faith-based institutions will impact negatively upon academic performance is brought into question when we note that a number of Muslim girls' schools have performed well in the academic league tables and have now actively applied for state funding.[6] Moreover, it is also clear that other minority cultures in Britain are gaining in confidence, giving voice to their concerns and hopes for the future. Government decision-makers therefore may have to confront a range of controversial and potentially challenging cultural issues when deliberating on the pending applications for funding from faith-based schools.

Other schools will also look to the government to see that their religious and cultural convictions are not only respected but also financially supported. The government's choice of label 'foundation school' could equally have application to schools with a religious or philosophical ethos, and the recent government White Paper, which we discussed in Chapter 5, proposing an expansion of faith-based schools is also a sign of encouragement for minority groups. Notwithstanding nomenclature, Hindu and other groups who give expression to the reality of a multi-faith Britain may also wish to have equal access to state funding. As well as Sikh and Seventh Day Adventist schools now receiving state support, applications have also been made from other religious minority groups (*Times Educational Supplement* 2000, 2001g). These will also seek to see their religion embedded in the school along the lines developed in Muslim, Jewish and Sikh schools, whereby they are able to express their own particular beliefs, practices and sentiments.

It is too soon to try to analyse the impact of policy decisions regarding new faith-based schools and the support they will receive from state funding. At this point we can say that they have undergone a long struggle to be awarded equitable treatment, and their belief in the fairness of the state is now being rewarded. Clearly, if there are already established and accepted faith-based schools, formed on Christian or Jewish principles, then logically it is just and proper for schools centred on other faiths also to be permitted. If this is the case, they join the line of other religious minority groups now awarded funding in the tradition of denominationalism within the pluralist educational system of contemporary England and Wales. Legislation which has placed them in the 'voluntary aided status' category may also mean that a parity of esteem is established between all religious denominations in this country.

So far we have looked at the issue of faith-based schools within the context of social justice with reference to human rights, parity of treatment with other faith-based schools and single-sex schooling. There remains nevertheless the issue as to whether the expansion of faith-based schools is socially divisive? It is clear that the current New Labour government in the United Kingdom is beginning to give a renewed definition to what is meant by a multi-faith Britain. Along with other countries such as the Netherlands (Walford 2001a, 2001b) and Australia (Donohoue Clyne 2001) it has moved beyond the pious, rhetorical expressions of equality towards a more robust standpoint of justice and equity for all. In terms of social justice, therefore, whilst ever funding is available for some faith-based schools the same treatment should be accorded to other groups which meet the criteria regardless of whether they may be representative of a particular ethnic group.

Government plans to increase faith-based schools came at exactly the same time as racial tensions increased in some northern areas, exacerbated by poor housing and employment opportunities. Ignorance, misunderstanding and fear are said to be at the centre of the ill-feeling, made worse by policy at local government level which has done little to change the pattern of segregation. In Oldham, for example, it was said:

> there are a small number of deprived estates where white children have never made an Asian friend and vice versa. Most primary schools are single race, and many secondaries are 99% Asian. For many people, the first prolonged contact with different cultures comes at sixth-form college. By then, isolation, poverty and unemployment have already cemented attitudes on race.[7]

Reports on the race riots in Oldham, Burnley and Bradford in 2001 stated that segregation has left many communities marginalized. Over seventy recommendations have been made from these documents: for example, a national debate on the concept of citizenship, including an oath of allegiance; faith-based schools and monocultural schools to have no more than 75 per cent of pupils from one single ethnic or religious group; 'community cohesion' strategies to be developed by towns and cities; and regeneration funding not only for ethnic minority group needs but also for other groups in order to avoid inter-community envy.[8] Also at issue are the ideology of integration and the extent to which many people in multicultural Britain have retreated behind ethnic lines, a separation exacerbated by segregated schooling and housing.

Of the four reports on the riots, the largest, the Cantle Report (2001), highlights the 'depth of polarisation' between communities which rarely if ever overlap. Fears are expressed that an expansion in faith-based schools serves to fuel the tensions by reinforcing the polarization of a monocultural, educational experience in segregated communities and does nothing to open up communication, pull down barriers and challenge negative stereotyping. This comes at a time when race relations in some parts of the country are said to be at their worst and some groups in Britain, such as Muslim communities, are particularly vulnerable at a time of global conflict.[9] There are no easy answers to these problems of segregation and racism, and local communities themselves will have to become centrally involved in solutions. This was underscored by the head teacher of Oldham Church of England Secondary school, which received a lot of media attention during the riots, who said:

> we are perceived as being part of the problem in Oldham. We want to be part of the solution.[10]

As a response, the school has changed its admissions policy, and 15 per cent of its intake will now be from other than Anglican denominations, and governors are considering whether to extend this to include admitting other faiths. Further initiatives have been inter-school twinning, joint sport and cultural events, teacher exchanges, and opportunities created to enable different ethnic groups to mix. Leicester, for example, which was once deeply divided along race lines, has made headway in developing community cohesion. Similarly, three faith-based schools in Oldham are to open their doors to non-Christian pupils.[11]

Opposition to faith-based schools also comes from within religious communities; for example, Ghulum Shazad, a school governor of LEA schools and a member of the local RE standing advisory council, states:

> if we have faith schools I am concerned that it will not help the growth of children. If you live in a multi-cultural, multi-faith society there must be interaction.[12]

Despite their mono-faith composition, it is of course the fact that some faith-based schools have a wide range of nationalities and cultures; for example, Islamia

Primary School has over 23 different nationalities represented, non-Muslim staff, and is open to all faiths in terms of admissions policy. The school claims that new faith-based schools serve the community as well as their own faith, and they do not wish to be a ghetto.[13] A great deal has been done by religious communities themselves to break down barriers, and it is argued that a monocultural profile is the result of demographics.

It is right to acknowledge and have open debate about problems between ethnic communities, but what has not been openly acknowledged are the 'parallel lives' lived by communities in the same geographical area, and reinforced by patterns of schooling. The question is, how far can schools simply accommodate religious needs, and do they have an obligation to foster social cohesion? Whilst issues concerning legislative reform and racial tensions may lie outside the control of governors of faith-based schools, such institutions have a role to play in reducing barriers and developing a shared sense of citizenship.

Another point that should be made is that faith-based schools are said to provide quality education with a strong school ethos and high academic attainment. The evidence for this is ambiguous, as we noted in Chapter 5. Muslim schools appear to have done well in league tables, in the absence of state funding; however, Marks (2001) has questioned the generalization, saying that whilst there is some evidence that faith-based schools do better than community schools, this is not apparent across the board. It is for these reasons that the concept of community schools is promoted by Hargreaves (1994). His view is that the community school should become secular with citizenship education replacing religious education. This contrasts with the view that schools are, and should be, sensitive to religious diversity, a view reinforced by a Home Office study conducted by Derby University which found that schools were among the worst offenders of perpetrating religious prejudice (Weller et al. 2000). Similarly, Prince Charles has launched a 'Respect' project calling for dialogue between schools for children of religious backgrounds and for community schools to be encouraged to do more for inter-faith harmony.

When people talk about the expansion of faith-based schools, it is sometimes said that what they mean is the increase in the number of Muslim schools. This is an easy statement to make as, indeed, the increase in faith-based schools in this country has been led by those of an Islamic ethos, as documented earlier in Chapter 3, with over a hundred now established (Parker-Jenkins 2002). What is significant about this group of faith-based schools is that their congregations are drawn from a diversity of ethnic backgrounds, but in some geographical locations, due to demographic patterns, they are sometimes hugely representative of one group. Support for faith-based schools whose members are of different racial backgrounds also stems from concerns over racism. In the 1980s, the Conservative government was opposed to the expansion of voluntary aided schools, but evidence from documents such as 'Terror in our Schools', published by the Commission for Racial Equality, recorded high levels of racism experienced by minority ethnic pupils, and also raised the issue of parental rights in schooling. Certainly, many groups, such as the British

Pakistani-Muslim ethnic-religious one, are said to feel defensive and threatened as a community.

The issue of citizenship has also emerged as a central concern in educational debates today, particularly the core values upon which citizenship within a modern society should be based. The Cantle Report (2001) concluded that 'a meaningful concept of citizenship' which recognizes the contribution of all cultures to Britain's development needs to be established. One way of bringing this about is to end segregated schooling based on religion or colour, but, as we have noted throughout the book, this would appear to challenge very forcefully the government's decision to expand faith-based schools.

The question of swearing an oath of allegiance is particularly important in this discussion. Werbner (2001) posits the question, should a Muslim, for example, 'insist that his religio-cultural priorities, including the defence of jihad against America, override his civic duties of loyalty, tolerance, justice and respect for democracy?'[14] The counter-argument is that British Muslim support for the Taliban represents a tiny minority, and the 'loyalty debate' has been fuelled by David Blunkett's schemes for new immigrant education in citizenship. As Werbner continues, what does it mean to be a British citizen in a global world, and how would disloyalty be construed?[15] It is suggested there will have to be adaptation on all sides: English lessons for newly arrived immigrants, but also an obligation on the white community to recognize the changed and changing nature of Britishness. Clearly there are implications here also for the teaching of citizenship within the National Curriculum framework, as we highlighted earlier in Chapter 6, and the way(s) in which we define the concept of citizenship. Young (1990), for example, suggests we could have 'differentiated citizenship' applied to children, which would reflect the reality of multiple senses of identity which we discussed earlier in Chapter 4.

One of the most interesting issues to emerge from the recent debate on the expansion of faith-based schools is the composition of the school roll and the question of inclusion. In the past, schools based on a religious ethos have tended to recruit almost exclusively from their own religious community. This has been substantiated in terms of the need to develop and nurture a shared religious identity. Indeed, where admissions policy has been open, there has been care to ensure that those pupils from outside the faith constitute less than 10 per cent of the total school population in order to ensure that the '*raison d'être*' is not lost. This extends to the recruitment of staff also, where efforts are made to ensure teachers are not simply passive but active supporters of the faith (Parker-Jenkins 1985; *Times Educational Supplement* 2003a). In the absence of sufficient staff drawn from their own religious community, Muslim schools, for example, recruit teachers who are themselves of a religious background or who are sympathetic to the promotion of a religious ethos in schools (Parker-Jenkins and Haw 1996).

In order to defuse opposition to the expansion of faith-based schools, the government is attempting to change admissions policy concerning Church of

England schools. Anglican schools are to consult diocesan boards of education annually over their admissions policy. The support for greater inclusion comes from the Archbishop of Canterbury who called for Church of England schools to take children of other faiths or of none, even if it means rejecting pupils of practising Christians. Not all Anglican schools share this desire to improve inclusion rates and instead dismiss such moves as 'the façade of inclusivity' (*Times Educational Supplement*, 2002i, 2003c), in the name of political correctness. The Catholic Church has not to date announced changes to its admissions policy.[16]

It is by no means unanimous among faith-based schools in general that they should extend their policy on inclusion to foster social integration. Some leading clerics are unhappy about moves towards inclusivity. For example, the Reverend Peter Shepherd, writing in the *Church Times* (2002), condemned the call for Church of England schools to accept pupils from outside of their faith, and for the modification of legislation on church school admissions.[17] Difficulties have also been expressed by other groups. Deputy head teacher Akhmed Hussain of Al-Hijrah, the first co-educational Muslim secondary school in Britain to receive state funding, said: 'allocating places to non-Muslims would simply not work in this largely Asian community'.[18] Similarly, the Catholic Church was reported as saying that it could not afford more school places for children of other faiths or of none, due to poverty and staff shortages, adding: 'rejecting even more Catholics from the places that they have funded and nurtured over so many years would cause considerable pain'.[19]

Although it will not be obligatory at this stage to accept pupils of other faiths or indeed of none at all, this move towards inclusion is a signal that schools should consult with their governing bodies. From our research, we have found that Muslim schools often have an admissions policy open to others, but this appears to be rarely utilized, even for those achieving high academic attainment levels. The reverse is true of Catholic schools, which traditionally have often been oversubscribed (Grace 2002a). Overall, proof of a pupil's affiliation to a particular religious group in order to ensure their access to a faith-based school tends to be moderated by the popularity of the school in question. In other cases, a decrease in the religious community may cause a fall in roll, and only through recruiting outside the faith is the school able to remain viable, a point we made earlier in Chapter 2.[20] The propensity towards inclusion is affected by the popularity of a particular faith-based school, waiting lists and parents' commitment to join. Within admissions arrangements there tend to be stricter entrance criteria in oversubscribed schools and more theological conservatism. In the meantime, the government reiterates its plans to expand faith-based schools, adding that they would prefer new faith-based schools to be 'inclusive' or paired with a non-religious partner. There are a number of arrangements whereby schools voluntarily become 'twin-schools' and develop exchange opportunities, but generally many faith-based schools fail to demonstrate that they are open to the diverse communities within their geographic area.[21]

Also, there is in some cases little diversity within faith-based schools. This is attributed to the conservative/orthodox element within some religions which avoid 'outreach'. Now at Key Stages 3 and 4 of the National Curriculum there is a requirement that all children have knowledge and understanding of religious diversity in the country, as we noted earlier in Chapter 6, making it more difficult for schools to countenance a single-faith/monocultural perspective within teaching. Finally, support for greater inclusion comes from the view that the integration of minority groups into democratic life is a good thing. Lewis (1997) has documented this trend with regard first to Irish Catholics, and more recently to Muslims in Bradford who are engaging with the democratic process. Werbner (2002b) also makes this point with reference to Muslims in Manchester.

Thus far we have provided a critique of faith-based schools drawing on issues such as human rights and social effect. There is also the argument that religion should remain in the private domain – or what the American Constitution describes as separation of Church and state. Certainly, it is a promising way forward according to Polly Toynbee:

> the only way to treat all British races equally is to remove official recognition of any religion. The one third of state funded schools run by religions will be an ever greater problem, unless phased out now.[22]

She continues,

> Muslims have reminded us how dangerous all faiths are when passionately believed. They have made it a surrogate for race and so from now on there must be transparently equal treatment of all faiths if the resentment and division in towns like Oldham is not to grow. The only non-racist route is to remove religion from all functions of the state ... An entirely secular state can do more to tackle racial segregation in Oldham, Burnley and Bradford, demanding religious integration. Instead the government is digging a bigger hole, storing up worse trouble for the future, as atheist white middle classes demand more (selective) church schools while Muslims choose segregation too.[23]

Similarly, the secular argument is articulated by Gillard (2002) who states:

> my advice to Mr Blair ... is to close all faith-based schools ... and open them as secular state-maintained schools; to ban religious education, except in the context of socio-historical studies; and to disestablish the Church of England and create a secular state in which the practice of religion is protected by law *provided* it is an entirely private matter. (p. 22)

For Frank Dobson, MP for Holborn, the issue is about the impact on pupils:

> to separate children on the grounds of religion is bound to be divisive. At its most innocent a school develops the loyalties of its children. Children at their school are 'us'. Children at other schools are 'them'. Such fairly harmless rivalry can develop into

something much worse when race or religion are added to the mixture, reflecting and in turn reinforcing the bigotry of grown-ups. Just a glance at Northern Ireland, where children attend either Catholic or Protestant schools, shows what can happen. Growing up together is what really counts.[24]

A counter-argument is that secular humanism is itself a faith-based philosophy. The British Humanist Association has, however, been very proactive in trying to develop a model of school which accommodates different values and beliefs, which we will be reviewing in the next chapter.

Despite opposition to faith-based schools, plans for expansion of this category of schools continue. As of May 2002, proposals for 15 new faith schools were awaiting approval, including two Islamic, two Roman Catholic and nine Church of England primaries, and an Anglican secondary school (*Times Educational Supplement* 2002b). Geographically they are concentrated in the London boroughs, with smaller numbers in Blackburn, Coventry, Dorset, Leicester and Wigan. There are also plans for two existing schools to convert to Islam and Sikhism.[25] This would be the first time a state school has been 'converted', with the children of those parents who opposed the change being housed in a new building on site.

David Blunkett is reported as saying that he wants to 'bottle the success and ethos of faith schools', creating 13 more with 60 awaiting approval.[26] He is also encouraging the introduction of legislation which would make illegal 'incitement to religious hatred', within a terrorist bill (Weller et al. 2000). Increasingly faith is becoming a political football. For example, the former Education Secretary Estelle Morris said:

> I think that what you get in any good school is a solid value base, a sense of purpose, a sense of mission, a sense of being. I do feel that faith schools find it easier to express that value base.[27]

It is clear that the New Labour government has given fresh definition to what is meant by a multi-faith Britain and, along with other countries such as the Netherlands and Australia, has moved beyond the pious, rhetorical expressions of equality to the reality of equal opportunity in practice. In the context of a second term of office for 'New Labour', it is now timely that we revisit debates on social justice, but with greater sophistication concerning the intersections between race, ethnicity and religion; and consideration of which may be the dominant variable in terms of understanding personal identity. 'Equal opportunities' as understood in the 1980s was high on simplistic slogans but often disappointing in practice. The implications of policy and legislation are complex and problematic, and this needs to be recognized if equal opportunities are to be made a reality, with subtleties and sensitivities of the argument understood in order to put in place good practice. Moreover, the tension between nurturing social cohesion and accommodating freedom of religion within an educational setting will continue to test the government in its determination to push through its policy agenda on faith-based schools.

Parents Rights Versus Children's Rights?

The government's decision to expand faith-based schools can be seen as a victory for parental choice, yet will it infringe the rights of children and lead to further segregation and cultural alienation? This question is of central importance as it highlights a potential dilemma that could result in conflict and disharmony within families and communities. Article 15(1) of the United Nations Convention on the Rights of the Child (1989) calls for: 'the right of the child to education ... with a view to achieving the full realisation of this right on the basis of equal opportunity'. Further, Article 10 of the document provides for:

> the right of the child to freedom of thought, conscience and religion ... [and] ... the liberty of the child and his [sic] parents ... to ensure the religious and moral education of the child in conformity with the convictions of their choice. (10:3)

In part this takes us back to our earlier discussion about how the language of equality has been utilized, as equality of opportunity may not result in an outcome that is socially just. Moreover, exactly whose rights are being supported here – those of the parent or the child's? This lack of clarity serves to perpetuate a certain ambiguity concerning the legal relationship between parent and child. The European Charter on the Rights of the Child meanwhile, which was enacted in 1979, is much clearer about this, stating that: 'children must no longer be considered as parents' property, but must be recognised as individuals with their own rights and needs' (Children's Legal Centre 1986, p. 4). This view is also espoused in the Children Act (1989), which requires social services to take into account children's views when making decisions about their futures, although, as Mayall (2002) points out, 'compliance with this requirement is patchy' (p. 174). Whilst there continues to be much discussion and debate about the allocation of rights to children, the issue itself remains contentious as, notes Smith (2000a):

> the notion of children having rights tends to be interpreted as being permissive and giving them too much power and control, while at the same time taking power and control away from parents and others in authority over children. (p. 14)

The extent to which these 'rights' might be exercised if they conflict with those of their parents, whether children's voices will be heard, and how this might impact on faith-based schools, remains unclear and requires further examination.

Parents' rights and responsibilities for the welfare of their child are affirmed in many international and national documents. For example, the First Protocol to the European Convention on Human Rights 91951) stipulates:

> in the exercise of any functions which it assumes in relation to education and teaching, the state shall respect the rights of parents to ensure such education and teaching is in conformity with their own religious and philosophical convictions.

Because of a lack of available places, or due to the inability of minority groups to maintain a school with small numbers of pupils, not all parents can choose schools that reflect their religious or philosophical convictions. A case in point is that of the development of Muslim schools in Britain which, as we have noted earlier in Chapter 3, have a tendency to open and close at random due to financial difficulties (Parker-Jenkins 2002). Muslim organizations in particular have been voicing concerns about issues affecting the moral and spiritual development of children in community schools, and have shown that they are prepared to make substantial sacrifices to ensure their children are educated in Muslim schools. There is also a feeling that the current multi-faith approach to religious education is inadequate, failing to provide for the spiritual and moral development of children (Mukadam 1998). Conversely, the British Humanist Association (BHA) argues that it is difficult for parents to find 'an ordinary *non-church* maintained primary school' (Humanist Philosophers' Group 2001, p. 33, emphasis added), nor is it satisfied with the content of the religious education syllabus, which it sees as compromising parental beliefs.

The new Human Rights Act adds a useful dimension to discussions about the rights of parents (and children). It clearly states that:

> everyone has the right to freedom of thought, conscience and religion; this right includes freedom to change his [*sic*] religion or belief, and freedom either alone or in community with others and in public or private, to manifest his religion or belief, in worship, teaching, practice and observance. (Article 9:1).

'Freedom of thought, conscience and religion' and 'the manifestation of belief' could provide ample opportunities for ethnic minority and religious groups to pursue equitable educational provision. The clause 'manifestation of belief' is particularly useful for communities whose religious identity is expressed in terms of dress, such as the wearing of turbans, skullcaps, 'burkhas', 'hijabs' or headscarves. Alternatively, 'freedom of conscience' provides for the individual child *not* to wear such clothing. Overall, the legal articles contained in this document take an holistic and inclusive approach to the development of the child. Children are expected to develop social and moral responsibility in terms of tolerance and understanding of others, regardless of religion and ethnicity, and to be reared in accordance with their parents' cultural identity and values. For children who belong to ethnic, religious or linguistic minorities:

> they shall not be denied the right, in community with other members of his or her group, to enjoy his or her own culture, to profess and practice his or her own religion, or to use his or her own language.[28]

At the same time, children should be fully prepared to live an individual life in society, and be brought up in the spirit of the ideals proclaimed in the Charter of the United Nations, which include the spirit of peace, dignity, tolerance, freedom and equality. There are clearly potential contradictions in this. Although the legislation's use of the term 'everyone' includes children, this right is operationalized more by parents, and gives recognition to a parent's right to have their child educated in a faith-based school. As parents make decisions about other aspects of a child's life it could be argued that:

> religious parents obviously want to pass on to their own offspring values, doctrines, and practices that they regard as of the first importance. (Humanist Philosphers' Group 2001, p. 29)

A persuasive argument against faith-based schools pertains to the extent to which they will infringe the rights of the child. Neither the BHA nor the National Secular Society (NSS) 'accepts education in schools that has a basis in one of the faiths' (cited in Archbishop's Council Church Schools Review Group 2001, p. 1). Similarly, Gillard (2002) argues that:

> religion and education are mutually incompatible. Indeed, religion is the antithesis of education. (p. 22)

For him, religion should be a matter of private conscience and choice rather than something supported from public funds, and he advocates that we change to the American model which ensures the separation of state and religion. Such an amendment to the Constitution is unlikely, and, rather than disestablishing the Church of England, there are plans to expand Anglican schools. The BHA argues that: 'a proliferation of religious schools will increase discrimination in favour of Christians' (British Humanist Association 2002, p. 28). Another interesting argument put forward by the Association is one that derives from the Race Relations (Amendment) Act (2000). The Act states that public authorities:

> shall, in carrying out its functions, have a due regard to the need (a) to eliminate unlawful racial discrimination and (b) to promote equality of opportunity and good relations between persons and different racial groups.

Faith-based schools which have a high number of pupils from the same ethnic-religious group cannot, it is argued, assist this process and in fact they actively divide children on the basis of ethnicity (BHA 2002). The same can also be said, for example, of some community schools – in Cambridgeshire for instance – that primarily represent one cultural group as a result of the demographic population spread, and which therefore could be described as monocultural (*Times Educational Supplement* 2003b). Moreover, as discussed earlier in Chapter 6, the monocultural and Eurocentric nature of the National Curriculum does little to counterbalance this or encourage a multicultural 'feel' (Gundara 2000).

Opponents of faith-based schools also maintain that the autonomy of the child is ignored as a child's 'adoption of the school's preferred religion may not be truly voluntary, depending on the methods used' (Humanist Philosophers' Group 2001, p. 10). They express the view that, as children are vulnerable to 'suggestion' and lack the sophistication to freely consent, their exposure to religious instruction may act as a form of indoctrination, leading to unquestioning acceptance of particular belief systems (ibid., pp. 10–11). This is highlighted in their concern that children in faith-based schools will only receive selective information that is likely to reflect the teachings and values of a particular religion. Further, as well as these concerns about indoctrination and an absence of self-determination and children's autonomy, teachers in faith-based schools are portrayed by such critics as indoctrinators rather than educators. In short:

> parents do have rights to bring up their children. But it should not be thought that parents have these rights in virtue of somehow owning their own children … The crucial question is not whether it is best for the parents that their children be given a religious schooling but whether it is best for the children themselves that they are. (ibid., p. 30)

Under the United Nations Convention on the Rights of the Child (1989) highlighted earlier, it is stipulated that the child should be protected against all forms of discrimination on the basis of expressed opinions, or beliefs of the child's parents, legal guardians or family members. In addition:

> the education of the child shall be directed to the preparation of the child for responsible life in a free society, in the spirit of understanding, peace, tolerance, equality of sexes, and friendship among all peoples, ethnic, national and religious groups. (Article 29:1d)

The BHA maintain that the expansion of faith-based schools will result in children receiving a limited type of education which is the preference of parents but not necessarily in the child's best interests. This view has also been echoed in the Cantle Report (2001), which expressed concern about the apparent segregation of faith-based schools from the wider community. Humanists question whether these schools can really commit to a 'free society', 'equality of the sexes' and 'tolerance' (British Humanist Association 2002, p. 33). Careful consideration must be given to this viewpoint if the imposition of a form of cultural elitism that further contributes to the oppression of ethnic and religious groups whose views are 'different' to those espoused by the majority society is to be avoided. Wood and Tuohy (2000) succinctly capture this dilemma, writing:

> the values of personal autonomy and self-determination and privacy have different meanings in different cultures. Individual independence is highly valued in European society, but in some other cultures the value of parenthood is something realised more completely through collectivity. (p. 214)

This suggests that, for some communities, the cultural imperative is a desire to achieve collective harmony that acknowledges the importance of order and obligation. Mayall (2002) found from her research with children in England that

Muslim pupils were aware of how their religion acted to shape their lives, and voiced an understanding of the importance attached to obedience to, and respect for, family. Clearly there is scope for conflict here in relation to the expectations of those who promote the rights of children in isolation of cultural and religious considerations. Our own research suggests that faith-based schools, such as those with a Jewish, Muslim, Hindu or Sikh ethos, are very much aware of wider concerns, consider themselves to be part of local communities and actively engage with social issues through their teaching. This does not negate the responsibility of government to safeguard the right of the child to express their own views freely in all matters, and that such views are given due weight in accordance with age and maturity, as noted in Article 21 of the UN Convention.

Interestingly the voice of the child is seldom heard in schools generally, whether community or faith-based, or even within the children's rights movement itself (Smith 2002a). Similarly, the Humanist Philosophers' Group (2001) asks whether local children are to be consulted about the desirability of faith-based schools. As it stands, not only are children rarely consulted on such issues, they are even denied the right to remove themselves from acts of collective worship and religious education in schools, as this can only be exercised by parents. Yet there are a number of studies which suggest that children do not favour school assemblies (Economic and Social Research Council 1999), nor cultural segregation (Save the Children, as reported in 'Young sceptics say faith schools breed racism', *Times Educational Supplement*, 17 August 2001, p. 9). Furthermore, in the aftermath of the 'race' riots in northern England, The Ouseley Report (2001) put forward a strong argument that there is a need to break down cultural and religious barriers in order that young people have the opportunity to mix more freely.

Finally on this point of children's rights, Article 13 of the Convention states that:

> the child shall have the right to freedom of expression; this right shall include freedom to seek, receive and impart information and ideas of all kinds.

The BHA agree that this sounds educationally uncontroversial, and would be supported by inclusive school assemblies and 'beliefs and values' education which it advocates as an alternative to that being offered in faith-based schools. There is also a growing literature that advocates more agency for children in matters of religion in schools, such as that of Ipgrave (2001) and Jackson (2003a). (We return to this point later in Chapter 9.) The BHA add:

> it is also questionable whether children in all faith-based schools have this freedom. Some doubtless do, but some faith-based schools exist in order to protect children from ideas that are different from those of the parental faith group, or disapproved of by that group. (British Humanist Association 2002, p. 33)

If children's voices are to be heard, and their rights respected, it is imperative that faith-based schools give careful thought to the challenges presented by the BHA and others who oppose their development. Yet this is not just an issue for faith-based schools, as those that retain a 'secular' approach may also need to review their existing practices if they are to become culturally inclusive. Through the provision of opportunities for children, parents and educators to critically explore, examine and discuss the complexities of their worlds in inter-faith settings and contexts, enhanced awareness and understanding may help them to identify both commonalities and differences in the way their lives are constructed and played out. We have noted in earlier chapters that faith-based schools share commonalities of family, culture and community, and the same can be said of many community schools. Moreover, enabling them to look 'through an alternative and more plausible lens is likely to provoke changes in the racist construction of the way things are' (Troyna 1993, p. 128), resulting in a clearer understanding of the arguments in favour of faith-based schools. It will also help to illuminate why parents and/or children may have chosen this type of education in preference to one that is perceived to be secular in nature. The development of a culturally appropriate curriculum for *all* schools, faith-based or community, is a key aspect of this. Such a curriculum, however, should not impinge on the rights of children, nor restrict opportunities for them to participate freely in the multiple worlds they occupy. Taafaki (2000) succinctly captures this cultural challenge, writing that:

> existing culture curricula must be expanded beyond the narrow scope of how people behaved in the past ... No one can deny the right to preserve what is sacred ... However, there are aspects of all cultural behaviours that most agree are best relegated to the past. (p. 109)

Clearly, if faith-based schools are to sit comfortably alongside each other, and community schools, there is a need to review the ways in which education is organized and delivered. Without openness and dialogue, fears that faith-based schools will indoctrinate pupils, forcing them into a religious strait-jacket (Hare 1992; Davies 1990), restrict children's rights (Humanist Philosophers' Group 2001), or normalize 'traditional gender roles' (Bhatti 1999), will remain unaddressed. The involvement of children and families from *all* ethnic backgrounds, in *all* aspects of the educational process and in *all* schools, whether faith-based or community, will help to ensure that the values, beliefs and world-views the schools transmit remain culturally relevant to the communities they serve (Liévano 2000). This will also enable students and educators, 'white and non-white', and of whatever faith, to feel culturally secure in their surroundings, whilst safeguarding the rights of parents *and* children.

Conclusion

There is a need to explore the broader issues emerging from the decision to expand faith-based schools. The government's agenda assumes that diversity and parental choice of these schools will increase confidence in the state school system, especially at secondary level. In rejecting the concept of the 'standardized' comprehensive school, faith-based schooling is seen as one of the ingredients of success, and private sponsors are encouraged to become partners in this new vision. In the climate of a 'new deal' for *all* citizens living in Britain, and a second term of office for the New Labour party, religion has become an important aspect of politics. It is now timely to revisit the concept of equal opportunities, but with greater sophistication concerning the intersections between 'race', ethnicity, religion and gender. Further consideration must also be given to the constructions of both individual and group identity, along with a clearer understanding of how these shape behaviours and attitudes to fairness, justice and state governance.

The concept of 'equal opportunities', as understood in the 1970s and 1980s, has run its course. Although well intentioned, overall the long-term effects of existing 'equality' legislation have been disappointing in practice. In its defence, it has served to bring issues of inequality to the fore, and sought to challenge these in a limited way. Unfortunately there has been a tendency for legislation to focus on *individual* cases of discrimination at the expense of *collective* disadvantage and discrimination. Moreover, whilst attempts to promote 'equality of opportunity' in schools and the workplace have been strong on rhetoric, they have often relied on simplistic analysis and solutions, resulting overall in ineffectual action and little fundamental social change, such as in the scope of the Race Relations Act (2000). The implications for policy and legislation are complex and problematic, and this must be recognized if a more equitable society, founded on principles of justice, fairness, difference and diversity, is to become a reality. Yet, if this is to be achieved, the subtleties and sensitivities of *all* cultural groups will have to be exposed, discussed, debated and understood. Given the developing 'citizenship' curriculum that has been introduced into all state-funded British schools, and the pro-equity initiatives of the European Union, the unfolding 'equality' agenda promises much. This is particularly true for faith-based schools where, it is argued, the rights of the parent are being given primacy over the rights of the child, particularly in terms of access to knowledge outside of the religious cultural group.

When considering issues of equity and justice, it would be easy to conclude simply that faith-based schools have a right to exist within a pluralist society. This development, however, should not be accepted blindly, nor supported universally, as the key question to be addressed by *all* faith-based schools is how far they will use their interpretation of religion and culture to generate open minds and open opportunities for both sexes. Clearly faith-based schools face many challenges as they seek to establish a legitimate future within the state education sector in the 21st century. We suggest that the focus should not only be on the development of publicly funded faith-based schools but also on ensuring that such schools can provide an education that is socially just. By displaying an openness about ways in which particular religious beliefs impact on the ethos of the school, admissions procedures, curriculum content, social learning and engagement with the wider community, faith-based schools may go some way to alleviating concerns that they will simply become repositories for religious dogma. This leads us to our final chapter which looks forward at what changes may be possible in our understanding of faith-based schooling.

Notes

1 As cited in Solomos (1993).
2 See, for example, Griffiths (2003).
3 See Young (1990).
4 Crick (1998).
5 Department for Education and Skills (2003b).
6 See, for example, Inspection Report (2002b), for the Leicester Islamic Academy results.
7 *The Guardian* (2001b), 12 December, p. 5.
8 *The Guardian*, 'Religion must be removed from all functions of state', 12 December 2001, p. 18; *The Guardian* (2001f), 12 December, p. 19.
9 *Times Higher Educational Supplement* (2001), 14 December, pp. 30–31.
10 *Times Educational Supplement* (2002a), 18 January, p. 7.
11 *The Guardian* (2001a), 12 December, p. 5.
12 *Times Educational Supplement* (2002b), 3 May, p. 27.
13 Mr Abdulah Treverne, head teacher, 'Faith Schools After Bradford' seminar, Warwick in London seminar series, London, 28 May 2002.
14 *Times Higher Educational Supplement* (2001), 14 December, pp. 30–31.
15 Ibid.
16 Catholic Education Service website (2002), http://www.ces.org.schools; see also *Times Educational Supplement* (2002i), 3 May, p. 3, and 'Little faith in church policy', *Times Educational Supplement*, 17 May 2002, p. 25.
17 *Church Times* (2002), 8 February.
18 Ibid.
19 Ibid.
20 See, for example, King David School in Liverpool.
21 See Parker-Jenkins (1995) on 'twinning schools' of different religious backgrounds, and 'For the benefit of all', *Times Educational Supplement*, 31 January 2003, p. 31 and its coverage of the Education Act (2002) on opening up admissions.
22 *The Sunday Times* (2002c) 19 May, p. 8.
23 'Religion must be removed from all functions of state', *The Guardian*, 12 December 2001, p. 18/
24 *The Sunday Times* (2002b) 14 April, p. 11.
25 *The Sunday Times* (2002c), 19 May, p. 8.
26 'Religion must be removed from all functions of state', *The Guardian*, 12 December 2001, p. 18.
27 Ibid.
28 See Human Rights Act (1998).

* We wish to acknowledge Professor Bob Jackson's introductory talk at the Warwick in London seminar on 'Faith Schools After Bradford', May 2002, which informed background details to aspects of this discussion.

Chapter 9

A Future for Faith-Based Schooling: Final Thoughts

Throughout our discussions we have seen that the proposed expansion of state-funded faith-based schools reflects political and cultural issues about the nature of education and the significance of religious identity within some communities. Moreover, we have sought to raise questions about whether a secular or community-based approach to education could meet the needs of those committed to the further development of faith-based schools. Here we provide concluding comments looking at:

- the cumulative arguments contained in our discussion concerning faith-based schooling;
- the extent of human rights in a society; and
- the possible way forward in responding to competing demands in education.

Cumulative Arguments in the Discussion of Faith-Based Schools

We have seen in Chapter 2 that faith-based schools are not a new phenomenon as they have been with us for several centuries. Historically, those within the state sector and supported by government funding have been primarily Christian, reflecting the influence of the Church on the development of the educational system in England and Wales. The disproportionate provision of faith-based schools by just Christian denominations still continues but Jewish schools have established their presence in variety and numbers, as we saw in Chapter 3, and demands for their own publicly funded institutions from Muslim, Sikh and Greek Orthodox school communities, which in the past have tended to be marginalized from the state sector, have also realized success. Many minority ethnic parents also express a desire for their children to be educated not only in accordance with a particular set of religious values but also, as we saw in Chapter 4, in a climate that is free from racism, and they see faith-based schools as providing this environment. We have also argued that it is important to locate the demands for faith-based education within a wider socio-political context if they are to be fully understood. Ranjit Sondhi (1998), a former commissioner at the Commission for Racial Equality (CRE), comments that:

we have a responsibility to develop a vision of a pluralist society which maximises opportunities for ethnic minorities to participate while also preserving their autonomy. (p. 10)

The current New Labour government clearly shares this view, and presents the expansion of faith-based schools as a concrete and visible commitment to the development of an inclusive multicultural society in which *equal* recognition and opportunity is given to all religious communities. Further, it also reflects the view of the Prime Minister that *all* schooling should be founded on, and promote, sound moral principles. In February 2001, the commitment to increase the number of schools run by churches and other religious groups was announced, where there was clear local demand from parents and the community.[1] This was followed by a White Paper in September 2001 with an emphasis on encouraging diversity in educational provision. Collectively, policy statements in that year show a number of themes and policy alignments notes Chitty (2001):

> in the Government's view, 'raising standards', 'promoting diversity' and 'achieving results' are all synonymous aspirations, [and its] modernising agenda assumes that choice, diversity and the promotion of specialist schools will lead to greater public confidence in the state system, particularly at secondary level. (p. 13)

Added to this, he argues, is 'a creeping obsession with the "virtues" of privatisation', and 'a rejection of the outdated principles of the "one size fits all" comprehensives'. The government is concerned to see the promotion of diversity within the secondary sector allied to the extension of autonomy for 'successful' schools; and there is a desire for private and voluntary sector sponsors to play a greater role in the organization of schools. As such, he concludes:

> all the privatising measures contained within the white paper and the Bill can be seen as small but significant steps towards the construction of a new education market on terrain which has traditionally belonged to the State as the dominant provider of schooling in a democratic society. (ibid., p. 14)

The array of schools also includes plans for specialist schools, beacon schools, city academies, those sponsored by the private and voluntary sectors, and faith-based schools, with targets set for 1 500 specialist schools being in operation by 2005 (Department for Education and Employment 2001a; West 2001). Debate over the proliferation of Catholic, Church of England and Muslim schools has been widespread (Baumfield 2003). Further, city academies, for example, which are intended to replace struggling community schools, thus far number 12 with plans for a total of 34 by 2006 (*Times Educational Supplement* 2003j). The issue is not solely about numbers, however, but also concerns the principle of expanding faith-based and specialist schools as opposed to having confidence in community schools, which have disparagingly been described as 'bog-standard'.[2] The government announcement was greeted with approval by those schools anxious to expand, while others expressed the view that such institutions were divisive in a multicultural society. Short (2002) notes the unease centring on the allegedly divisive nature of faith-based schools, but instead argues that rather than undermining social cohesion, they are a force for unity.[3] Certainly the government has espoused such sentiment and the proposed policy implies that it will listen to any faith group wishing to establish a school and be supported with state funding, which might include Montessori, Steiner, Zoroastrian and Wicca groups and communities (Brown 2003).

The debate over faith-based schooling has also had a renewed intensity since the September 11 events. For example, MP Tony Wright, warned:

> before September 11th, it looked like a bad idea; it now looks like a mad idea. (*Times Educational Supplement* 2001f)

Conversely, faith-based schools are also seen to act as a moral compass for the nation as a whole, and provide ostensibly a better school ethos than that which pertains in community schools (Donnelly 2000). As part of a strategy to attract votes, the New Labour government's attempts to expand religious education, and the number of faith-based schools, have been embraced by many politicians on both sides of the political spectrum. The New Labour view is that it will contribute to the development of a pluralistic society and help to legitimize the cultural identity of ethnic groups, whilst for the Conservatives it is regarded as being an example of parental choice and an aid to moral education.

Academically, faith-based schools are also said to deliver good examination results, hence their popularity with parents, and it would seem that the government does not mind what religious beliefs are being espoused as long as attainment is high. Yet, as we have seen in Chapter 5, the view that faith-based schools achieve academically is not entirely true. Marks, for example, maintains that 'church schools often over emphasize their pastoral care to hide their academic weakness'.[4] Similarly, the view that all community schools cannot deliver academically, or morally in the form of values and ethos, is equally untrue.

A further issue in the argument is the perception of increased secularization in schools today. Locke (2001) maintains that

> since the 1960's education has become significantly secularised – too readily equated with 'professionalism'. To avoid any unprofessionalism many Christian teachers have felt obliged to play down their faith – even in RE and corporate worship ... Secular meaning 'non-RE' has become secular meaning (purportedly) 'objective neutral'. Modernism rules OK! Even at its best, forty minutes of RE per week is small antidote to 15,000 hours of compulsory secular schooling supplemented by 15,000 hours of secular TV.

He continues that whilst there is 'a new pick-and-mix kaleidoscope', the principle of spirituality and values in education is, however, back on the agenda, finding expression in schools' mission statements and inspected by Ofsted.

As noted throughout the book, the existence and proposed expansion of faith-based schooling are highly controversial, and it is important to ensure that opposing voices are heard. A major consideration, when exploring our understanding of oppression and disadvantage, relates to those 'structural inequalities founded upon race, gender and religious beliefs', as these serve to reinforce social divisions (Irving et al. 2003, p. 108). The London Development Education Centre (2002) highlights these issues in the concerns they raise about single-faith-based schools. It questions whether such schools can contribute to the overcoming of racism, and asks what will happen to those minority ethnic children and families who do not hold religious beliefs, or construct their identity around their religion. Furthermore, the extension of single-faith-based schools, it is argued:

> will cause deeper divisions in the Black communities, and a greater stranglehold of the most conservative, anti-women and communal individuals over our children's education and over communities as a whole. (p. 4)

We noted earlier in Chapter 4 the overlap between race and religion and that, for some groups, religion rather than ethnic background may be the key marker of identity. There is concern that an expansion of faith-based schools will contribute to the deepening of cultural, religious and economic divisions in society, whereby, in a 'voluntary apartheid' system (Halstead 1995b), children of different faiths are educated separately (Chitty 2001). Added to this, statements made in the Ouseley Report (2001) into race relations in Bradford suggest that fragmentation of schools on cultural, racial and religious lines has played a key role in heightening racial tensions: ethnic loyalties, cemented at segregated primary schools, remain fixed through the years of secondary schooling.[5] Similarly, Wood of the British Secular Society states that:

> children of all races and creeds need to mix if we are ever to eradicate racism and religious prejudice.[6]

Without social mixing, it is argued, communities become suspicious of each other, fearful and hostile.[7] This is felt to be true especially in the light of such events as the dispute at the Holy Cross Primary School in Belfast and the concern over religious diversity and social cohesion (Judge 2001; Hewer 2001b). Yet the assertion that simply enabling children from diverse backgrounds to be taught together and mix socially through the provision of community-based schooling will serve to combat racism is open to question. Troyna and Hatcher (1992) challenge this notion, suggesting that the 'contact hypothesis' does little to change the structural and institutional racism prevalent in schools and embedded within the wider society. Nor does it necessarily impact on the views and attitudes of teachers and others who work within schools. It was also noted that the death of an Asian pupil at Burnage High School, who was murdered by a fellow pupil, had taken place in 'a racist culture and context' (Macdonald et al. 1989, p. 45). Although Burnage School had an anti-racist policy, there is little evidence that it had the full support of *all* staff, pupils and parents. The issue, therefore, goes beyond that of simply valuing difference or implementing policy from above. It centres on the need for an effective anti-racist education that is holistic in nature, whether in relation to a community school, faith-based school or independent school. This is echoed in the Macpherson Report (Macpherson 1999), and the Race Relations (Amendment) Act (2000) requires schools to develop race-equality policy.

The particular nature of faith-based schools seeking public funding has also come under scrutiny. Roy Hattersley raises concerns that it will be 'religious fundamentalists' particularly who will seek to have their schools expand. He hypothesizes:

> will the Department of Education endorse the creation of a Christian Science, a Scientology or a Mormon school? If not, it will have to take the intolerable step of nominating state-approved religions.[8]

Very importantly, he adds:

> people who support a Christian's right to be ridiculous will expect the government to step in when an Islamic school tells its science class that the sky is Allah's blue carpet. Fundamentalism is less acceptable when it is not white.[9]

This concern has been at the crux of debates about the expansion of state-funded, faith-based schooling, as we said at the beginning of our discussions, because those newly introduced schools are highly representative of pupils from minority ethnic backgrounds. Children's skin colour rather than their religion *per se* is seen as the main factor of identity and the idea of 'racial' segregation does not sit well in modern-day Britain. Yet, as a result of demographics and local education development, there are community schools in existence which are predominantly Muslim, for example, and with pupils of similar ethnic backgrounds (Department for Education and Skills 2003b).

The government states that new faith-based schools can only be created in response to parental demand, but, it is argued, demand can be artificially stimulated. The intention to promote the concept of faith-based schooling was advocated during a period of economic prosperity and high support for the New Labour Party being recorded in opinion polls. It is in this earlier climate of New Labour's popularity and of economic prosperity and in the area of 'image-manipulation' that continuing support for faith-based schools is said to exist.[10]. In the light of the current protracted presence of troops in Iraq, and declining public support for the government,[11] however, it will be interesting to see if there is any backtracking on the commitment to faith-based schools in the immediate future. At the present time, despite arguments being raised in opposition to faith-based schools along the lines we have discussed, there is little sign of any policy change, or the likelihood of them being abolished or reduced in number. This could happen through legislative change, but the current New Labour government has signalled its intention to support their expansion. Yet it would be churlish to suggest that, as a result, there is no need to engage further in debate about their internal management, educational practices, and external monitoring and inspection processes. If faith-based schools are to respond to the challenges identified throughout this book then they will need to give much careful thought to how they will ensure that they do not become insular, introverted and dogmatic. Moreover, respect for cultural diversity and religious difference must not be allowed to feed into a perverse form of inverse racism and/or sexism that disregards the views and opinions of those who do not share the same faith. Without such safeguards, there is a danger that there will be a drift into a further escalation of social divisions, and racially motivated resistance in particular, as a consequence of heightened ignorance and mistrust (Chronicle Comment 2003).

Furthermore, the challenges are not for state-funded faith-based schools alone. Community schools also need to consider *why* there have been calls for an increase in faith-based schooling, particularly from minority ethnic groups. Closer examination suggests that this demand is not simply due to the desire of minority ethnic parents to see children educated within a particular faith: for many such schools are viewed as a means by which they might protect their children from institutionalized racism. Moreover, the choice can also be seen as an attempt by parents to ensure that their children are exposed to a curriculum that respects and reflects their cultural and religious heritage, as we discussed in Chapter 6, in preference to one which continues to present a monocultural view of the world with a limited, ethnocentric curriculum.

Government policy embraces cultural pluralism and religious tolerance. Yet turning this view into a reality will take much more than floral rhetoric or piecemeal change. An enhanced understanding of the complex nature of 'difference' and 'diversity' will serve to inform what is required. Action is now long overdue concerning the updating of government policies, educational provision, school-based practices and the accommodation of 'minority' religious rights. There may be hope in the new Employment Equality (Religion or Belief) Regulations (2003), which are a way forward in implementing the UK's obligations in relation to discrimination on the grounds of religion or belief, establishing a general framework for equal treatment in the field of employment within the European Communities. As we saw earlier in Chapter 4, UK domestic legislation does not currently extend anti-discrimination legislation on these grounds. Whilst British society is generally becoming more secular, for many citizens religion remains a key organizing principle for their lives, as we have noted throughout our discussions, and it is also evident that religious belief continues to be an influential social force in the shaping of contemporary Britain (Modood et al. 1997; Modood 2003).

Attempts to address inequalities in the education system must therefore take place at both the socio-political (macro) and institutional/community (micro) levels if they are to permeate throughout (Gillborn and Youdell 2000). Time and thought are needed to ensure that what it means to be 'British' becomes inclusive and dynamic. Opportunities to explore how we are to live with each other, how our differences can be mediated, and how a collective sense of community can be developed, are of central importance. The citizenship curriculum, as we saw in Chapter 6, has been introduced at secondary level and may help in part to promote greater openness and facilitate the process of change. This should be reflected in opportunities for cultural interplay, through the embedding of a process of critical-constructive dialogue within our educational provision that enables and encourages the voices of all, committed and critical alike, to be heard and acknowledged.

It is important to recognize, however, that faith-based schools alone will not provide a 'cure' for racism or the 'answer' to social exclusion, as this requires much more direct action on the part of government. As the London Development Education Centre (2002) notes, whilst government uses the language of multiculturalism, it is failing to address many of the fundamental causes of racism by not 'changing the laws on immigration, reining in the rhetoric about asylum seekers [and] tackling widespread institutional racism' (p. 10). Engagement with, and the active involvement of, Britain's diverse communities in the reconstruction of a new nation-state is long overdue, and the establishment of faith-based schools may prove to be one major step forward in this. As we begin to recognize and acknowledge competing human, religious and cultural rights, an acceptance of 'difference' and a valuing of diversity may follow. From this a critical social justice agenda might thus be instigated, to ensure fairness and equity for all, as we highlighted in the previous chapter.

It is evident that there are many arguments put forward as to whether it is right, proper and just to expand faith-based schools, and thus support them with public funding. From a financial point of view, for example, state-funded faith-based communities are presently contributing 10 per cent of the costs of education for their children of compulsory school age, money which would have to be provided by the government if they were abolished. Jackson (2003b) provides a useful overview, suggesting that further arguments in favour of faith-based schools are predicated on the fact that they:

- provide a positive response to racism;
- promote social justice for pupils, parents and community;
- offer high-quality education; and
- promote social cohesion and the integration of minority communities into the democratic way of life.

Conversely, they are seen by their critics to:

- limit the personal autonomy of children;
- erode social cohesion through sustaining the segregation of children on the basis of religion;

- impose a restricted view of religion promoted by the sponsoring bodies using state finance to fund proselytization or mission; and
- disadvantage other schools through selection procedures that pick the most able pupils.

The debate is therefore complex and, at times, riddled with potential contradictions, as 'secular' schooling is subject to continual, implicit and at times overt influence from an Anglo-Christian ethos, embedded within the state and reinforced through the education process. Any discussion about faith-based education is further exacerbated by considerations of individual rights, the impact of racism, and the potential perpetuation of gender inequalities that are perceived to be a feature of some ethnic minority cultures.[12] Moreover, there are also concerns that the expansion of faith-based education will lead to increasing cultural divisions and social fragmentation. Responding to these many issues is no easy task, and we have endeavoured to produce a balanced perspective that allows for the airing of diverse views. As faith-based schools expand their cultural, social and political impact will be much clearer, with many more opportunities for ongoing development in terms of where they 'fit' in today's society, and what they have to offer, which will ensure parental support and ultimately their own survival. As we saw in Chapter 7, there is a particular challenge in newly funded faith-based schools in terms of special needs and how provision for these is to be developed within a religious context (Broadbent and Brown 2003).

It is arguable to assert that there is no such thing as a Jewish, Muslim or Catholic child, but rather there are only children of religious parents. Children do not make theological decisions; they believe what they are told, at least in the early stages of their lives and educational experience. Therefore, it could be argued that it is the state's obligation to ensure that children are provided with alternative views, and if this should be the case, where does that leave faith-based schools exactly? Conversely, if the rights of parents who strongly hold particular faith teachings are to be supported, should there be an obligation for the state to pay for this mono-faith perspective? Historically, as we have seen, there has been such a provision and it has now been extended to encompass a range of new faith-based schools. Yet mono-faith need not be equated with an education that is isolated and segregated. Pupils from different faith-based schools may welcome the opportunity to join together (Scholefield 2001) but with arrangements more substantial than occasional twinning activities. Ipgrave (2001), for example, reports on a scheme whereby dialogue between children from faith-based and community schools is taking place, using e-mail as a form of communication.

Further, concerns that faith-based schools may use religion to exclude others could be regarded as clearly unacceptable, just as it would be for other schools if selection criteria, for example, were based on colour (*Times Educational Supplement* 2003a). Therefore, propping up what may appear to be a divisive system requires clear justification and coherent arguments, as we have highlighted throughout the book. Children do not automatically see religious difference unless we teach it, and it is arguable that we can no longer afford the present system on moral grounds. In this case, as we noted in the previous chapter, parental rights may be set against, and be taking primacy over, children's rights.

The Extent of Human Rights?

The right to a religious identity in this country and elsewhere is perpetuated and sustained in religious education. New faith-based schools have been established along similar lines to those of other faith groups, such as Catholic and Jewish ones, reflecting community settlement patterns. In some cases, as in that of Muslim schooling, the role of the convert has been instrumental in providing leadership, as we saw in Chapter 4.

In the past, the issue has been about equality before the law and equity in funding rather than the alternative view, namely that we should have a common school for all. For Muslim communities particularly, who have established the largest number of new faith-based schools, it took over a decade for these institutions to be successful in gaining public funding. Here race, ethnicity and religion have overlapped to an extent not demonstrated in the development of other state-funded faith-based schools. And this can be seen to sit uncomfortably with the desire to foster racial harmony. Some religious parents also have misgivings about the growth of a discrete educational system that separates rather than unifies children from different ethnic, cultural, linguistic and religious backgrounds. It could be argued that the current New Labour government has gone beyond what it needed to do to satisfy the Muslim voters of the last election. Then they looked to the Labour party to make good its electoral promises of ensuring equity in funding along the lines of that afforded to other groups.[13] The recent New Labour commitment to encourage the expansion of faith-based schools generally reinforces support for Muslim schools and others such as Sikh and Greek Orthodox. Basically, the supporters of Muslim and other faith-based schools see their patience rewarded, whereas supporters of a common schooling for all fear that this development means that children will have less opportunity to learn first hand about each other on a day-to-day basis. Separation and segregation such as that which occurs in Northern Ireland does not bode well for the future, whilst around the world there has been increasing hostility towards groups and individuals based on their religious identity. These concerns highlight the fear amongst many educationalists and others that the development of discrete faith-based schools is not a good thing.

As such, although the argument has been constructed in terms of equality of treatment before the law and the right to freedom of religion, it could be contended that in any society there is a limit to the extent to which individual rights and collective rights can and should be supported before social cohesion and harmony are placed in jeopardy. Human rights, as we said in Chapter 4, are never absolute:

they are dependent on time, place and circumstance. Therefore, the notion of state funding for any faith-based school could be seen as undermining the collective good of society as a whole. Yet to deny the children of religious parents the right of access to faith-based education also implies that moral values and ethical codes can be universally determined and applied to all, regardless of community desires.

The Way Forward

What then is the way forward? Should the development of faith-based schools continue unabated, and unhindered, yet supported by the state? What might alternative models look like, and, if there are none which are feasible, how do we improve on what we already have?

If the government is really serious about faith-based schooling, perhaps the ill-fated 'four-faith school model' might be revised. This was proposed by a group of Anglicans, Jews, Muslims and Hindus; a visionary and radical move which has not yet been achieved. It is, however, worth revisiting if only because it marries issues of religious schooling and is one way of addressing the question of how a faith-based school can be more inclusive.[14] As we saw in Chapter 2, Catholic schools, for example, were set up to educate the children of one faith, but they also enrol children of other religions. The current push for greater inclusion, however, is not shared by all. For example, Oona Stannard, Director of Catholic Education Services, rejects the idea that new faith-based schools should be obligated to take in a certain percentage of children of other faiths, or of none at all, unless it is the wish of the community or promoters (Stannard 2001). There are concerns about the pressure being placed on faith-based schools to be more inclusive of children who hold other, or potentially no, religious beliefs. The Church of England, on the other hand, has signalled its decision to commit to greater inclusion and many Muslim schools have an open enrolment policy towards children of faiths other than Islam, although the take-up has usually been marginal.[15] Policy alone does not appear to lead to greater inclusion unless it occurs in the context of falling rolls when schools are financially required to recruit from outside their own religious group.[16] Yet financial viability should not be regarded as the precursor for the implementation of an inclusive strategy. As an alternative to the traditional mono-faith school, the above 'four-faith' model may have some appeal as it satisfies the criterion that faith-based schools should provide a religious education but with a greater sense of inclusion. Practically this may be a difficult model to sustain but it is an interesting way forward in trying to reconcile the twin needs.

Currently, the phasing out of faith-based schools is not contemplated by the present government; rather the opposite is the case, as we have been discussing. Neither is it likely that any future alternative government formed by the Conservative or Liberal Democratic Parties would change direction. As choice and diversity in education has become an expectation of parents, it is now feared that any reverse in this policy may not attract votes. Yet a move away from faith-based education and a return to community-based schooling is what some groups actively advocate. The British Humanist Association, for example, has proposed a model of inclusive community schools, which provides opportunities for all faiths to exist in an environment that acknowledges all religious and philosophical views. Such a model, the BHA maintains, would provide '"reasonable accommodations" to meet the legitimate wishes of religious parents and pupils' (British Humanist Association 2002, p. 4), and as such would do away with the need for separate faith-based schools as we know them and as they have been traditionally established. This model reflects the American Communitarian approach, 'Diversity within Unity', in which there is a 'neutral common framework' in which all children whether or not they subscribe to a particular faith are educated together. One key aspect of this approach would be the introduction of inclusive assemblies, and a reformed Religious Education providing more balance and representation than exists now, as it would include the teaching of philosophical viewpoints.[17] There is, as we saw in Chapter 6, a tendency to teach the principal religions of Christianity, Islam, Judaism, Hinduism and Buddhism, whilst ignoring, or simply failing to give recognition to, alternative views. A number of polls suggest that religion is no longer embraced by large numbers of people in our society, the exception being among some minority ethnic groups (Modood et al. 1997; Modood 2003). Yet it is argued that the alternative, secular view is not provided for in schools.[18] Moreover, as Religious Education presently exists:

> when it states or implies that religion is the sole basis of morality, RE excludes and offends the non-religious. (British Humanist Association 2002, p. 39)

The BHA model therefore presents 'a third way', moving beyond what could be described as the government's fragmented, diverse approach towards the development of faith-based schooling, to one based on integration and inclusion. Importantly, within this model, the complete secularization of schools is not being suggested as, for example, on the lines of the French or Turkish models, which may be seen to marginalize people. Instead, space is to be provided for those pupils who wish to engage in religious study and worship. For those religious parents who do not wish their children to be educated in isolation of other children, or for those who wish to have their secular or philosophical convictions recognized, this suggests a promising way forward.

To summarize, the New Labour government under Tony Blair has stated its commitment for community life, which it sees played out in faith-based schools and as part of active citizenship. It also views faith-based schools as academically successful, and feels that together these points will result in a quick, politically acceptable and inexpensive way of getting results: selection via faith-based schools equating with high levels of achievement. Also, calling such institutions a 'faith school' is seen to bring a winning image and status. In other words, if you make every school a faith-based school or a specialist school it can be a cheap way of providing excellence. Religious communities help support the funding, and by taking the cachet and lustre of faith-based schools and spreading it, the government hopes it will work elsewhere. It would be churlish to suggest that this is the only motivation, as the government has also expressed an interest in promoting a return to moral codes of behaviour, social harmony and the establishment of a multi-ethnic Britain. Yet to assume that this can be achieved through the establishment of faith-based schools represents a misunderstanding of their nature and history, and focuses only on their perceived outcomes. As such they are not a simple answer to the problem of raising attainment.

Faith-based schools have been criticized for a number of things, as we have signalled: deliberate proselytization in schools, the forcing of identities on children, the removal of means of easy communication with children from other backgrounds, the suppression of knowledge and the stereotyping of others. However, these criticisms are not intrinsic to faith-based schools (Jackson 2003b). All schools need to examine their work in the area of prompting understanding and practice of social justice, social cohesion and appropriate pupil autonomy. In its promotion of faith-based schools the government has played down the potential of the community school to provide these things, along with its potential to be re-formed as a plural school (ibid.), not one devoid of both religion and religious education as contemplated by Hargreaves (1994). By focusing narrowly on the importance of religion in the instilling of moral codes of conduct, and placing emphasis on the raising of academic standards and achievement, there is a risk that these wider challenges, and potential gains, may be overlooked. The importance of community recognition and support, along with the pursuit of broader faith-based goals, is also an important aspect of such schools.

Faith-based schools that are in receipt of state funding may also need to change. Whilst some may wish to reject what they consider to be the polluting influences of the outside world, a sense of estrangement from society does not in itself constitute a threat to that society. Yet it risks denying the lived realities likely to be encountered by many of their pupils. As Cush (2003) observes, maybe we ask too little of faith-based schools in return for the money invested, and, we might add, perhaps we should demand their commitment to the wider community, and a demonstration of socially just educational practices. Given that, in the immediate future, a diversity of educational provision will continue to exist, the ideals noted above should be regarded as a part of the principles and practices of both community and faith-based schools. Clearly this will need to be embedded in the educational practice and inspection criteria, along with a visible demonstration of their engagement with, and support from, the *whole* community, not only from those who have a vested interest in the existence of the school itself.

Conclusion

What is most telling in the support for faith-based schools is the lack of confidence in community schools in terms of adequate cultural sensitivity or high academic attainment. The support for faith-based schools, therefore, tells us something about present perceptions of community schools particularly by the government, as well as from minority ethnic parents. The expansion of these schools can also be seen as a challenge to the teaching of Religious Education presently taking place in community schools, and as a demand for more robust provision for the inclusion of both religious and secular viewpoints in a wider manner than presently contemplated, in order to acknowledge and respond to the 'dignity of difference'.[19] Church of England and Catholic schools are also being challenged to demonstrate the inclusiveness of their selection practices with reference to ethnic diversity and socio-economic class. Due to their traditional position as education providers, they are in a strong position to initiate change from within. As such, both traditional and new faith-based schools need to define their distinctive character more clearly if they are to counter the negative criticisms attached to these institutions. They must visibly demonstrate how they will contribute to social cohesion and provide evidence that they are actively promoting an educational process that is not only relevant to their faiths but also prepares their pupils for life in a multi-ethnic, multi-faith world. Moreover, this will require a firm commitment to practices and principles that are socially just, and which respect differences in views and values.

Whilst there are serious concerns expressed about the wisdom of expanding schools which select pupils on the basis of religion there is little likelihood of change in the system. The realities of British educational history suggest that a compromise position could be pursued. There needs to be a pragmatic response that addresses the reality of the influence and success of faith-based schools among some communities, but one which also recognizes the views of those who advocate for better accommodation of their views and beliefs within reconstructed and culturally sensitive community schools. Good schools are popular and poor schools are not, regardless of whether they have a religious character.[20] So the challenge for the future will be that of sustaining within each school what is academically and morally acceptable to both the school itself and the outside community. This will require each school to be open to constructive critique, acknowledge the potential for change, demonstrate an active commitment to social justice and make a positive contribution to the pursuit of social harmony.

A common strand throughout this book has been to reaffirm the view that education be regarded as a collective act, with individual schools existing as part of a wider social and political community. Clearly the introduction of new faith-based schools in receipt of state funding presents an opportunity to those who believe that there should be not only diversity in provision, but also a much closer formal and informal relationship between different categories of schools. Added to this is a desire to see the development of closer working relationships between teachers and pupils across a range of diverse educational institutions. Although the path ahead may be strewn with obstacles, many of these are of our own making. There has never been a better time to review and renew our commitment to an education for all.

Notes

1 See Department for Education and Employment (2001a) *Schools: Building on Success.*
2 This reference to community schools being 'bog-standard' is attributed to Alastair Campbell, the Prime Minister's former official spokesman: The former Minister of Education, Estelle Morris, also stated she 'would not touch them with a bargepole'. See 'Minister's "bargepole" jibe at comprehensives causes row', *Daily Telegraph*, 25 June 2002, p. 2, and 'Fury at Minister's attack on schools', *The Independent*, 25 June 2002, p. 1.
3 See, for example, Short and Lenga (2002).
4 *The Guardian* (2002a), 18 March, p. 18.
5 Cantle Report (2001). There is, however, work being done in some schools to counter the image of 'white highlands'. See, for example, *Times Educational Supplement* (2003b), 'Diversity triumphs in the Dales', 31 January, p. 19.
6 National Secular Society (2002).
7 Cantle Report (2001).
8 *The Guardian* (2002), 18 March, p. 18.
9 Ibid.
10 Ibid.
11 'Blair: the Voters' Verdict', *The Guardian*, 20 July 2004, p. 1.
12 See, for example, Haw (1998).
13 *Labour election manifesto* (1997), London: Labour Party.
14 See, for example, Brown (1997).
15 Reports from Muslim schools in our study.
16 King David School in Liverpool is a case in point.
17 This is particularly relevant given statistical data concerning non-affiliation to religious groups. See, for example, 'Religion must bee removed ffrom all functions of state', *The Guardian*, 12 Deccember 2001, p. 18.
18 The BHA have been very active in this area, as demonstrated in, for example, their publications (Humanist Philosophers' Group 2001; British Humanist Association 2002). See also criticism of discriminatory practices against non-religious groups in *The Sunday Times* (2002d), 'Atheists in legal fight for God slot', 15 December, p. 7.
19 Sacks (2002).
20 Brown (2003) makes this point very forcefully.

Bibliography

Primary References

Aaronovitch, D. (2003), 'Lies, damned lies', *The Observer*, 26 June, p. 9.

Ahmed, L. (1992), *Women and Gender in Islam: Historical Roots of Modern Debate*, New Haven: Yale University Press.

Ainscow, M. (1995a), 'Education for all: making it happen', *Support for Learning*, vol. 10, no. 4, pp. 147–54.

—— (1995b), 'School Improvement and Special Needs: what's the connection?', *Educational Review*, vol. 9, no. 1, pp. 27–30.

—— (1997) 'Towards Inclusive Schooling', *British Journal of Special Education*, vol. 24, no. 1, pp. 3–6.

Albisetti, J. (1999), 'Catholics and Coeducation: Rhetoric and Reality in Europe Before *Divini Illius Magistri*', *Pedagogica Historica,* vol. 35, no. 3, pp. 667–96.

Alderman, G. (1999), 'British Jews or Britons of the Jewish persuasion', in S. Cohen and S. Horenczyk (eds), *National Variations in Jewish Identity*, New York: State University Press.

Alexander, H. (1995), *Jewish Education and the Search for Authenticity: a study of Jewish identity*, Los Angeles: University of Judaism.

Al-Furquan School, *School Prospectus (2003–2004)*, Reddings Lane, Tyseley, Birmingham B11 3EY.

Al-Muntaba Islamic School, *School Prospectus (2003–2004)*, 7 Bridges Place, off Parsons Green Lane, London SW6 4HW.

Anwar, M. (1993), *Muslims in Britain: The 1991 Census and Other Statistical Sources*, Paper 9, Centre for the Study of Christian and Muslim Relations, Selly Oak Colleges, Birmingham B29 6LE.

Apple, M. W. (1996), *Cultural Politics and Education*, Buckingham: Open University Press.

—— (2000), *Official Knowledge: Democratic Education in a Conservative Age*, 2nd edn, London: Routledge.

—— (2001), *Educating The "Right" Way: Markets, Standards, God, and Inequality*, New York: Routledge/Falmer.

Archbishop's Council Church Schools Review Group (2001), *The Way Ahead: Church of England Schools in the New Millennium*, chaired by Lord R. Dearing, London: Church House Publishing.

Archer L. (2001), 'Muslim brothers, black lads, traditional Asians: British Muslim young men's constructions of "race", religion and masculinity', *Feminism and Psychology*, vol. 11, no. 1, pp. 79–105.

Armitage, W. H. G. (1964), *Four Hundred Years of English Education*, London: Cambridge University Press.

Arthur, J. (1995), 'Government Education Policy and Voluntary-aided Schools', *Oxford Review of Education*, vol. 21, no. 4, pp. 447–55.

Ashraf, A. S. (1993), 'The Role of Muslim Youth in a Multi-Religious Society', *Muslim Education Quarterly*, vol. 11, no. 1, pp. 3–13.

—— (1994), 'Faith-Based Education: A Theoretical Shift from the Secular to the Transcendent', *Muslim Education Quarterly*, vol. 11, no. 2, pp. 3–8.

Association of Muslim Schools (2003), *Muslim Schools in Britain*, AMS, 5 Bishopsgate Street, Edgbaston, Birmingham B15 1ET.

Association of Muslim Schools School Centred Initial Teacher Training (2000), *Course Handbook*, Cheltenham: Cheltenham and Gloucester College of Higher Education.

Ball, E. W. and Harry, B. (1993), 'Multicultural education and special education: parallels, divergences and intersections', *The Educational Forum*, vol. 57, pp. 430–37.

Ball, S., Maguire, M. and Macrae, S. (2000), *Choice, Pathways and Transitions post-16: New Youth, New Economies in the Global City*, London: Routledge/Falmer.

Ballard, R. (1990), 'Migration and Kinsship: the differential effects of marriage rules on the process of Punjabi migration to Britain', in C. Clark, C. Peach and S. Vertovec (eds), *South Asians Overseas: Migration and Ethnicity*, Cambridge: Cambridge University Press.

—— (2000), 'The growth and changing character of the Sikh presence in Britain', in J. Hinnells (ed.), *The South Asian Religious Diaspora in Britain, Canada and the United States*, Albany, New York: State University of New York Press.

Ballard, R. and Kalra, V. S. (1994), *The Ethnic Dimensions of the 1991 Census: A preliminary report*, Manchester: University of Manchester.

Banks, J. A. and Lynch, J. (eds) (1986), *Multicultural Education in Western Societies*, London: Holt, Rinehart and Winston.

Barker, V. and Irving, B. A. (2003), 'Citizenship for all: engaging Muslim girls in the career education process', in A. Edwards (ed.), *Career Education and Citizenship: an Inclusive Agenda,* Canterbury: Canterbury Christ Church University College.

Barrell, G. and Partington, J. (1985), *Teachers and the Law*, 6th edn, London: Methuen.

Barrow, J. (1995), 'Children's Nurture at Clifton Road Gurdwara', *Sikh Bulletin*, vol. 12.

Bartels, E. (2000), 'Dutch Islam: young people, learning and integration', *Current Sociology*, October, vol. 48, no. 4, pp. 59–74.

Barth, F. (1969), *Ethnic Groups and Boundaries: the social organisation of cultural difference*, London: George Allen and Unwin.

Bastiani, J. (1989), *Working with Parents: A Whole School Approach*, Windsor: NFER-Nelson.

Baumann, G. (1994), 'Contextual Indeterminacy', *Religion and Society*, vol. 25, no. 1, pp. 3–9.

—— (1996), *Contesting Cultures: Discourses of identity in multi-ethnic London*, Cambridge Cambridge University Press.

Baumfield, V. (2003), 'The Dignity of Difference: Faith and Schooling in a Liberal Democracy', *British Journal of Religious Education*, vol. 25, no. 2, pp. 86–8.

Beishon, S., Modood, T. and Virdee, S. (1998), *Ethnic Minority Families*, London: Policy Studies Institute.

Bennett, C. (1995), *Yugoslavia's Bloody Collapse: Causes, Course and Consequences*, New York: New York University Press.

Berger, J. (1982), *Religion in West European Politics*, London: Cassell.

Berliner, W. (1993), 'Muslims Stand Their Ground', *Education Guardian*, 23 March, pp. 6–7.

Bernstein, B. (1990), *The Structuring of Pedagogic Discourse*, New York: Routledge.

Bhatti, G. (1999), *Asian Children at Home and at School*, London: Routledge.

Bigger, S. (2000), 'Religious education, spirituality and anti-racism', in M. Leicester, C. Modgil and S. Modgil (eds), *Spirituality and Religious Education*, London: Falmer Press.

Bilton, T., Bonnett, K., Jones, P., Sheard, K., Stanworth, M. and Webster, A. (1981), *Introductory Sociology*, London: Macmillan Press Ltd.

Binns, J. (2002), *An Introduction to the Christian Orthodox Churches*, Cambridge: Cambridge University Press.

Black, J. (1998), *JFS: The History of the Jews' Free School, London since 1732*, London: Tymsder Publishers.

Blair, M. and Cole, M. (2000), 'Racism and Education: The Imperial Legacy', in M. Cole (ed.), *Education, Equality and Human Rights*, London: Routledge/Falmer.

Blaylock, L. (1999), 'RE for all, because we are all human', *Resource*, vol. 22, no. 1, pp. 21–3.

Bolton, J. (1991), 'Catholic Aided Schools – The Special Relationship', *The International Journal of Educational Management*, vol. 5/6, pp. 14–20.

Booth, T., Ainscow, M., Black-Hawkins, K., Vaughan, M. and Shaw, L. (2000), *Index for Inclusion: Developing Learning and Participation in Schools*, Bristol: CSIE.

Borowitz, E. (1985), *Explaining Reform Judaism*, New York: Behrman House.

Bourdieu, P. (1985), 'The Social Space and the Genesis of Groups', *Theory and Society*, vol. 14, pp. 723–44.

Bower, C. A. and Palmer, J. (1996), 'Educating for an ecologically sustainable culture', *British Journal of Educational Studies*, vol. 44, no. 2, pp. 144–56.

Boyle, K. and Sheen, J. (eds) (1997), *Freedom of Religion and Belief: A World Report*, London: Routledge.

Bradley, H. (1996), *Fractured Identities: Changing Patterns of Inequality*, Cambridge: Polity Press.

Bradney, A. (1993), *Religions, Rights and Laws*, Leicester: Leicester University Press.

Brah, A. (1996), *Cartographies of Diaspora: Contesting Identities*, London: Routledge.

British Columbia Court of Appeals (1979) in Margaret Caldwell vs. Ian Charles Stuart, Principal, St. Thomas Aquinas High School and the Catholic Public Schools of Vancouver Archdioceses, Official Court Reporters, Box 34, Courthouse, 800 Hornby St, Vancouver, BC V8Z 2C5.

British Humanist Association (1998), 'Collective Worship and School Assemblies: What is the law?', London: BHA.

British Humanist Association (2002), *A Better Way Forward,* London: BHA.

British Muslims Monthly Survey (1999a), 'Yusuf Islam Interview', vol. 7, no. 11, 20 December, p. 3.

—— (1999b), 'State Funding for Feversham College', vol. 7, no. 11, 20 December, p. 10.

—— (2000a), 'Prince Charles Visits Islamia', vol. 8, no. 5, 20 June, pp. 1–2.

—— (2000b) 'Lord Ahmed Calls for More Involvement', vol. 8, no. 5, 20 June, p. 9.

Broadbent, L. and Brown, A. (2003), *Issues in Religious Education*, London: Routledge/Falmer.

Brown, A. (1992), *The Multi-faith Church School*, London: The National Society.

—— (1997), *The Multi-faith Church School*, 2nd impression, London: The National Society.

—— (2003), 'Church of England Schools: Politics, Power and Identity', *British Journal of Religious Education*, vol. 25, no. 2, pp. 103–16.

Brown, B. (1996), *Unlearning Discrimination in the Early Years*, Stoke: Trentham Books.

Brownlie, I. (1981), *Basic Documents in International Law*, 2nd edn, Oxford: Clarendon Press.

Brownlie, I. and Goodwin, G. S. (2002), *Basic Documents on Human Rights*, 4th edn, Oxford: Oxford University Press.

Bruner, J. (1987), 'The Transactional Self', in J. Bruner and H. Haste (eds), *Making Sense: the Child's Construction of the World*, London: Methuen.

Buckley, S. (1991), *Bridge of Light: The Struggle of an Islamic Private School in Australia*, New South Wales: Muslim Service Association.

Burke, J., Bright, M., Barnett, A., Walsh, N. and Burhan, W. (2002), 'How the Bin Ladin network spread its tentacles', *The Observer*, 20 January, p. 3.

Butler, R. (1993), *Themes in Religion: Sikhism*, London: Longman.

Cairns, J. and Gardner, R. (2002), 'Assessment in Citizenship', in L. Gearon (ed.), *Learning to Teach Citizenship in the Secondary School*, London: Routledge/Falmer.

Calderhead, J. (1992), 'The nature and growth of knowledge in student teaching', *Teaching and Teacher Education*, vol. 7, pp. 531–5.

Cameron, R. J., Owen, A. J. and Tee, G. (1986), 'Curriculum Management (Part 3) Assessment and Evaluation', *Educational Psychology in Practice*, vol. 2, no. 3, pp. 3–9.

Cantle Report (2001), *Community Cohesion: A Report of the Independent Review Team*, London: Home Office.

Carrington, S. (1999), 'Inclusion needs a different school culture', *International Journal of Inclusive Education*, vol. 3, no. 3, pp. 257–68.

Carrington, S. and Elkins, J. (2002), 'Bridging the gap between inclusive policy and inclusive culture in secondary schools', *Support for Learning*, vol. 17, no. 2, pp. 51–7.

Castles, S. (1996), 'The racisms of globilisation', in S. Castles and E. Vasta (eds), *The Teeth are Smiling: the persistence of racism in multicultural Australia*, Sydney: Allen and Unwin.

Catholic Education Service (1996), *Learning from Ofsted and diocesan inspections: the distinctive nature of education in Catholic primary and secondary schools*, London: CES.

—— (1997), *The Catholic Schools and Other Faiths Report*, London: CES.

—— (1998), *Education for Love*, London: CES.

—— (1999), *Evaluating the Dinstinctive Nature of the Catholic School*, 4th edn, London: CES.

—— (2000), *Performance Management*, London: CES.

—— (2001), *Handbook for Clerks*, London: CES.

—— (2003), *Ethnicity, Identity and Achievement in Catholic Education*, London: CES.

Centre for the Study of Islam and Christian–Muslim Relations (1985), *Report of Seminar held at Westhill College, Selly Oak, Birmingham, 'Citizenship and Religious Education: Multi-Faith and Denominational Schools'*, Birmingham: CSIC.

Chadwick, P. (2001), 'The Anglican Perspective on Church Schools', *Oxford Review of Education*, vol. 27, no. 4, pp. 475–87.

Chambers, C. (1995), *Beliefs and Cultures: Sikh*, London: Watts Books.

Children's Legal Centre (1986), *Children's Charter, London: CLC*.

Chitty, C. (2001), 'The 2001 White Paper and the New Education Bill', *Forum*, vol. 44, no. 1, pp. 13–14.

Choudhury, M. A. (1993), 'A Critical Examination of the Concept of Islamization of Knowledge in Contemporary Times', *Muslim Educational Quarterly*, vol. 10, no. 4, pp. 3–34.

Christensen, C. A. and Dorn, S. (1997), 'Competing notions of social justice in special education reform', *Journal of Special Education*, vol. 31, no. 2, pp. 181–98.

Chronicle Comment (2003) 'No hiding the truth', *Oldham Evening Chronicle,* Monday, 3 February, p. 4.

Church Times (2002), Friday, 8 February.

Clerkin, C. (1996), *Challenging Disabling Attitudes and Policies: the integration of deaf and partially hearing pupils into mainstream education, a study of Inclusive Education in the London Borough of Newham,* London: University of East London.

Clore Shalom School, *Brochure (2002–2003),* Hugo Gryn Way, Shenley, Hertfordshire WD7 9BL.

Cohen, A. P, (1986), *Symbolising Boundaries: Identity and Diversity in British Cultures,* Manchester: Manchester University Press.

—— (1996), 'Foreword', in D. S. Tatla, *The Sikh Diaspora: The Search for Statehood,* London: University College Press.

Cole, M. (1998), 'Racism, Reconstructed Multiculturalism and Antiracist Education', *Cambridge Journal of Education,* vol. 28, no. 1, pp. 37–48.

Commission for Racial Equality (1990), *Schools of Faith,* Elliot House, 10–12 Allington Street, London SW1E 5EH.

Connell, R. W. (1993), *Schools and Social Justice,* Toronto: Our Schools/Our Selves Educational Foundation.

Conroy, J. C. (1999), *Catholic Education: inside-out and outside-in,* Dublin: Veritas.

Corbett, J. (1998), *Special Educational Needs in the Twentieth Century: A Cultural Analysis,* London: Cassell.

Council of Europe (1972), *Selected Texts (the European Convention on Human Rights),* Strasbourg: Council of Europe.

—— (1999), *European Social Charter: the charter, its protocols, the revised Charter,* Strasbourg: Council of Europe.

Coward, H., Hinnells, J. R. and Williams, R. B. (eds) (2000), *The South Asian Religious Diaspora in Britain, Canada, and the United States,* Albany, New York: State University of New York Press.

Cox, E. (1966), *Changing Aims of Religious Education,* London: Routledge and Kegan Paul.

Craft, M. and Bardell, G. (eds) (1984), *Curriculum Opportunities in a Multicultural Society,* London: Harper Educational.

Crick, B. (1998), *Education for citizenship and the teaching of democracy in schools,* London: Qualifications Curriculum Authority.

—— (2000a), *Education for Citizenship and the Teaching of Democracies: Final Report of the Advisory Group on Citizenship (Crick Report),* London: QCA.

Crick, R. D. (2002), *Transforming Visions – Managing Values in School: a Case Study,* Middlesex: Middlesex University Press.

Cummins, J. (1986), 'Empowering minority students: a framework for intervention', *Harvard Educational Review*, vol. 56, no. 1, pp. 342–5.

Cumper, D. (1990), 'Muslim Schools: Implications of the Education Reform Act 1988', *New Community*, vol. 16, no. 3, pp. 379–89.

Cunningham, C. and Davis, H. (1985), *Working with Parents: Frameworks for Collaboration*, Milton Keynes: Open University Press.

Curtis, S. J. and Boultwood, M. E. (1966), *An Introductory History of Education Since 1800*, 4th edn, London: University Tutorial Press.

Cush, D. (2003), 'Should the State Fund Schools with a Religious Character?', *Religious Education (PCfRE)*, Spring, vol. 25, no. 2, pp. 10–15.

Dadzie, S. (2000), *Toolkit for Tackling Racism in Schools*, Stoke-on-Trent: Trentham Books.

Daly, P. (1995), 'Public Accountability and the Academic Effectiveness of Grant-Aided Catholic Schools', *School Effectiveness and School Improvement*, vol. 6, no. 4, pp. 367–79.

Daniel, N. W. (1968), *Racial Discrimination in Britain*, Harmondsworth: Penguin.

Davies, L. (1990), *School Management in an International Context*, London: Falmer.

Deakin, R. (1989), *New Christian Schools: The Case for Public Funding*, Bristol: The Regius Press Ltd.

—— (1994) 'Frameworks for Thinking about Values and Religious Beliefs', *Spectrum*, vol. 26, no. 1.

—— (2002), *Transforming Visions – Managing Values in Schools*, Middlesex: Middlesex University Press.

Dearing, R. (1994), *The National Curriculum and its Assessment, Dearing Report*, London: School Curriculum and Assessment Agency.

Deen, H. (1998), *Broken Bangles,* Moorebank: Anchor.

Department of Education and Science (1977), *Education in Schools: A Consultative Document (Green Paper, Cmnd 6869)*, London: HMSO.

Department for Education and Employment (1998), *The National Literacy Strategy: Framework for Teaching*, London: DfEE.

—— (1999), *The National Numeracy Strategy*, Sudbury, Suffolk: DfEE.

—— (2000), *Schools: Building on Success, Government Green paper, CM 505*, London: DfEE.

—— (2001a), *Schools: Building on Success*, Norwich: HMSO.

—— (2001b), *Schools: Achieving Success, White Paper*, London: HMSO.

—— (2001c), *Special Educational Needs and the Disability Act*, London: HMSO.

Department for Education and Employment and the Home Office (1997), *School Security with Troublemakers: Wearing Kirpans in Schools, annex F*, London: DfEE/HO.

Department for Education and Employment and Qualifications and Curriculum Authority (1999a), *Science: The National Curriculum for England*, London: DfEE and QCA.

—— (1999b), *The National Curriculum: Handbook for Primary Teachers in England*, London: DfEE and QCA.

Department for Education and Skills (1999), *Guidance on Statutory Proposals EE, 457 0E2*, London: HMSO.

—— (2001), *Special Educational Needs Code of Practice*, London: DfES.

—— (2002), *Raising Standards*, London: DfES.

—— (2003a), *Aiming High: Raising the Achievement of Minority Ethnic Pupils*, London: DfES.

—— (2003b), *Statistics for Education: Schools in England*, London: HMSO, http://www.dfes.gov.uk/rsgateway/DB/vol/rooo417/index.shtml.

Derby City (2003), *All Our Worlds: Derby City Religious Education Agreed Syllabus*, Derby: Derby City Education Service, LEA.

Dialogue (1997), 'The Challenge of Islamophobia', November, London: Public Affairs Committee for Shi'a Muslims, Stone Hall, Chevening Road, London NW6 6TN.

Diamant, A. and Cooper, H. (1991), *Living a Jewish Life*, New York: Harper Collins.

Dijkstra, A. and Veenstra, R. (2001), 'Do Religious Schools Matter?: Beliefs and Life-Styles of Students in Faith-based Secondary Schools', *International Journal of Education and Religion,* vol. 2, pp. 182–206.

Diniz, F. A. (1997), 'Working with families in a multi-ethnic European context', in B. Carpenter (ed.), *Families in Context: Emerging Trends in Family Support*, London: David Fulton.

—— (1999), 'Race and special educational needs in the 1990s', *British Journal of Special Education*, vol. 26, no. 4, pp. 213–17.

Donald, J. and Rattansi, A. (eds) (1992), *Race, Culture and Difference*, London: Sage.

Donnelly, C. (1999), 'Differences in Schools: a question of ethos?', paper presented to the British Educational Research Association Annual Conference, Brighton, http://leeds.ac.uk/educol/documents/00001274.htm

—— (2000), 'In pursuit of school ethos', *British Journal of Education Studies*, vol. 48, no. 2, pp. 134–54.

Donohoue Clyne, I. (2001), 'Educating Muslim Children in Australia', in *Muslim Communities in Australia*, by A. Saeed and S. Akbarzadeh (eds), Sydney : University of New South Wales.

Dooley, P. (1991), 'Muslim Private Schools', in G. Walford (ed,), *Tradition, Change and Diversity*, London: Paul Chapman.

Drury, B. D. (1991), 'Sikh girls and the maintenance of an ethnic culture', *New Community*, vol. 17, no. 3, pp. 387–99.

Dyson, A. (1992), 'Innovatory mainstream practice: what's happening in the schools" provision for special needs?', *Support for Learning*, vol. 7, no. 2, pp. 51–7.

Economic and Social Research Council (1999), *Children 5–16 Research briefing: Civil Rights in School*, Swindon: ESRC.

Eggleston, J. (1990), 'Can anti-racist teaching survive the 1988 Education Act', *Multiculture Teaching*, vol. 8, no. 3, pp. 9–11.

Erricker, C. and Erricker, J. (2000), *Reconstructing Religious, Spiritual and Moral Education*, London: Routledge/Falmer.

European Convention on Human Rights (1951), http://www.hri.org./docs/ECHR50.html

Evangelical Times (2003), 'Emmanuel College Ethos to Expand', http://www.evangelical-times.org/ETNews/June03/jun03n20.htm

Falaturi, U. and Tworuschka, A. (1991), 'Islam in Instruction', paper presented at the Intercultural Education in Europe, Conference, Frankfurt.

Feheney, M. (ed.) (1999), *Beyond the Race for Points: Aspects of Pastoral Care*, Dublin: Veritas.

Felenstein, D. (2000), *Inspecting Jewish Schools*, London: Board of Deputies.

Flyn, M. and Mok, M. (1998), 'Effects of Catholic school culture on students' achievement in High School exams: a multilevel path analysis], *Education Psychology*, vol. 18, no. 4, pp. 409–32.

Francis, L. (2000), 'The Domestic and General Function of Anglican Schools in England and Wales', *International Journal of Education and Religion,* vol. 11, pp. 100–121.

Francis, L. and Egan, J. (1993), *Christian Perspective on Church Schools: a reader*, Leominster: Gracewing.

Francis, L. and Lankshear, D. (eds), (1993), *Christian Perspectives on Church Schools*, Leominster: Gracewing Books.

—— (2001), 'The relationship between church schools and local church life: distinguishing between aided and controlled', *Education and Studies*, vol. 27, pp. 425–38.

Franklin, J. (1998), 'Introduction: Social Policy in Perspective', in J. Franklin (ed.), *Social Policy and Social Justice*, Cambridge: Polity Press.

Frederickson, N. and Cline, T. (20020, *Special Educational Needs, Inclusion and Diversity, a textbook*, Buckingham: Open University Press.

Freire, P. (1999), *Pedagogy of Hope: Reliving Pedagogy of the Oppressed*, trans. Robert R. Barr, New York: Continuum.

Friedenberg, E. Z. (1980), *Deference to Authority: The Case of Canada*, New York: M. E. Sharpe Inc.

Fullan, M. (1992), *The Meaning of Educational Change*, London: Cassell.

—— (2000), *Change Forces: the Sequel*, London: Falmer press.

Gaine, C. (1996), *Still No Trouble Here*, Stoke-on-Trent: Trentham Books.

Gale, T. (2000), 'Rethinking social justice in schools: how will we recognise it when we see it?', *International Journal of Inclusive Education*, vol. 4, no. 3, pp. 253–69.

Gale, T. and Densmore, K. (2000), *Just Schooling: explorations in the cultural politics of teaching*, Buckingham: Open University Press.

Gallagher, D. J. (2001), 'Neutrality as a moral standpoint, conceptual confusion and the full inclusion debate', *Disability and Society*, vol. 16, no. 5, pp. 637–54.

Gallagher, M. (1997), 'New Forms of Cultural Unbelief', in P. Hogan and K. Williams (eds), *The Future of Religion in Irish Education*, Dublin: Veritas.

Gartner, L. (1960), *The Jewish Immigrant in England 1870–1914*, London: Wayne State University Press.

Geaves, R. (2000), *The Sufis of Britain: An Exploration of Muslim Identity,* Cardiff: Cardiff Academic Press.

General Synod (1998), *Church of England Schools in the New Millennium.* London: General Synod of the Church of England.

Gerwitz, S. Miller, H. and Walford, G. (19910, 'Parents' Individualist and Collectivist Strategies at the City Technology College, Kingshurst', *International Studies in Sociology of Education*, vol. 1, no. 1/2, pp. 173–91.

Ghuman, P. A. (1980), 'Bhattra Sikhs in Cardiff: Family and Social Organisation', *New Community,* vol. 8, no. 3, pp. 308–16.

Giddens, A. (1995), *Politics, Sociology and Social Theory: Encounters with classical and contemporary social thought*, Cambridge: Polity Press.

—— (2001) *Sociology*, 4th edn, Cambridge: Polity Press.

Gillard, D. (2002), 'The Faith Schools Debate: Glass in their snowballs', *Forum*, vol. 44, no. 1, pp. 15–22.

Gillborn, D. (1995), *Racism and Antiracism in Real Schools*, Buckingham: Open University Press.

—— (1996a), *Recent research on the achievement of ethnic minority pupils*, London: HMSO.

—— (1996b), 'Student Roles and Perspectives in Antiracist Education: a crisis in white ethnicity?', *British Educational Research Journal*, vol. 22, no. 2, pp. 165–79.

—— (1997), 'Racism and Reform: new ethnicities/old inequalities', *British Educational Research Journal*, vol. 23, no. 3, pp. 345–60.

—— (1998), 'Racism and the politics of qualitative research: learning from controversy and critique', in Connolly, P. and Troyna, B. (eds), *Researching Racism in Education: Politics, Theory and Practice*, Buckingham: Open University Press.

Gillborn, D. and Mirza, M. (2000), *Educational Inequality: mapping race, class and gender: a synthesis of research evidence*, London: Ofsted.

Gillborn, D. and Youdell, D. (2000), *Rationing Education: Policy, Practice, Reform and Equity*, Buckingham: Open University Press.

Gillman, N. (1993), *Conservative Judaism*, New York: Behrman House.

Gilroy, P. (1987), *There Ain't No Black in the Union Jack*, London: Hutchinson.

—— (1993) *The Black Atlantic: Modernity and Double Consciousness,* London: Verso.

—— (2000a), 'Joined-up Politics and Post-colonial Melancholia', *Journal of Contemporary African Art*, vol. 11/12, pp. 48–55.

Gipps, C. (1994), *Beyond Testing: Towards a Theory of Educational Assessment*, London: Falmer Press.

Gipps, C. and Murphy, P. (1994), *A Fair Test?*, Philadelphia: Open University Press.

Giroux, H. A. (1992), *Border Crossings*, New York: Routledge.

Gledhill, R. (19980, 'Sunday Schools Crisis in Faith', *The Times*, 10 January, p. 18.

Goodin, R. E., Headey, B., Muffels, R. and Dirven, H. (1999), *The Real Worlds of Welfare Capitalism*, Cambridge: Cambridge University Press.

Grace, G. (2001), 'The state and Catholic schooling in England and Wales politics, ideology and mission integrity', *Oxford Review of Education*, vol. 24, no. 4, pp. 489–500.

—— (2002a), *Catholic Schools : Mission, Markets, and Morality*, London: Routledge/Falmer.

—— (2002b), 'Replacing Prejudice with Evidence-Based Argument: A Research Agenda for Faith-Based Schooling', paper presented at the Faith Schools: Conflict or Consensus Conference, the Institute of Education, University of London, June 2002.

Greek Association Language Enhancement Organisation (GALE) (2003), http://www.enostos.net/grk_org1.html

Griffiths, M. (2003), *Action for Social Justice*, Milton Keynes: Open University.

Grimmitt, M. (2000), *Pedagogies of Religious Education*, Great Wakering: McCrimmons.

Grugeon, E. (1992), 'Ruled out or rescued? A statement for Balbinder', in T. Booth, W. Swan, M. Masterton and P. Potts (eds), *Policies for Diversity in Education*, London: Routledge/Open University Press.

The Guardian (2001a), 'Faith in the System', 12 December, p. 5.

—— (2001b), 'Mean Streets divided', 12 December, p. 5.

—— (2001c), 'Blunkett's blunder puts the clock back', 12 December, p. 18.

—— (2001d), 'It's not about cricket', 14 December, p. 21.

—— (2002a), 'Blair wears his faith on his shirt cuff', 18 March, p. 18.

—— (2002b), 'Beyond Belief', 8 January, p. 2.

—— (2003a), 'The violation of a place of worship or a vital blow in the war against terrorism', 21 January, p. 3.

—— (2003b), 'Fear and Loathing', 21 January, p. 17.

—— (2003c), 'French angry at veil move', 22 April, p. 15.

—— (2003d), 'On the buses: should religion determine which children receive free schools transport, 7 October, p. 6.

The Guardian Education (2002) 'Dutch Politician Pim Fortuyn Assassinated', 6 May, p. 9.

—— (2003), 'Friends, Pupils, Citizens', 9 September, p. 2.

Guibernau, M. and Rex, J. (eds) (1997), *The Ethnicity Reader: Nationalism, Multiculturalism and Migration*, Cambridge: Polity Press.

Gundara, J. S. (2000), *Interculturalism, Education and Inclusion*, London: Sage.

Guru Nanak Sikh Secondary Voluntary Aided School, *School Prospectus (2001–2002)*, Spring Field Road, Hayes, Middlesex UB4 0LT.

Hahn, C. (1999), 'Citizenship education: an empirical study of policy, practices and outcomes', *Oxford Review of Education*, vol. 25, nos 1 and 2, pp. 231–50.

Hall, S. (1992), 'New Ethnicities', in J. Donald and A. Rattansi (eds), *'Race', Culture and Difference*, London: Sage.

Hall, S., Ozerk, K., Zulfiqar, M. and Tan, J. (2002), 'This is our school: provision, purpose and pedagogy of supplementary schools in Leeds and Oslo', *British Educational Research Journal*, vol. 28, no. 3, pp. 399–418.

Hall, T., Coffey, A. and Williamson, H. (2000), 'Young people, citizenship and the third way: a role for the youth service?', *Journal of Youth Studies*, vol. 3, pp. 461–72.

Hallgren, C. (2002), 'Working Harder to be the Same: experiences of young men and women in Sweden from minority ethnic backgrounds', paper submitted to the European Educational Research Association Conference, Lisbon, 11–14 September.

Hallgren, C. and Weiner, G. (2002), 'Why here? Why now? The Web, Antiracism, Education and the State of Sweden', paper presented to the European Educational Research Association Conference, Lisbon, 11–14 September.

Halstead, J. M. (1986), *The Case for Muslim Voluntary-Aided Schools: Some Philosophical Reflections*, Cambridge: The Islamic Academy.

—— (1988), *Education, Justice and Cultural: An Examination of the Honeyford Affair*, London: Falmer Press.

—— (1995a) 'Should Schools Reinforce Children's Religious Identity?', *Religious Education*, vol. 90, nos 3/4, pp. 360–76.

Halstead, M. (1995b) 'Voluntary Apartheid? Problems of Schooling for Religious and other Minorities in Democratic Societies', *Journal of Philosophy of Education*, vol. 29, no. 2, pp. 257–72.

Halstead, M. and Taylor, M. (2000), *The Development of Values, Attitudes and Personal Qualities*, Basingstoke: NFER.

Haneef, S. (1979), *What Everyone Should Know About Islam and Muslims*, Lahore: Kazi Publications.

Hare, R. M. (1992), *Essays on Religion and Education*, Oxford: Clarendon Press.

Hargreaves, D. (1994), *The Mosaic of Learning: Schools and Teachers for the New Century*, Demos Paper 8, London: Demos.

Harris, M. (2001), 'Some practical considerations for teaching music to Muslims', *NAME* (National Association of Music Educators), vol. 5, no. 1, pp. 27–31.

Hartman, W. and Fay, T. (1996), 'Cost effectiveness of institutional support', *Journal of Education Finance*, vol. 21, pp. 555–80.

Harvey, C. D. H. (2001), *Maintaining our Differences: Minority families in multicultural societies*, Aldershot: Ashgate Publishing Ltd.

Haw, K. (1998), *Educating Muslim Girls: Shifting Discourses*, Buckingham: Open University Press.

Helweg, A. W. (1986), 2nd edn, *Sikhs in England: The Development of a Migrant Community*, Delhi: Oxford University Press.

Hewer, C. (1992), 'Muslim Teacher Training in Britain', *Muslim Education Quarterly*, vol. 9, no. 2, pp. 21–34.

—— (2001a), *The Essence of Islam*, London: RP Publishing.

—— (2001b), 'Schools for Muslims', *Oxford Review of Education*, vol. 27, no. 4, pp. 515–28.

Hewitt I. (1998), 'Final Report', *Report: The Magazine from the Association of Teachers and Lecturers*, April.

Hickman, M. (1995), *Religion, Class and Identity: the state, the Catholic church and the education of the Irish in Britain*, Aldershot: Avebury.

Hillery, (1955) G. "Definitions of Community", *Rural Sociology,* vol. 20, no. 2.

Hinnells, J. R.(1995), *Dictionary of Religions*, London: Penguin Books.

—— (ed.) (1997), *A New Handbook of Living Religions*, London: Penguin Books.

Holmes, R., Jones L. and McCreery, E. (2002), 'The Phenomenon of Muslim-only Nurseries: Why are Parents Choosing Them?' paper presented at the *Faith Schools: Consensus or Conflict* Conference, the Institute of Education, University of London, June 2002.

Home Office (2001), *Schools Achieving Success*, White Paper, September, London: HMSO.

Hopkins, D. and Reynolds, D. (2001), 'The past, present and future of school improvement: towards the third age', *British Educational Research journal*, vol. 27, no. 4, pp. 459–75.

Hornsby-Smith, M. (2000), 'The Changing Social and Religious Content of Catholic Schooling in England and Wales', in M. Eaton, J. Longman and A. Naylor (eds), *Commitment to Diversity: Catholics and Education in a Changing World*, London: Cassell.

Howard, V. (1987), *A Report on Afro-Caribbean Christianity in Britain*, Community Religions Project Research Papers, Leeds: Leeds University.

Huddleston, T. and Rowe, D. (2002), 'Citizenship and the role of language', in L. Gearon (ed.), *Learning to Teach Citizenship in the Secondary School*, London: Routledge/Falmer.

Hull, J. M. (1984), *Studies in Religion and Education*, Lewes: Falmer.

Hulmes, E. (1989), *Education and Cultural Diversity*, London: Longmans.

Humanist Philosophers' Group (2001), *Religious Schools: the Case Against*, London: British Humanist Association.

Hurst, J. (2000), 'Religious Requirement: The Case for Roman Catholic Schools in the 1940s and Muslim Schools in the 1990s', *Journal of Beliefs and Values*, vol. 21, no. 1, pp. 87–97.

Husain F. and O'Brien M. (1999), *Muslim Families in Europe: Social Existence and Social Care*, report for ED-DGV, London: University of North London.

—— (2001), 'South Asian Muslims in Britain: Faith, Family and Community', in C. D. H. Harvey (ed.), *Maintaining our Differences: Minority families in multicultural societies*, Aldershot: Ashgate.

Husain, S. S. and Ashraf, S. A. (1979), *A Crisis in Muslim Education*, Sevenoaks: Hodder and Stoughton.

Hussain, F. (1984), *Muslim Women*, New York: St Martin's Press.

Hussain, Z. (1996) *al-Madaris Newspaper*, no. 5, Winter, p. 5.

Hutchinson, J. and Smith, A. D. (1996), *Ethnicity*, Oxford: Oxford University Press.

The Independent (2002), 'More "creationist" schools revealed', 17 March, p. 15.

Independent Schools Inspectorate (2002), www.isi.org.uk

Inspection Report (2000a), *Islamia Primary School*, London: HMI.

—— (2000b), *Waltham Church of England School*, London: HMI.

—— (2001a), *Emmanuel City Technology College*, London: HMI.

—— (2001b), *Hartstone Church of England Primary School*, London: HMI.

—— (2001c), *John Loughborough School*, London: HMI.

—— (2001d), *St Edward's Catholic Primary School*, London: HMI.

—— (2002a), *Al-Muntada Islamic School*, London: HMI.

—— (2002b), *Leicester Islamic Academy*, London: HMI.

—— (2003a), *Guru Nanak Sikh Secondary School*, London: HMI.

—— (2003b), *King David School*, London: HMI.

—— (2003c), *St Cyprian's School*, London: HMI.

—— (2003d), *The Swaminarayan Independent Day School*, London: HMI.

Ipgrave, J. (2001), *Pupil to Pupil Dialogue in the Classroom as a Tool for Religious Education*, Warwick Religions and Educational Research Unit Occasional Papers 11, Warwick: Institute of Education, University of Warwick.

Irving, B. A. (2000), 'Compulsory Education: No place for the lifelong learner in *Australian Journal of Career Development*, vol. 9, no. 2, Winter, pp. 8–13.

Irving, B. and Marris, L. (2002), 'A context for Connexions', in Institute of Career Guidance (ed.), *Constructing the Future – 2002. Social Inclusion: Policy and Practice*, Stourbridge, Institute of Career Guidance.

Irving, B. A., Barker, V., Jones, S. and Woolmer, D. (2002), *Muslim Girls Careers Education Pack*, Reading: Centre for British Teachers.

Irving, B. A., Barker, V., Parker-Jenkins, M. and Hartas, D. (2000), 'In Pursuit of Social Justice career guidance provision for Muslim girls in England', *Revista Espanola De Orientacion Y Psicopedagogia*, vol. 11, no. 20, pp. 175–86.

—— (2003), 'Choice and Opportunity: Supporting Young Muslim Women's Career Aspirations', in H. Jawad and T. Benn (eds), *Muslim Women in the United Kingdom and Beyond: Experiences and Images*, Leiden: Brill.

Islamia: National Muslim Education Newsletter (1992), 'Under-education not underachievement of Muslim Children in the UK', vol. 20, November, pp. 6–8.

—— (1994), 'A Muslim Boyss' Secondary School', vol. 23, March, pp. 6–7.

Islamia School, *School Prospectus (2003–2004)*, London: Islamic School Centre.

Islamic Educational Trust (1991), *Muslims in Britain: A Statistical Survey*, Education and Training Unit No. 8, 3–11 Keythorpe Street, Leicester.

Jacobs, R. (1987), 'Cultural differences clarification for young children', *Early Child Development and Care*, vol. 28, no. 2, pp. 163–5.

Jackson, R. (1997), *Religious Education and An Interpretive Approach*, London: Hodder and Stoughton.

—— (2001), 'Faith Based Schools and Religious Education within the State System in England and Wales', Editorial, *British Journal of Religious Education*, vol. 24, no. 1, pp. 2–6.

—— (ed.) (2003a), *International Perspectives on Citizenship, Education and Religious Diversity*, London: Routledge.

—— (2003b), 'Should the State Fund Faith Based Schools?: A Review of the Arguments', *British Journal of Religious Education*, vol. 25, no. 2. pp. 89–102.

Jackson, R. and Nesbitt, E. (1993), *Hindu Children*, Stoke-on-Trent: Trentham Books Ltd.

—— (2000), *Sikh Children in Coventry*, Leeds: Community Religions project, Everington.

Jeffcoate, R. (1981), 'Why Multicultural Education?', *Education, 3–13*, vol. 9, no. 1, pp. 4–7.

Joly, D. (1989), *Muslims in Europe, Ethnic Minorities and Education in Britain: interaction between the Muslim community and Birmingham schools*, Research Papers No. 41, Centre for the Study of islam and Christian–Muslim Relations, Selly Oak Colleges, Birmingham B29 6LE.

Judge, H. (2001), 'Faith-based schools and state funding: a partial view', *Oxford Review of Education*, vol. 27, no. 4, pp. 463–74.

—— (2002), *Faith-based Schools and the State :Catholics in America, France and England*, Oxford: Symposium Books.

Kallistos, W. (1995), *The Orthodox Way*, London: St Vladimir's Seminary Press.

Kalsi, S. S. (1992), *The Evolution of the Sikh Community in Britain: Religious and Social Change among the Sikhs of Leeds and Bradford*, Leeds Community Religions Project, University of Leeds.

Kanitkar, H. and Jackson, R. (1982), *Hindus in Britain*, London: School of Oriental and African Studies.

Kapitzke, C. (1995), *Literacy and Religion: the textual politics and practice of Seventh Day Adventism*, Amsterdam: John Benjamins.

Kay, W. and Francis, L. (eds) (1998), *Religion in Education, volume 2*, London: Fowler Wright.

Kay, W. K. and Linnet Smith, d. (2000), 'Religious Terms and Attitudes in the Classroom', Part 1. *British Journal of Religious Education*, vol. 22, no. 2, pp. 81–9.

Keiner, J. (1996), 'Opening up Jewish Education to Inspection: the impact of the Ofsted Inspection System in England', *Education Policy Analysis Archives*, vol. 4, no. 5 (electronic joournal).

Kelly, A. V. (1986), *Knowledge and curriculum planning*, London: Harper and Row.

Kelly, P. (1986), *Catholic Schools*, Salford: Salford Diocese.

Kelley-Laine, K. (1998), 'Parents as partners in schooling: the current state of affairs', *Childhood Education*, vol. 74, no. 6, pp. 342–5.

Keogh, B. K., Gallimore, R. and Weisner, T. I. (1997), 'A sociological perspective on learning and learning disabilities', *Learning Disabilities Research and Practice*, vol. 12, no. 2, pp. 107–13.

Kerr, D. (2003), 'Citizenship: local, national and international, in L. Gearon (ed.), *Learning to Teach Citizenship in the Secondary School*, London: Routledge/Falmer.

Kerr, H. T. (1999), 'Spiritual Discipline', *Theology Today*, vol. 49, no. 4.

Khan-Cheema, M. A. (1996), 'Muslim and religious education in state schools', paper presented at the National Muslim Education Council Conference, London: UMO.

Kincheloe, J. L. and Steinberg, S. R. (1997), *Changing Multiculturalism*, Buckingham: Open University Press.

King, U. (1984), *A Report on Hinduism in Britain*, Community Religions Project Research Papers, Leeds: Leeds University Press.

King, V. (1989), 'Support Teaching', *Special Children*, vol. 33, pp. 1–4.

Kirby, M., Kidd, W., Koubel, F., Barter, J., Hope, T., Kirtan, A., Madry, N., Manning, P. and Trigg, S. (1997), *Sociology in Perspective*, Oxford: Heinemann Educational Publishers.

Klein, I. (1979), *A Guide to Jewish Religious Practice*, New York: JTS.

Klein, J. (2001), *Citizens by Right: Citizenship Education in Primary Schools*, Stoke-on-Trent: Trentham Books.

Knott, K. (1986), *Hinduism in Leeds: a Study of Religious Practice in the Indian Hindu Community and in Hindu-Related Groups*, Community Religious Project Monograph, Leeds: University of Leeds.

—— (2000), 'Hinduism in Britain', in J. Hinnells (ed.), *The South Asian Religious Diaspora in Britain, Canada and the United States*, Albany, NY: State University of New York Press.

Kotsoni, K. (1990), *The Greek Orthodox Community in Leeds*, Community Religious Project Monograph, Leeds: University of Leeds.

Kuper, A. and Kuper, J. (1985), *The Social Science Encyclopaedia*, London: Routledge and Kegan Paul.

Labour Party (1989), *Multicultural Education: Labour's Policy for Schools*, The Labour Party, 150 Walworth Road, London SE17 1JT.

—— (1997), *Building the Future Together: Labour's policies for partnership*, London: LP.

Lankshear, D. W. (1996), *Churches Serving Schools*, London: The National Society.

—— (2000), *Governing and Managing Church Schools*, London National Society.

—— (2001), 'The relationship between church schools and local church life dinstinguishing between aided and controlled status', *Educational Studies*, vol. 27, no. 4, December, pp. 425–38.

—— (2002), *Churches Serving Schools*, London: The National Society.

—— (2003), 'What about Church Schools?', http://www.churchschools.co.uk/
subscribers/churches.Q5/06/0302

Larsen, T. (1999), *Friends of Religious Equality: Nonconformist Politics in Mid-Victorian England*, London: Boydell Press.

Law, J., Lindsay, G., Peacey, N., Gascoigne, M. and Soloff, N. (2000), *Provision for children with speech and language needs in england and Wales: facilitating communication between education and health services*, London: DfEE.

Lawton, C. (2000), 'Purim spiels and peace deals', *London Jewish News*, 17 March.

Lawton, D. (1980), *The Politics of the School Curriculum*, London: Routledge and Kegan Paul.

Leeman, Y. and Volman, M. (2001), 'Inclusive Education: recipe book or quest? On diversity in the classroom and educational research', *International Journal of Inclusive Education*. vol. 5, no. 4, pp. 367–79.

Leicester, M. C. (1989), *Multicultural Education: from Theory to Practice*, Windsor: NFER-Nelson.

Leicester Islamic Academy (2003), *Quality Education for a Quality of Life and Success*, Leicester Rd, Leicester LEZ 2PJ.

—— *School Prospectus (2003–2004)*. London Road, Leicester: LIA.

Leo Baeck College – Centre for Jewish Education (1998), *Focusing on Judaism (the Kesher Project Group)*, London: Leo Baeck College.

Lepkowska, D. (1998), 'Muslims gain funding', *Times Educational Supplement*, 16 January, p. 18.

Levin, L. (2002), 'Through the Looking Glass: Religion, Identity and Citizenship in a Plural Culture, from the Viewpoint of the Modern Orthodox Jewish School', paper presented at the conference Faith Schools: Conflict or Consensus: A National Conference, Institute of Education, University of London, 27–28 June.

Lewis, B. and Schnapper, D. (1994), *Muslims in Europe*, London: Pinter Publishers.

Lewis, P. (1994), *Islamic Britain: religion, politics and identity among British Muslims*, London: I B Tauris.

Lipner, J. (2000), 'Lowering the drawbridge: are Hinduism and Christianity compatible?', in M. Forward, S. Plant, J. White and S. White (eds), *A Great Commission*, London: Peter Lang.

Locke, G. (2001), 'Church Schools', *Light and Salt: The Care Review*, vol. 9, no. 1, http://www.care.org.uk/resources/Is/ Is070601.htm

London Development Education Centre (2002), *Undermining Education: New Labour and Single Faith Schools*, London: LONDEC.

Longmore, J., Naylor, A. and Eaton, M. (2000), *Commitment to Diversity: Catholics and the Changing World*, London: Continuum International Publishing Group.

Lustig, R. (1990), 'Fath Schools Hope for More Charity', *The Independent*, 17 March, p. 5.

Lynch, J. (1988), *Prejudice Reduction and Schools*, London: Cassell.

Mabud, S. A. (1992), 'A Muslim Response to the Education Reform Act of 1988', *British Journal of Religious Education*, vol. 14, pp. 88–98.

Macdonald, I., Bhavani, T., Khan, L. and John, G. (1989), *Murder in the Playground: The Report of the Macdonald Inquiry into Racism and Racial Violence in Manchester Schools*, London: Longsight Press.

Macpherson, W. (1999), *Inquiry into the Circumstances Leading to the Death of Stephen Lawrence*, London: HMSO.

Mahalingham, R. and McCarthy, C. (2000), 'Rethinking Multiculturalism and Curricular Knowledge for the Twenty-first Century', in R. Mahalingham and C. McCarthy (eds), *Multicultural Curriculum: New Directions for Social Theory, Policy and Practice*, New York: Routledge.

Manchester Islamic High School, *School Prospectus 2003–2004*, 10 Strathmore Avenue, Denton, Chorton-cum-Hardy, Manchester M34 7TT.

Mansell, J. and Slater, J. (2002), 'Faith law will press inclusion on schools', *Times Educational Supplement*, 3 May, p. 3.

Mansell, W. and Barnard, N. (2001), 'Faith schools opposition multiplies', *Times Educational Supplement*, 5 October, p. 1.

Marks, J. (2001), 'Standards in Church of England, RC and LEA Schools in England', in J. Burn, J. Marks, J. Pilkington and P. Thompson (eds), *Faith in Education*, London: Civitas.

Marmur, D. (1994), *On Being a Jew*, Toronto: Holy Blossom.

Marzec, J. (1988), *The Role of the Polish Catholic Church in the Polish Community of the UK: a case study in ethnic identity and religion*, Community Religions Project Research Papers, Leeds: Leeds University Press.

Massey, I. (1991), *More than Skin Deep*, London: Hodder and Stoughton.

Mavrogordatoson, G. T. (2003), 'Orthodoxy and Nationalism in the Greek Case', *West European Politics*, January, vol. 26, no. 1, pp. 117–36.

Mayall, Berry (2002), *Towards a Sociology for Childhood: thinking from children's lives*, Buckingham: Open University Press.

McCartney, E. (1999), 'Barriers to collaboration: an analysis of systematic barriers to collaboration between teachers and speech and language therapists', *International Journal of Language and Communication Disorders*, vol. 34, no. 4, pp. 431–40.

McGee, P. (1992), *Teaching Transcultural Care*, London: Chapman and Hall.

McGlynn, C. (2003), 'Education for Peace in Integrated Schools: A Priority for Northern Ireland?', paper presented to the Annual Conference of the European Educational Research Association, 17–20 September.

McLaughlin, T. (1996), 'The Dinstiveness of Catholic Education', in T. McLaughlin, J. O'Keefe and B. O'Keefe (eds), *The Contemporary Catholic School: Context and Identity*, London: Falmer Press.

Menter, I., Muschamp, P., Nichools, P., Ozga, J. and Pollard, A. (1997), *Work and Identity in the Primary School*, Philadelphia: Open University Press.

Mercer, N., Wegeriff, R. and Dawes, L. (1999), 'Children's talk and the development of reasoning in the classroom', *British Educational Research Journal*, vol. 25, no. 1, pp. 95–111.

Midgeley, S. (1989), 'Muslims turn to separate schools to preserve Islamic faith', *The Independent*, 20 January, p. 9.

Miller, H. (2001), 'Meeting the Challenges: the Jewish schooling phenomenon in the UK', *Oxford Review of Education*, vol. 27, no. 4, pp. 501–13.

Miller, H. and Shire, M. J. (2002), *Jewish Schools – A Value Added Contribution to Faith Based Education*, London: Leo Baeck Centre College for Jewish Education, 80 East End Road, Finchley, London N3 2SY.

Milner, D. (1983), *Children and Race Ten Years On*, London: Ward, Lock.

Mirza, M. (1998), 'Same voices, same lives?: revisiting black feminist standpoint epistemology', in Connolly, P. and Troyna B. (eds), *Researching Racism in Education: Politics, Theory and Practice*, Buckingham: Open University Press.

Modood, T. (1989), 'Religious anger and minority rights', *Political Quaarterly*, July, pp. 280–84.

—— (1992), *Not Easy Being British: Colour, Culture and Citizenship*, Stoke-on-Trent, Trentham Books.

—— (2003), 'Muslims and European Multiculturalism', *Open Democracy*, vol. 15, no. 5, %20multicult.htm

Modood, T. and Werbner, P. (1997), *The Politics of Multiculturalism in the new Europe racism, idientity and community*, London: Zed Books.

Modood, T., Berthoud, R., Lakey, J., Nazroo, J., Smith, P., Virdee, S. and Beishon, S. (1997), *Ethnic Minorities in Britain: Diversity and Disadvantage*, London: Policy Studies Institute.

Morris A. B. (1994), 'The Academic Performance of Catholic Schools', *School Organisation*, vol. 14, no. 1, pp. 81–9.

Mortimore, P., Sammons, P. and Ecob, R. (1988), *School Matters: The Junior Years*, Salisbury: Open Books.

Mukadam, M. H. (1998), 'Spiritual and Moral Education of Muslim Children in State Schools', unpublished Ph.D., Birmingham University.

Mullard, C. (1981), *Racism, Society and Schools*, London: University of London.

Murphy, R. L. J. (1982), 'Sex differences in objective test performance', *British Journal of Educational Psychology*, vol. 52, pp. 231–9.

Mustafa, B. (1999), 'Education for integration: case study of a British Muslim High School for Girls, *Journal of Muslim Minority Affairs*, vol. 19, pp. 291–8.

—— (2001), 'Public Education and Muslim Voluntary Organisations in Britain', *Westminster Studies in Education*, vol. 24, no. 2, pp. 129–35.

NALDIC Working Group (1998), *Provision in Literacy Hours for Pupils Learning English as an Additional Language*, Watford: NALDIC.

National Curriculum Council (1989), *Consultative Report on Technology*, London: DFES.

224   *Bibliography*

—— (2000), *The national Curriculum*, London: DFES.

National Foundation for Educational Research (2002), *The LEA Role in Data Collection, Analysis and Use and its Impact on Pupil Performance*, London: NFER.

National Secular Society (2002), 'Paper for the Institute of Education Faith Schools Conference', www.secularism.org.uk

—— (2004), www.secularism.org.uk

National Society (2003a), *Governing and Managing Church Schools*, London: National Society.

—— (2003b), 'Latest News', Church House, Great Smith Street, London, SW1P 3NZ, www.natsoc.org.uk

National Statistics Online-Census 2001-Profiles-UK, http://www.statistics.gov.uk/census2001/profiles/uk.asp

National Union of Teachers (1984), *Religious Education in a Multi-Faith Society: A Discussion Paper*, London: NUT.

Nehaul, K. (1996), *The Schooling of Children of Caribbean Heritage*, Stoke-on-Trent, Trentham Books.

Nelson, N. W. (1987), *Introduction to Islam and Religious Education in England*, Research Papers No. 3, Centre for the Study of Islam and Christian–Muslim Relations, Selly Oak Colleges, Birmingham B29 6LE.

—— (1992), 'Targets of curriculum-based language assessment', in W. A. Second and J. S. Damico (eds), *Best Practices in School Speech-Language Pathology*, Austin, TX: The Psychological Corporation.

Nesbitt, E. (1994), 'Valmikis in Coventry: The Revival and Reconstruction of a Community', in R. Ballard (ed.), *Desh Pardesh: The Asian Presence in Britain, The Religious Lives of Sikh Children*, London: Hurst and Co.

—— (2000), *The Religious Lives of Sikh Children*, Monograph Series, Leeds: Leeds Community Religions Project, University of Leeds.

Nesbitt, E. and Henderson, A. (2003), 'Religious organisations in the UK and Values Education Programmes for Schools', *Journal of Religious Beliefs*, vol. 24, no. 1, pp. 75–88.

Nesbitt, E. and Kaur, G. (1999), *Guru Nanak*, Norwich: Canterbury Press.

Nielsen, J. S. (1987), *Introduction to Islam and Religious Education in England*, Europe Research Papers, No. 3, Centre for the Study of Islam and Christian–Muslim Relations, Selly Oak Colleges, Birmingham B29 9LE.

—— (1989) 'Muslims in English Schools', *Journal of Muslim Minority Affairs*, vol. 10, no. 1, pp. 223–45.

—— (1995), *Muslims in Europe*, Edinburgh: Edinburgh University Press.

Nottingham Diocese (2002), *Guidelines for Section 23 Inspections in the Catholic Schools of the Diocese*, Nottingham: Nottingham Diocese.

Nottingham Evening Post (2003), 'Muslim kids doing well', 10 July, p. 23.

Nottingham Islamia School, *School Prospectus (2003–2004)*, Bentinck Road, Nottingham.

O'Cuanachain, C. (2003), 'Human Rights in an Irish Primary School, paper presented to the Annual Conference of the European Educational Research Association, 17-20 September.

O'Hear, P. (1994), 'An alternative national curriculum', in S. Tomlinson (ed.), *Educational Reform and its Consequences*, London: IPPR/Rivers Oram.

O'Keefe, B. (1999), 'Reordering Perspectives in Catholic Schools', in M. Hornsby-Smith (ed.), *Catholics in England 1950–2000*, London: Cassell.

—— (2000), 'Fidelity and Openness: A Christian Response to Pluralism', *International Journal of Education and Religion*, vol. 1, pp. 122–34.

O'Keefe, J. (1997), 'The Changing Role of Catholic Schools in England and Wales: From Exclusiveness to Engagement', in J. McMahon et al. (eds), *Leading the Catholic School*, Victoria NSW: Spectrum Publications.

O'Sullivan, D. (1996), 'Cultural Exclusion and Educational Change: Education, Church and Religion in the Irish Republic', *Compare*, vol. 26, no. 1, pp. 35–49.

Oberoi, H. (19994), *The Construction of Religious Boundaries*, Oxford: Oxford University Press.

Ofsted (1996), *Recent Reseaarch on the Achievements of Ethnic Minority Pupils*, London: HMSO.

—— (1999), *Raising the Attainment of Minority Ethnic Children: School and LEA responses*, London: Ofsted.

—— (2002a), *The Achievement of Black Caribbean Pupils: Good Practice in Primary Schools*, London: HMSO.

—— (2002b), *The Achievement of Black Caribbean Pupils: Good Practice in Secondary Schools*, London: HMSO.

—— (2002c), *Ofsted Subject Reports, Primary Religious Education*, London: Ofsted.

—— (2002d), *Ofsted Subject Reports, Secondary Religious Education*, London: Ofsted.

Ofsted Report (2003a), *Guru Nanak School*, London: HMI.

—— (2003b), *St Cyprian's Greek Orthodox School*, London: HMI.

O'Kagaki, L. and Frensch, P. A. (1998), 'Parenting and children's school achievement: a multi-ethnic perspective', *American Educational Research Journal*, vol. 35, no. 1, pp. 123-44.

Osler, A. (2002), 'The Crick Report and the future of multi-ethnic Britain', in L. Gearon (ed.), *Learning to Teach Citizenship in the Secondary School*, London: Routledge.

Osler, A. and Hussain, Z. (1995), 'Parental Choice and Schooling: some factors influencing Muslim mothers' decisions about the education of their daughters', *Cambridge Journal of Education*, vol. 25, no. 3, pp. 327–47.

Osler, A. and Starkey, H. (2003), 'Learning for Cosmopolitan Citizenship: theoretical debates and young people's experiences', *Educational Review*, vol. 55, no. 3, pp. 243–54.

Osler, A. and Vincent, K. (2002), *Citizenship and the Challenge of Global Education*, Stoke-on-Trent, Trentham Books.

Ouseley Report (2001), *Community Pride and Prejudice: Making Diversity Work in Bradford*, Bradford: Bradford City Council.

Parekh, Bhihu (2000), *Rethinking Multiculturalism: Cultural Diversity and Political Theory*, Basingstoke: Macmillan Press.

Parker-Jenkins, M. (1985), 'Rights in Conflict: The Case of Margaret Caldwell', *Canadian Journal of Education*, vol. 10, no. 1, pp. 66–76.

—— (1990), 'Accommodating Muslim Needs', *Canadian School Executive*, vol. 10, no. 5, pp. 13-19.

—— (1991), 'Muslim Matters: An Exploration of the Educational Needs of the Muslim Child', *New Community Journal of Research and Policy of Ethnic Relations*, July, pp. 569–82.

—— (1992), 'The Educational Needs of Muslim Children in Contemporary Britain', *American Journal of Islamic Social Sciences*, vol. 9, no. 3, pp. 351–69.

—— (1993), *Social Justice: Educating Muslim Children*, 2nd edn, Nottingham: School of Education, University of Nottingham.

—— (1995), *Children of Islam: A Teachers' Guide to Meeting the Educational Needs of Muslim Children*, Stoke-on-Trent: Trentham Books.

—— (1996), 'Muslims Down Under Come into Mainstream Funding', *Times Educational Supplement*, 19 January, p. 13.

—— (1998), 'UK: State Funding for Muslim Schools', *International Directions in Education*, May, p. 4.

—— (1999a), 'No Comfort for Caners in Court', *Times Educational Supplement*, 10 September, p. 21.

—— (1999b), *Sparing the Rod: Schools, Discipline and Children's Rights*, Stoke-on-Trent: Trentham Books.

—— (2002), 'Equal Access to State Funding: The Case of Muslim Schools', *Race, Ethnicity and Education*, vol. 5, no. 3, pp. 273–89.

—— (2004), 'The Legal Framework for Faith-based Schools and the Rights of the Child', in R. Gardiner (ed.), *Faith Schools: Conflict or Consensus*, London: Routledge (forthcoming).

Parker-Jenkins, M. and Hartas, D. (2000), 'Child Rearing Practices: A Cross Cultural Perspective', in A. A. Hosin (ed.), *Issues in Applied Developmental Psychology and Child Psychiatry*, Lampeter, Wales: Edwin Mellen Press.

Parker-Jenkins, M. and Haw, K. (1996), 'Equality Within Islam Not Without It: The Perspectives of Muslim Girls', *Muslim Educational Quarterly*, no. 3, pp. 17–34.

—— (1997), 'The Education of Muslim Children in Britain: Accommodation or Neglect?', in S. Vertovec (ed.), *Muslims, Europeans, Youth: Reproducing Religious and Ethnic Cultures*, London: Macmillan.

Parker-Jenkins, M., Haw, K. F. and Irving, B. A. (1998a), 'Bringing Muslim Schools Into The Mainstream', *Discernment*, vol. 4, no. 3, pp. 34–8.

—— (1998b), 'Career, Culture and Closing Doors', *The Experience of Muslim Women in Britain*, paper presented at the British Association of Educational Research Conference, Belfast, August 1998.

Parker-Jenkins, M., Hartas, D., Irving, B. and Barker, V. (2002), 'Choice and Opportunity: Supporting Muslim Girls' Career Aspirations', in H. Jawad and T. Benn (eds), *Muslim Women in the UK and Beyond: Experiences and Images*, Leiden-Boston: Brill.

Parsons, G. (1993), *The Growth of Religious Diversity: Britain from 1945*, vol. 1: *Traditions*, London: Routledge.

Passmore, B. and Barnard, N. (2001), 'Voters oppose expansion of faith schools', *Times Educational Supplement*, 30 November, p. 1.

Paterson, L. (2000), 'Catholic Education and Scottish Democracy', *Journal of Education and Christian Beliefs*, vol. 4, no. 1, pp. 37–49.

Peters, J. E. (2001), 'The Old Order Mennonites: Application of Family Life Cycle Stages', in C. D. H. Harvey (ed.), *Maintaining our Differences: Minority families in multicultural societies*, Aldershot: Ashgate.

Pittau, G. (2000), 'Education on the Threshold of the Third Millennium: Challenges, Mission and Adventure', *Catholic Education*, vol. 4, no. 2, pp. 139–52.

Popper, K. (1945), *The Open Society and its Enemies, vol. 1*, London: Routledge and Kegan Paul.

Poyntz, C. and Walford, G. (1994), 'The New Christian School: A Survey', *Educational Studies*, vol. 20, no. 1, pp. 127–43.

QCA (1999), *National Curriculum Review: Developing the School Curriculum*, London: QCA.

—— (2000), *The National Curriculum: Revised 2000*, London: QCA.

—— (2003), *A Non-Statutory Framework for Religious Education: Report of a Feasibility Study*, London: QCA.

Qureshi, S. and Khan J. (1989), *The Politics of Satanic Versus: Unmasking Western Attitudes*, Leicester: Muslim Communities Studies Institute.

Race Relations (Amendment) Act (2000), London: The Stationery Office Ltd., www.hmso.gov.uk./acts/acts2000/200000/34.htm

Rafferty, F. (1991), 'Muslim Boarding Schools Planned', *Times Educational Supplement*, 6 December, p. 5.

Rampton Committee (1981), *West Indian Children in Our Schools*, Cmnd 8263, London HMSO.

Rattansi, A. (1992), 'Changing the Subject? Racism and Education', in J. Donald and A. Rattansi (eds), *Race, Culture and Difference*, London: Sage Publications.

Raza, M. S. (1993), *Islam in Britain: Past, Present and Future*, 2nd edn, Loughborough: Volcano Press Ltd.

Rendel, M. (1997), *Whose Human Rights?*, Stoke-on-Trent: Trentham books.

Reynolds, M. C. (1989), 'An historical perspective: the delivery of special education to mildly disabled and at-risk students', *Remedial and Special Education*, vol. 10, no. 6, pp. 7–11.

Rex, J. (1993), *Religion and Ethnicity in the Metropolis*, Kampen: Kok Pharos.

Riddell, S., Baron, S. and Wilson, A. (2001), *The Learning Society and People with Learning Difficulties*, Bristol: Policy Press.

Riley, K. (1994), *Quality and Equality: promoting opportunities in schools*, London: Cassell.

Rizvi, F. and Christensen, C. (eds) (1996), *In Disability and the Dilemmas of Education and Justice*, Buckingham: Open University Press.

Roberts, G. and Williams, C. (2003), *Welsh Medium Education*, Bangor: University of Wales.

Robertson, A. H. (1982), *Human Rights in the World: An Introduction to the Study of the International Protection of Human Rights*, 2nd edn, Manchester: Manchester University Press.

Robertson, R. and Chirico, J. (1985), 'Humanity, Globalization and Worldwide Religious Resurgence: A Theoretical Exploration', *Sociological Analysis*, vol. 46, no. 3, pp. 219–42.

Robinson, F. (1988), *Varieties of South Asian Islam*, Research Paper No. 8, Centre for Ethnic Relations: Warwick University.

Robson, A. (1989), 'Special needs and special educational needs', unpublished paper, London: Inner London Education Authority.

Rocker, S. (2000), 'Jewish Schools on an Unstoppable Roll', *Jewish Chronicle,* 15 December.

Romain, J. (1985), *The Jews of England*, London: Michael Goulston Educational Foundation.

Rouse, M. and Florian, L. (1996), *School Reform and Special Educational Needs: Anglo-American Perspectives*, Cambridge: University of Cambridge, Institute of Education.

Rowe, D. (1992), 'The Citizen as a Moral Agent – the Development of a Continuous and Progressive Conflict-based Citizenship Curriculum', *Curriculum*, vol. 13, no. 3, pp, 23–36.

Runnymede Trust (1997), *Islamophobia: a challenge for us all*, London: Runnymede Trust.

Sacks, J. (1994), *Will We Have Jewish Grandchildren?*, London: Valentine Mitchell.

—— (2002), *Dignity of Difference*, London: Continuum.

Saeed, A. and Akbarzadeh, S. (2001) *Muslim Communities in Australia*, Sydney: University of New South Wales Press.

Said, E. (1978), *Orientalism: Western Perceptions of the Orient*, London: Penguin.

—— (1993), *Culture and Imperialism*, London: Chatto and Windus.

Sawar, G. (1983), *Muslims and Education in Britain*, London: Muslim Educational Trust, 130 Stroud Green Street, London N4 3AZ.

—— (1989), *Sex Education: The Muslim Perspective* London: Muslim Educational Trust.

—— (1992), *Islam Beliefs and Teachings*, 4th edn, London: Muslim Educational Trust.

—— (1994), *British Muslims and Schools*, London: Muslim Educational Trust.

Scarfe, J. (2001), 'Primary School Music: The Case of British Punjabi Muslims', unpublished Ph.D. dissertation, University of Derby.

Scarman, L. G. (1981), *Reports on the Inquiry into the Brixton Disorders*, Cmnd 8427, London: HMSO.

Schagen, S., Davies, D., Rudd, P. and Schagen, I. (2002), *The Impact of Specialist and Faith Schools on Performance*, Slough: NFER.

Schiff, A. (1966), *The Jewish Day School in America*, New York: Jewish Education Committee Press.

—— (1988), *Jewish Supplementary Schooling: an educational system in need of change*, New York: Board of Jewish Education.

Schlesinger, E, (2003), *Creating Community and Accumulating Social Capital: Jews associating with other Jews in Manchester*, London: Institute for Jewish Policy Research.

Schmool, M. and Cohen, F. (1998), *A Profile of British Jewry: patterns and trends at the turn of the century*, London: Board of Deputies of British Jews.

Scholefield, L. (2001), 'The Spiritual, Moral, Social and Cultural Values of Students in a Jewish and a Catholic Secondary School', *International Journal of Children's Spirituality*, vol. 6, pt 1, pp. 41–53.

Sebba, J. (1993), 'Implementing the national curriculum in special schools: how might the Dearing review help?' *Education Review*, vol. 7, no. 2, pp. 21–4.

Sewell, T. (1996), *Black Masculinities and Schooling*, Stoke-on-Trent: Trentham Books.

Shackle, C., Singh, G. and Mandair, A. S. (eds) (2001), *Sikh Religion, Culture and Ethnicity*, Richmond, Surrey: Curzon Press.

Sherkat, D. E. (2001), 'That they be Keepers of the Home: the Effect of Conservative Religion on Early and Late Transitions into Housewifery', in C. D. H. Harvey (ed.), (2001), *Maintaining our Differences: Minority families in multicultural societies*, Aldershot: Ashgate Publishing Ltd.

Short, G. (2003), 'Faith Schools and Social Cohesion: Opening up the Debate', *British Journal of Religious Education*, vol. 25, no. 2, Spring, pp. 129–41.

Short, G. and Lenga, R. A. (2002), 'Jewish primary Schools in a Multicultural Society and Responding to Diversity', *Journal of Beliefs and Values*, vol. 23, no. 1, pp. 43–54.

Shulman, L. (1987), 'Knowledge and teaching: Foundations of the new reform', *Harvard Educational Review*, vol. 63, pp. 161–82.

Simpson, M. (1997), 'Developing differentiation practices: meeting the needs of pupils and teachers', *The Curriculum Journal*, vol. 8, no. 1, pp. 85–104.

Simpson, P. (1992), 'Governors in Church of England Voluntary Aided Primary Schools', *Education Today*, vol. 43, no. 3, pp. 26–32.

Singh, B. (2000), 'Further attempts to balance liberal views with claims for cultural identity within traditional non-liberal communities: A reply to Neil Burtonwood', *Educational Studies*, vol. 26, pp. 213–28.

Siraj-Blatchford, I. and Siraj-Blatchford, J. (1999), ' "Race", Research and Reform: the impact of the three Rs on anti-racist pre-school and primary education in the UK', *Race, Ethnicity and Education*, vol. 2, no. 1, pp. 127–48.

Slee, R. (2001), *The Inclusive School*, London: Falmer.

Smart, N, (1964), *The Teacher and Religious Belief*, Edinburgh: James Clarke.

—— (1968), *Secular Education and the Logic of Religion*, London: Faber and Faber.

—— (1971), *The Religious Experience of Mankind*, London: Fontana.

Smith, A. B. (2000a), 'Children's Rights: An overview', in A. B. Smith, M. Gollop, K. Marshall and K. Nairn (eds), *Advocating for Children: International Perspectives on Children's Rights*, Otago: University of Otago Press, pp. 13–18.

Smith, A. (2001), 'Religious Segregation and the Emergence of Integrated Schools in Northern Ireland', *Oxford Review of Education*, vol. 27, no. 4, pp. 559–74.

Smith, W. C. (1978), *The Meaning and End of Religion*, London: SPCK.

Smooha, S. (1985), 'Ethnic Groups', in A. Kruper and J. Kruper (eds), *The Social Science Encyclopaedia*, London: Routledge and Kegan Paul.

Solomos, J. (1993), *Race and Racism in Britain*, 2nd edn, Basingstoke: Macmillan Press.

Solomos, J. and Back, L. (1996), *Racism and Society*, Basingstoke: Macmillan Press.

Sondhi, R. (1998), 'Diversity and equality', in *Connections*, Spring, pp. 10–11.

Stannard, O. (2001), 'A statement from the Catholic Education Service on the Expansion of Faith Schools as Proposed in the Education Bill', 26 November, Catholic Education Service: http://www.cesew.org.uk/news/index.htm

Starkey, H. (2000), 'Citizenship Education in France and Britain: evolving theories and practices', *The Curriculum Journal*, vol. 11, no. 1, pp. 39–54.

St Cyprian's Greek Orthodox Primary Voluntary Aided School, *School Prospectus (2003–2004)*, Springfield Road, Thornton Heath, Surrey CTZ 8DZ.

The Sunday Telegraph (2002), 'How did it all begin then, Sir?', 24 March, p. 16.

The Sunday Times (2002b), 'Oh me of little faith', 14 April, p. 11.

—— (2002c), 'Primaries get go-ahead to embrace Islam', 19 May, p. 8.

—— (2002d), 'Atheists in legal fight for God slot', 15 December, p. 7.

—— (2003a), 'Girl in headscarf goes central stage in Dutch election', 19 January, World News, p. 28.

—— (2003b), 'Kabbalah-lite', 26 January, News Review, p. 5.

—— (2003c), 'And now, a little local jihad', 26 January, News Review, p. 9.

Sunier, T. and van Kuuijeren, M. (2002), 'Islam in the Netherlands', in Y. Y. Haddad (ed.), *Muslims in the West: from sojourners to citizens*, Oxford: Open University Press.

Swaminarayan Secondary School, *School Prospectus (2002–2003)*, 260 Brentfield Road, Neasden, London LNW10 8HE.

Swann, M. (1985), *Education for All: A Summary of the Swann Report on the Education of Ethnic Minority Children*, Windsor: National Foundation for Educational Research-Nelson.

Taafaki, I. J. (2000), 'Cultural Rights: A curriculum and pedagogy for praxis', in M. Wilson, and P. Hunt (eds), *Culture, Rights and Human Rights: Perspectives from the South Pacific*, Wellington: Huia Publishers.

Talcott, G. (2000), *The Context and Risk of Organised Illegal Immigration to New Zealand*, Centre for Strategic Studies Working Paper 15/00, Wellingon: Victoria University of Wellington.

Tatla, D. S. (1999), *The Sikh Diaspora: The Search for Statehood*, London: University College Press.

Taylor, P., Richardson, J., Yeo, A., Marsh I., Trobe, K., Pilkington, A., Hughes, G. and Sharp, K. (2002), *Sociology in Focus*, Ormskirk, Lancashire: Causeway Press.

Taylor, S. and Hegarty, S. (1985), *The Best of Both Worlds ...? A Review of Research into the Education of Pupils of South Asian Origin*, Windsor: NFER-Nelson.

Teacher Training Agency (1998), *Initial Teacher Training National Curriculum for Primary Science* (annex E of DfEE circular 4/98), London: TTA.

—— (2002), *Qualifying Teacher Status*, London: TTA.

Thomas, G. (1997), 'Inclusive schools for an inclusive society', *British Journal of Special Education*, vol. 24, no. 3, pp. 103–7.

Times Educational Supplement (1997), 'Muslims threaten to desert Labour', 4 July, p. 14.

—— (1998a), 'Muslims gain equality to funding', 16 January, p. 18.

—— (2000), 'Uniquely Sikh', 28 April, pp. 10–13.

—— (2001a), 'Faith bid sparks Commons rebellion', 8 February, p. 6.

—— (2001b), 'Schools accused of racial segregation', 22 June, p. 3.

—— (2001c), 'Is greater diversity healthy?' 3 August, p. 13.

—— (2001d), 'Faith schools' opposition multiplies', 5 October, p. 1.

—— (2001e), 'Jewish faith schools' popularity soars', 5 October, p. 23.

—— (2001f), 'Labour fails to convert the public', Religious School News, 30 November, p. 6.

—— (2001g), 'Faith facts', Religious School News, 30 November, p. 7.

—— (2002a), 'Church seeks to outlaw religious bias', 18 January, p. 7.

—— (2002b), 'Determined to keep the faith', 3 May, p. 27.

—— (2002c), 'The Christian response is to help people', 19 April, p. 9.

—— (2003a), 'Miracle needed to recruit Catholic heads', 10 January, p. 2.

—— (2003b), 'Diversity triumphs in the Dales', 31 January, p. 19.

—— (2003c), 'Rise of covert selection', 7 February, p. 5.

—— (2003d), 'Catholic "Eton" wants the girls', 7 February, p. 10.

—— (2003e), 'Confusion about citizenship', letters page, 18 July, p. 20.

—— (2003f), 'Concern over spy cameras in class', 25 July, p. 3.

—— (2003g), 'Jewish schools fearful of attacks', 1 August, p. 3.

—— (2003h), 'The fake aristocrat who ran a school', 1 August, p. 9.

—— (2003i), 'Unfair fare deal', letters page, 1 August, p. 14.

—— (2003j), 'Academies of excellence', 12 September, p. 5.

—— (2003k), 'City academies target rich pupils, says union', 10 October, p. 16.

—— (2003l), 'Too many admissions obstacles', 17 October, p. 26.

—— (2003m), 'School crucifix banned in latest protest from Muslim minority', 31 October, p. 2.

Times Higher Educational Supplement (2000), 'Midlands Mix of Koran, Kant and Kashmir', 3 August, pp. 18–19.

—— (2001), 'God will not forsake us …', 14 December, pp. 30–31.

Tomlinson, S. (1984), *Home and School in Multicultural Britain*, London: Batsford.

—— (1990), *Multicultural Education in White Schools*, London: Batsford.

—— (2000), 'Ethnic minority and education: new disadvantages', in T. Cox (ed.), *Combating Educational Disadvantage: Meeting the Needs of Vulnerable Children*, London: Falmer Press.

Tomlinson, S. (2001), *Education in a post-welfare society*, Buckingham: Open University Press.

Tonnies, F. et al. (2001), *Community and Society*, Cambridge: Cambridge University Press.

Tooley, J. and Howes, A. (1999), *The Seven Habits of Highly Effective Schools*, London: Technology Trust.

Trepp, L. (1980), *The Complete Book of Jewish Observance*, New York: Behrman House.

Tropp, A. (1957), *The School Teachers: The Growth of the Teaching Profession in England and Wales from 1800 to the Present Day*, London: Heinemann.

Troyna, B. (1986), 'Beyond Multiculturalism: towards the enactment of anti-racist education in policy, provision and pedagogy', *Oxford Review of Education*, vol. 13, no. 3, pp. 301–20.

—— (1993), *Racism and Education*, Buckingham: Open University Press.

Troyna, B. and Ball, S. (1987), *Views from the Chalkface*, 2nd edn, Warwick: University of Warwick Press.

Troyna, B. and Carrington, B. (1990), *Education, Racism and Reform*, London: Routledge.

Troyna, B. and Hatcher, R. (1992), *Racism in Children's Lives: A Study of Mainly White Primary Schools*, London: Routledge/National Children's Bureau.

Troyna, B. and Williams, J. (1986), *Racism, Education and the State: the racialisation of education policy*, Beckenham: Croom Helm.

Tucker, J. A. (1980), 'Ethnic proportions in classes for the learning disabled: issues in non-biased assessment', *Journal of Special Needs*, vol. 14, pp. 83–105.

TVNZ (2003), *One News Report*, 22nd April.

United Nations (1989), *Convention on the Rights of the Child*, Geneva: United Nations.

UNESCO (1994), *Salamanca Statement and Framework for Action*, Paris: UNESCO.

Vakatale, T.(2000), 'Multiculturalism vs Indigenous Cultural Rights', in M. Wilson and P. Hunt (eds), *Culture, Rights and Human Rights: Perspectives from the South Pacific*, Wellington: Huia Publishers.

Valins, O., Kosmin, B. and Goldberg, J. (2002), *The Future of Jewish Schooling in the United Kingdom*, London: Institute for Jewish Policy Research.

Valley, C. A. (1995) 'Managing Change in the Seventh Day Adventist Church: an interpretive study of the establishment of the John Loughborough School', unpublished MBA dissertation, Nottingham University.

Van Onderwijs (1999), [Netherlands (Ministerie van Onderwijs)], *Netherlands Educational Institutions*, 's-Gravenhage: Staatsuit geverij.

Vardy Foundation (2003), www.evangelical_times.org/ETNews/.htm

Virani-Ropei, Z. (2001), 'Bilingual Learning and Numeracy', in M. Gravelle (ed.), *Planning for Bilingual Learners: an Inclusive Curriculum*, Stoke-on-Trent: Trentham Books.

Vitello, S. J. and Mithaug, D. E. (1998), *Inclusive Schooling: National and International Perspectives*, Mahawah, NJ: Lawrence Erlbaum Associates.

Wadham, J., Mountfield, H. and Edmundson, A. (2003), *Blackstone's Guide to the Human Rights Act 1998*, 3rd edn, London: Blackstone Press.

Walford, G. (1991), *Private Schooling: Tradition, Change and Diversity*, London: Paul Chapman.

—— (1995a), 'The Christian Schools Campaign – a successful educational pressure group?', *British Educational Research Journal*, vol. 21, no. 4, pp. 245–57.

—— (1995b), *Educational Politics: Pressure Groups and Faith-based Schools*, London: Avebury.

—— (2000), *Policy, Politics and Education: Sponsored Grant-Maintained Schools and Religious Diversity*, Aldershot: Ashgate

—— (2001a), 'Evangelical Christian Schools in England and the Netherlands, *Oxford Review of Education*, vol. 27, no. 4, pp. 529–41.

—— (2001b), 'Funding for Religious Schooling in England and the Netherlands: can the piper call the tune?', *Research Papers in Education*, vol. 16, no. 4, pp. 359–80.

Wang, M. C. and Reynolds, M. C. (1995), *Making a Difference for Students at Risk: Trends and Alternatives*, London: Sage.

Wardle, D. (1976), *English Popular Education 1780–1975*, 2nd edn, London: Cambridge University Press.

Watson, I. J. (1977), *Between Two Cultures: Migrants and Minorities in Britain*, Oxford: Basil Blackwell.

Webber, J. (ed.) (1994), *Jewish Identities in the New Europe*, London: Littman Library of Jewish Civilization.

Weber, M. (1961), *From Max Weber: Essays in Sociology*, London: Routledge and Kegan Paul.

Weiner, G. (1994), *Feminisms in Education: an introduction*, Buckingham: Open University Press.

Weldon, F. (1989), *Sacred Cows*, London: Chatto and Windus.

Weller, P. (ed.) (1997), *Religions in the UK: a Multi-Faith Directory*, Derby: University of Derby/the Inter Faith Network for the UK.

—— (ed.) (2001), *Religions in the UK: Directory 2001–3*, Derby: Derby University/Multi-Faith Centre for the UK.

—— (2003), 'Identity, Politics and the Future(s) of Religion in the UK: The Case of the Religion Questions in the 2001 Decentennial Census', *Journal of Contemporary Religion*, vol. 19, no. 1, pp. 3–21.

Weller, P. et al. (2000), *Religious Discrimination in England and Wales: Interim Report*, London: Home Office.

Weller, P., Feldman, A. and Purdham, K. (2001), *Religious Discrimination in England and Wales*, Research Study 220, London: Home Office.

Werbner, P. (2001), 'The vulnerabilities of the Muslim population in Britain', *Times Higher Educational Supplement*, 14 December, pp. 30–31.

—— (2002a), *The Migrant Process: Capital, Gifts and Offerings Among Manchester Pakistanis*, Oxford: Berg Publishers.

West, A. (2001), 'Choice and Diversity: The Case for Small Specialist Schools', *New Economy*, vol. 8, pp. 208–212.

West, A. and Pennell, H. (2003), *Underachievement in Schools*, London: Routledge.

Westby, C. (1996), 'Assessment of pragmatic competence in children with psychiatric disorders', in D. Rogers-Adkinsoon and P. Griffith (eds), *Communication Disorders and Children with Psychiatric and Behavioural Disorders*, San Diego: Singular Publishing Group.

Western Australian Curriculum Council (1988), *Curriculum Frameworks*, Osborne Park: Western Australian Curriculum Council.

Whitty, G. (1997), 'Creating quasi-markets in education', in M. W. Apple (ed.), *Review of Research in Education 22*, Washington, DC: American Education Research Association.

Wickliffe, C. (2000), 'Culture Rights, Culture and Human Rights Education', in M. Wilson and P. Hunt (eds), *Culture, Rights and Human Rights: Perspectives from the South Pacific*, Wellington: Huia Publishers.

Williams, G. (1991), *The Welsh and their Religion*, Cardiff: University of Wales Press.

Wilson, M. (2000), 'Cultural Rights: Definitions and Contexts', in M. Wilson and P. Hunt (eds), *Culture, Rights and Human Rights: Perspectives from the South Pacific*, Wellington: Huia Publishers.

Wilson, S. and Wineburg, S. S. (1998), 'Peering at history with different lenses: the role of disciplinary perspectives in teaching history', *Teachers College Record*, vol. 89, pp. 525–39.

Wolfendale, S. (1992), *Empowering Parents and Teachers: Working for Children*, London Cassell.

Wolfe, J. (ed.) (1994), *The growth of Religious Diversity: Britain from 1945*, Newcastle: Open University Press.

Wood, A. (1960), *Nineteenth Century Britain*, London: Longmans.

Wood, B. and Tuohy, P. (2000), 'Consent in Child Health: Upholding the participation rights of children and young people', in A. B. Smith, M. Gollop, K. Marshall and K. Nairn (eds), *Advocating for Children: International Perspectives on Children's Rights*, Otago: University of Otago Press.

Wright, A. (1966), 'Language and experience in the hermeneutics of religious understanding', *British Journal of Religious Education*, vol. 18, no. 3, pp. 166–80.

Wright, C. and Weekes, D. (1999), *Improving Practice: a whole school approach to raising the achievement of Asians?*, London: Runnymede Trust.

Wrigley, T. (2002), *The Power to Learn: stories of success in the education of Asian and bilingual pupils*, Stoke-on-Trent: Trentham Books.

Young, I. (1990), *Justice and the Politics of Difference*, Princeton: Princeton University Press.

Yuval-Davis, N. (1992), 'Fundamentalism, Multiculturalism and Women in Britain', in J. Donald and A. Rattansi (eds), *Race, Culture and Difference*, London: Sage Publications.

Zipfel, R. (1996), 'Who do e serve and what do we offer?': Race, equality and Catholic schools', in T. McLaughlin, J. O'Keefe and B. O'Keefe (eds), *The Contemporary Catholic School*, London: Falmer Press.

Websites

www.churchschools.co.uk
www.christianpublications.co.uk/emmanuel
www/Eurokideng.html
www.virtualclassroom.co.uk

Further Reading

Abbas, T. (1997), 'British South Asian Youth: A New Diaspora', *Dialogue*, December, pp. 4–5.

Ahmad, I. (2002), 'Multi-faith plan is a secularist plot', The London School of Islamics Trust', 63 Margery Park Road, London E7 (e-mail article, also placed in *Times Educational Supplement*, 2 August 2002, p. 14).

Anwar, M. (1982), *Young Muslims in a Multicultural Society: Their Needs and Policy Implications*, Leicester. The Islamic Foundation.

Apple, M. W. and Beane, J. A. (1999), 'The case for democratic schools', in M. W. Apple and J. A. Beane (eds), *Democratic Schools*, Buckingham: Open University Press.

Bailey, J. (2002), 'Religious Education in Church Schools', in L. Broadbent and A. Brown (eds), *Issues in Religious Education*, London: Routledge-Falmer.

Barot, R. (ed.) (1993), *Religion and Ethnicity: Minorities and Social Change in the Metropolis*, Kampen, the Netherlands: Kok Pharos Publishing House.

Barrel, G. and Partington, J. (1970), *Legal Cases for Teachers*, London, Methuen.

Baumfield, V. M. (1996), 'Hindu Schools', paper presented at the Hindi Studies Committee Conference, Newcastle.

Bennett, C. (2001), 'Genres of Research in Multicultural Education', *Review of Educational Research*, vol. 71, no. 2, pp. 171–217.

Brown, A. (1994), *The Multifaith Church School*, London: National Society.

—— (1996), 'Science and religion at the chalkface: where it all goes wrong', *Spectrum*, vol. 28, no. 2, Summer, pp. 119–30.

Castles, S. (1984), *Here for Good: Western Europe's New Ethnic Minorities*, London: Pluto.

—— (1998), *The Teeth are Smiling: Persistence of Racism in Multicultural Australia*, London: Allen and Unwin.

—— (2000), *Citizenship and migration*, Basingstoke: Macmillan.

Clogg, R. (ed.) (1999), *The Greek Diaspora in the 20th Century*, Basingstoke: Macmillan.

Cohen, A. (1994), *Frontiers of Identity: the British and Others*, London: Longman.

—— (1996b), *Symbolising Boundaries: Identity and Diversity in Britain*, Manchester: Manchester University Press.

Collective Worship in Schools in England and Wales: Circular 3/98 (1988), 12 February, London: The InterFaith Network for the UK.

Commission for Racial Equality (2002), *A place for us all – Learning from Bradford, Oldham and Burnley*, London: CRE.

Commission on Social Justice (1994), *Social Justice: Strategies for National Renewal*, London: Vintage.

Coutts, J. (1990), *Living the Faith: Sikh Lives*, Harlow: Oliver and Boyd.

Crick, B. (2000b), *Essays on Citizenship*, London: Continuum.

Cummins, J. (1996), *Negotiating Identities: Education for Empowerment in a Diverse Society*, Los Angeles: California Association for Bilingual Education.

Curti, E. (2001), 'A Church School for Muslims', *The Tablet*, vol. 255, no. 8404, 6 October, pp. 1412–13.

Dale, R. (1989), *The State and Education Policy*, Milton Keynes: Open University Press.

Department for Education and Skills (2003c), *Careers Education and Guidance in England: A National Framework 11–19*, London DfES.

Durham, M. (1989), 'The Religious Issues Won't Go Away', *The Guardian*, 4 March, p. 12.

Eaton, M. Longmore, J. and Naylor, A. (2000), *Commitment to Diversity: Catholic Education in a Changing World*, London: Cassell.

El-Droubie, R. (1997), *My Muslim Life*, London: Hodder Wayland.

Engineer, A. (1992), *The Rights of Women in Islam*, London: Hurst and Co.

Fitzgerald, J. (1995), 'English-as-a-second-language learners' cognitive reading processes: A review of research in the United States', *Review of Educational Research*, vol. 32, no. 1, pp. 145–90.

Francis, L. and Lankshear, D. (1991), 'The Impact of Church Schools of Urban Church Life', *School Effectiveness and School Improvement*, vol. 2, no. 4, pp. 324–35.

Franklin, J. (1998), 'Introduction', in J. Franklin (ed.), *Equality*, London: Institute for Public Policy Research.

Gallagher, A. M. (2002), 'Results of the Consultation on the Burns Report', seminar to the Graduate School of Education, Belfast University, December.

Gilroy, P. (2000b), *Without Guarantees: In Honour of Stuart Hall*, New York: Verso.

The Guardian (2001e), 'Loyalty pledge to Britain urged for all cultures', 12 December, p. 4.

—— (2001f), 'Behind the riot lines', 12 December, p. 19.

—— (2002b), 'Writing on the wall for "terror school"', 22 October, p. 3.

—— (2003e), 'French Muslims angry at veil move', 22 April, p. 3.

—— (2003f), 'What does Britain expect'?, 23 September, p. 50.

Hall, S. (2000a), 'From Scarman to Macpherson', *Society*, vol. 3, pp. 8–9.

—— (2000b), 'The multicultural question', Political Economy Research Centre Annual Lecture at www.sheff.ac.uk/uni/academic/N-Q/lectures/htm

Hornsby-Smith, M. P. (1978), *Catholic Education: The Unobtrusive Partner*, London: Sheed and Ward.

—— (ed.) (1999), *Catholics in England 1950–2000: Historical and Sociological Perspectives*, London: Cassell.

Kerr, D. A. (1992), *Religion, State and Ethnic Groups*, Comparative Studies on Governments and Non-Dominant Ethnic Groups in Europe, 1850–1940, vol. 11, Dartmouth: European Science Foundation/New York University Press.

Knott, K. (2000), 'In Every Town and Village', *International Review of Sociology of Religion*, vol. 47, no.2.

Labour Party (2000), *Building on Success*, London: Labour Party.

Liévano, B. M. (2000), 'Intercultural Competencies and Strategies in Guidance: Tools for Intervention in Schools', paper presented at the International Association of Educational and Vocational Guidance conference, Berlin, 31 August.

Lipner, J. (1984), *Hindus: their religious beliefs and practices*, London: Routledge.

McCarthy, C. (ed.), *Multicultural Curriculum: New Directions for Social Theory, Policy and Practice*, New York: Routledge.

McClelland, A. (1992), *The Catholic School and the European Context*, Aspects of Education Journal of the Institute of Education, no. 46, Hull: Hull University of Hull.

McLaughlin, T.(1997), 'Leadership in Catholic Schools: a touchstone for authenticity,' in J. McMahon, H. Niedhart and J. Chapman (eds), *Leading the Catholic School*, Richmond, Victoria: Spectrum Publications.

Mcleod, H. (1997), *Sikhism*, London: Penguin.

—— (2000), *Exploring Sikhism: Aspects of Identity, Culture and Thought*, Oxford: Oxford University Press.

Miller, A. (2002), 'Inside a Muslim School', *The Tablet*, 9 February, p. 16.

O'Keefe, B. (1992), 'Catholic Schools in an Open Society: the English Challenge', in A. McClelland (ed.), *The Catholic School and the European Context*, Aspects of Education Journal of the Institute of Education, no. 46, Hull: University of Hull.

Pettifer, K. (1993), *The Greeks: The Land and the People Since the War*, London: Viking.

Raphael, T. (1991), *The Role of the Church in a Multifaith City*, London: London Diocesan Board for Schools.

Said, E. (1980), *Covering Islam: how the media and the experts determine how we see the rest*, London: RKP.

Sander, W. (1997), 'Catholic Grade Schools and Academic Achievement', *Journal of Human Resources*, vol. 31, pp. 540–48.

Schmool, M. and Cohen, F. (2000), *A Profile of British Jewry: Patterns and Trends at the Turn of the Century*, 2nd edn, London: Board of Deputies of British Jews.

Short, G. (2002), *Responding to Diversity? An Initial Investigation into Multicultural Education in Jewish Schools in the UK*, London: Institute for Jewish Policy Research.

Short, G. and Carrington, B. (1995), 'Learning about Judaism: A Contribution to the Debate on Multi-Faith Religious Education', *British Journal of Religious Education*, vol. 17, pp. 157–67.

Smart, N. (1999), *World Religions*, London: St Mary's Press.

Smith, Z. (2000b), *White Teeth*, London: Penguin Books.

The Sunday Times (2001), 'All aboard Cat's peace train', 11 November, p. 6.

Taylor, D. (1987), 'The Sathya Sai Baba movement in Britain: aims and methods', in P. B. Clarke (ed.), *The New Evangelists: Recruitment, Methods and Aims of New Religious Movements*, London: Ethnographical Press.

Times Educational Supplement (1998b), 'Funding bid for Muslim secondaries, 25 September, p. 14.

—— (1998c), 'Inspectors fail Jewish primary', 25 September, p. 14.

—— (2000h), 'Outrageous timing of faith schools bill', 7 December, p. 8.

—— (2001i), 'The roots of racial conflict', 21 December, p. 19.

—— (2002d), 'Is faith a political football?', 8 February, p. 1.

—— (2002e), 'Faith bid sparks commons rebellion', 8 February, p. 6.

—— (2002f), 'Muslim dad's victory may cause chaos', 1 March, p. 9.

—— (2002g), 'Police beat girls who defy scarf ban' (Turkey), 22 March, p. 24.

—— (2002h), 'Charles wants schools to lead faith campaign', 26 April, p. 1.

—— (2002i), 'Faith law will "press" inclusion', 3 May, p. 3.

—— (2002j), 'Catholics good race news ignored', letters page, 18 July, p. 18.

—— (2002k), 'Muslim scarf banned' (Germany), 19 July, p. 12.

—— (2002l), 'Church loses faith in interview process', 27 September, p. 3.

—— (2002m), 'Dark ages ban on Muslim scarf', 13 December, p. 10.

—— (2004), 'Law bans hijab but permits crucifix' (Germany), 16 January, p. 20.

Times Higher Educational Supplement (2002), 'What it means to be a citizen', 15 February, p. 22.

Werbner, P. (2002b), *Imagined Diasporas Among Manchester Muslims: The Public Performed Performance of Transnational Identity Politics*, Oxford: James Currey Publishers.

—— (2002c), *Pilgrims of Love: The Anthropology of a Global Sufi Cult*, London: C. Hurst and Co Publishers.

Williams, J. D. (1992), 'Pride or Prejudice?: Opportunity structures and the effects of Catholic schools in Scotland', in A. Yogeev (ed.), *International Perspectives on Education and Society, A Research and Policy Annual*, vol. 2, Greenwich, CT: JAJ Press.

Williams, P. J. (1991), *The Alchemy of Race and Rights*, London: Harvard University Press.

Wilson, M. and Hunt, P. (eds) (2001), *Culture Rights and Human Rights: Perspectives from the South Pacific*, Wellington: Huia Publishers.

Wittenberg, J. (2000), 'From Visions to Realities: A Multi-faith School in Living Community', *Journal of the Shape Working Party on World Religions in Education*, pp. 89–90.

Websites

www.muhajabah.com/islamicblog/veiled4allah.php

Index

Anglican: 11, 13, 16, 17, 18, 21, 23, 27, 31, 33, 42, 45, 46, 179, 181, 184, 198
Australia: 7, 24, 48, 76, 80, 83, 98, 125, 175

Bali bombings: 8
board schools: 13, 14, 27, 28, 35

Catholic Church: 21–4, 179
Catholic schools: 1, 2, 11–13, 20–23, 25–7, 32, 35, 42, 43, 45, 47, 81, 96, 100, 104, 105, 109, 133, 139, 181, 200, 203
central reform schools: 19
charity schools: 12
Chedarim schools: 3, 28
Christian – Accelerated Christian Learning: 20
Christianity: 1, 11, 12, 15, 27, 74, 78, 96, 124, 130, 131, 132, 191
Christian ethos: 7, 97
Christian schools: 2, 20, 34, 106, 109, 140
children's rights: 7, 80, 142, 157, 159. 160, 163, 182, 186, 187
Church of England: 12, 16–18, 179
Church of England schools: 1, 2, 12–17, 21, 23, 26, 32, 35, 43, 83, 96, 97, 100, 104, 109, 131, 135, 139, 176, 181, 200, 203
church schools: 9, 16, 33, 34, 96, 193
citizenship: 7, 87, 92, 107, 115, 127, 128, 136, 141–5, 152, 163, 176–8, 188, 201
City Academies: 17, 192
City Technology Colleges: 15, 100, 140
Commission for Racial Equality (CRE): 191
'Common schools': 7, 46
community schools: 1, 4, 7, 8, 14, 16, 17, 27, 31, 34, 39, 47, 56, 59, 74, 79, 81, 92, 95, 97–9, 103–7, 109–11, 119, 120, 128–31, 133–5, 137, 139, 143, 144, 147, 148, 160, 162, 164, 165, 177, 183, 184, 187, 192, 193, 195, 196, 198, 202, 203
confessional schools: 14

Conservative Government: 23, 24, 101, 177
creationism: 7, 20, 139, 140, 141
culture: 3–6, 15, 35, 50, 52, 63, 65, 67, 68, 70–73, 76, 79, 82, 88, 89, 93–5, 106, 110, 113, 115, 116, 119, 124, 168, 171
cultural background: 56, 57, 83, 85, 97, 116, 121, 122
cultural diversity: 8, 24, 25, 29, 30, 89, 108, 112, 116, 170, 196
cultural groups: 25, 65, 69
cultural heritage: 5, 6, 63, 65, 68, 76, 79, 88, 94, 153, 155
cultural identity: 6, 7, 40, 56, 64, 66, 71, 85, 87, 151, 152–5, 161, 174
cultural pluralism: 72, 89, 90, 108, 112, 152, 164, 196
curriculum: 5, 7, 22, 32, 39–41, 43–5, 48, 58, 81, 82, 90, 91, 94, 103, 106, 110, 111, 115–17, 125, 130, 133, 144, 155, 161, 162, 165, 187

denominational schools: 8, 9, 11–14, 17, 27, 33, 43, 46, 96, 130
dual denominational schools: 19
Durham Report (1970): 15

Education Reform Act (1988): 16
Ethnicity: 4–6, 24, 36, 38, 56, 63, 66–9, 70, 71, 73–5, 84, 85, 87, 88, 94, 102, 151–4, 159, 168, 184, 199
ethnic background: 1, 25, 71, 77, 116, 121, 125, 155
ethnic diversity: 1, 24, 91, 116, 203
ethnic groups: 6, 25, 28, 44, 49, 53, 69, 70, 76
ethnic-religious identity: 68, 84, 152, 178
European Convention on Human Rights: 105, 123
evangelical Christian schools: 19, 20, 34